For your reading pleasure

LONDON'S
STRANGEST
TALES

Other titles in the STRANGEST series

For your reading pleasure

LONDON'S STRANGEST TALES

EXTRAORDINARY BUT TRUE STORIES

FROM OVER A THOUSAND YEARS OF LONDON'S HISTORY

TOM QUINN

PORTICO

This edition published by Portico Books
10 Southcombe Street
London
W14 0RA

An imprint of Anova Books Company Ltd.

ISBN 9781861059765

A CIP catalogue record for this book is available from the British Library.

20 19 18 17 16 15 14 13 12 11

Printed and bound by CPI Group (UK) Ltd, Croydon, CR0 4YY

This book can be ordered direct from the publisher at
www.anovabooks.com

D.A.Q.1958–1981.

Thanks to Charlotte Wadham for advice and inspiration,
to Katy, Alex and James for entertainment and to Barbara Phelan and
Malcolm Croft at Robson Books for encouragement and jolly emails.

Contents

Introduction

Like all ancient cities, London is an extraordinarily rich source of strange tales. From stories of human fat sold to anglers after the hanging days at Tyburn, to tales of one-legged escalator testers, unsolved murders, flying rivers, moving churches and human lavatories.

Then there are the tales of extraordinary London characters, oddballs and inventors, mavericks and madmen – like Stanley Green, who spent his life campaigning against peanut eating, or Walter Rothschild, who taught two zebras to pull his carriage down The Mall. And away from people and places, there are the ancient rules and systems of governance that have survived the centuries to baffle historians and create numerous bizarre anomalies – dusty traditions, archaic practices and ceremonies are kept on despite, on the face of it, no longer being necessary.

Bags of nails are still paid for long-vanished plots of land, medieval legacies are still honoured each year and the pursuivants at the College of Arms still initiate prosecutions against those who infringe the rules governing the use of gules, azure and archant.

London's wealth of bizarre tales can be attributed to the city's love of the old ways, which is why much that is odd and ancient in London's social and business life survives. In the City proper, for example, an ancient ordinance defines a road as a highway without houses – which is why, to this day, no thoroughfare in the city may be called a road; it's either a street or an alley. Even big multinational corporations haven't been able to change that.

Many of London's strangest and quirkiest tales are well known to scholars but have been unavailable to the general public until now.

This book is the result of several years spent digging in obscure and dusty archives and in the libraries of organisations whose continued existence in the modern world is itself astonishing, but the labour has been worth it, for whatever your interest, whether political, social, architectural or historical, you will find *London's Strangest Tales* a mighty feast of the mad, bad, dotty, eccentric and – at times – quite unbelievable.

WHY PART OF SCOTLAND IS IN LONDON

950

Scotland Yard is famous throughout the world but few people wonder why a police station in central London should have been given this curious name. Why Scotland? The answer takes us into one of those curious and inexplicable areas of long forgotten history.

From the late tenth century until the Act of Union of 1707 which brought Scotland and England together under one Crown, Scotland was an entirely separate country with its own tradition, rules and statutes – even today Scottish law differs markedly from English law in many respects.

During the period of independence Scotland, like most foreign countries, had a London embassy and the name Great Scotland Yard is the last echo of an independent Scotland's presence in London.

Originally there were three streets that covered this area – Little Scotland Yard and Middle Scotland Yard have long gone – but bizarrely the rules that apply to foreign embassies today still, in theory, apply to this small area of London. All embassies are in practice foreign territory – the police cannot enter a foreign embassy unless invited to do so and their jurisdiction doesn't include the territory of a foreign embassy.

After the Act of Union no one remembered to abolish the foreign status of Great Scotland Yard, which means that even today the little street running off Whitehall near Trafalgar Square is actually Scottish territory.

PUT OUT YOUR FIRE

1066

Many delightful traditions linger in London long after their practical usefulness has gone. The beadle who watches Burlington Arcade, for example, forbids running, umbrellas and whistling despite the fact that these are no longer evidence of a lack of gentility. In parliament an MP under certain circumstances may only interrupt a debate if he first dons a top hat. Ravens are still kept at the Tower of London for fear that if they depart the monarchy will fall.

But perhaps the oddest and longest lasting tradition is the curfew bell still rung each evening in South Square in Gray's Inn, a centre of the legal profession since 1370.

The curfew bell rung here would have been only one of dozens rung all over medieval London, for the word curfew comes from the Norman French *couvre le feu* – meaning put out your fire – and it was rung not to tell citizens that they must not leave their houses but rather to tell them (since it was bedtime) that they should make sure they had extinguished all their fires and candles. The fear – to be realised in the terrible fire of 1666 – was that without a reminder someone might forget a candle or fire and the result would be that the thousands of dry timber and thatch buildings would ignite.

Originally, apart from the bells rung here at Gray's Inn, all London churches rang the curfew – it was on the order of William the Conqueror (1028–87) – and as late as the beginning of the Second World War a dozen or more city churches still rang the

2

curfew. Today that thousand-year tradition is still held in two places – Gray's Inn, as we have seen, and the Tower of London.

THE BISHOP OF WINCHESTER'S GEESE

1171

To those of a religious cast of mind it may come as a shock to discover that for centuries the Christian church made a very good living from prostitution. As it happens the Church was also one of the world's most important and vicious slave owners.

But the church in London was particularly keen to make money from prostitutes since it was so easy – in fact the prostitutes of Southwark were known as the Bishop of Winchester's geese. With magnificent hypocrisy the Bishop of Winchester was able to collect rents from the numerous brothels he owned but then when a prostitute died in the diocese the church refused to allow her to be buried in consecrated ground.

A sad little reminder of this grim and astonishing history can still be glimpsed down a quiet street in Southwark even today. Red Cross Way runs parallel to Borough High Street and if you follow it almost as far as the junction with Union Street you come to a rusty iron gate and behind it a plot of land.

This is the remnant of Cross Bones Graveyard where the Bishop of Winchester's geese were buried when they could no longer earn money for the church.

A royal ordinance of 1171 allowed the Bishop of Winchester to license the brothels, or stews as they were known, and to collect the income. The Bishop's jurisdiction covered what was known as the Liberty of the Clink – the reference is to the Clink

4

Prison, part of which can still be seen in the Anchor Inn a few hundred yards along the riverbank west from Southwark Cathedral.

In 1833 a history of the area mentions the 'unconsecrated burial ground known as the Cross Bones at the corner of Redcross Street, formerly called the Single Woman's burial ground...'. The writer is clearly echoing the words of a much earlier author, John Stow (1525–1605), whose great *Survey of London* was published in 1598.

Stow refers to Cross Bones and 'these single women who were forbidden the rites of the church, so long as they continued that sinful life, and were excluded from Christian burial, if they were not reconciled before their death. And therefore there was a plot of ground called the Single Woman's Churchyard, appointed for them far from the parish church.'

The brothels, drinking houses, bear-pits and cock-pits of Southwark survived until the death of Charles I on the scaffold in 1649 and the arrival of Oliver Cromwell and a Puritan-dominated government, but when the prostitutes – or most of them – departed, the poor arrived in their droves and by the middle of the nineteenth century this was one of the foulest and most overcrowded parts of London. It was also dangerous – so dangerous in fact that even the police were reluctant to stray too far into its warren of filthy, rat-infested streets and alleys. Cross Bones Graveyard continued to be used until 1853 when the bodies were being buried so close to the surface that decaying hands and feet were often seen sticking through the soil. The government insisted it be closed.

But if proof were needed that the patch of ground that remains really was a burial ground for the Southwark geese, an excavation in 1990 discovered almost 150 skeletons, mostly women and one with the clear marks of syphilis.

With typical greed the authorities have tried again and again to build on the remaining plot of land but fierce local opposition has ensured that, at least for the time being, the old graveyard of Southwark's geese remains as a monument to a long-vanished part of London's medieval history.

SQUABBLING CHURCHMEN

1176

Even the earliest gospels were written almost a century after the death of Jesus, so it is no wonder that they are full of inconsistencies – some make no mention of Christ's supposed divinity, some make no mention of his brothers and sisters (the Catholic Church couldn't bear the idea that Mary had children other than Jesus) so it is perhaps not surprising that as the centuries passed the Christian religion had far more to do with the church and the authority of its members than with Christ himself. Endless squabbles about what Christ really meant and what he might have approved or disapproved led eventually to schism and the passionate desire of Christians of every persuasion to burn each other to death.

One of the most hilarious of these ancient squabbles took place in Westminster Abbey in the second half of the twelfth century. Until this time priests had been perfectly entitled to marry and it was an entirely arbitrary decision to forbid something that had been acceptable for more than a thousand years. Other disputes centred on the differences between the ancient rites of the church inherited through the Irish tradition and the growing authority of Rome, whose traditions were very different in many particulars.

The Archbishop of York (Irish tradition) was convinced that he was the senior English cleric, but this infuriated the Archbishop of Canterbury (Rome) who refused to accept that anyone should even think of taking precedence over him.

Things came to a head when a papal legate visited England in 1176. The legate decided to sort out the question once and for all by convening a synod at Westminster Abbey.

It took the Archbishop of York much longer to get to London for the synod than his co-religionist from Canterbury. When he arrived and entered Westminster Abbey he found the Archbishop of Canterbury already seated in the position of precedence on the right of the papal legate. He was so furious that he marched up to the papal legate and sat on his lap, to the astonishment of the other bishops!

According to contemporary reports a fight ensued with ecclesiastical supporters of Canterbury attacking supporters of York – even the papal legate could do nothing to quell the riot. But the legate was a clever man who quickly saw a way through the problem – following debate at the synod (after everyone had calmed down) he determined that the Archbishop of York should be Primate of England and the Archbishop of Canterbury should be Primate of All England. This master-piece of fudging has lasted down to the present day.

HUMAN LAVATORY

1190

As successive British governments have closed Britain's once great wealth of public lavatories – London's loos, until the 1950s, were famous the world over – so has the public been forced to dash in and out of restaurants and pubs where they have no intention either of eating or drinking.

The reason London's magnificent Victorian public loos were built in the first place was simply that governments of the time saw them as essential to the wellbeing of Londoners. Parliamentarians who knew their history far better than today's legislators no doubt remembered that right through the Middle Ages and well into the seventeenth century one of London's biggest problems was the lack of public loos.

In their houses people simply used a bucket or pot and then threw the contents into the gutter or the Thames. There is much evidence to suggest that many householders – this was certainly true in aristocratic households – simply relieved themselves in the corner of any room they happened to be in.

Out in the streets people relieved themselves wherever they liked, but the more delicate-minded and, of course, women found this unacceptable – the solution was provided by human loos.

These were men and women who wore voluminous black capes and carried a bucket. When you needed the loo you looked for the nearest man or woman with a cape and bucket and gave them a farthing. You then sat on the bucket while they stood above you still wearing the cape but also surrounding you with it.

The name of only one human lavatory has come down to us – the court rolls reveal that in 1190 one Thomas Butcher of Cheapside was fined 'and admonished' for overcharging his clients.

THE RIGHT TO BE HANGED BY SILK

1237

The first freedom of the city of London was given in 1237. In late medieval England being granted the freedom of the city was not a courtesy title nor a simple invitation to wander the city at will. Instead it had enormous practical importance. Once granted it meant the recipient was freed from his duty to his feudal lord – he was a free agent and under the terms of the granting of freedom it meant he could own land and earn money in his own right. He was also protected from feudal duties – the duty of military service for example – because he had rights under the charter of the city. These rights were so important that they could occasionally conflict with the rights of the monarch.

The city authorities were careful, however, to ensure that so far as possible the monarch was central to the granting of freedom. The freedom of the city is still granted today and those accepting it have to swear the following oath:

> I do solemnly swear that I will be good and true to our Sovereign; that I will be obedient to the Mayor of this City; that I will maintain the Franchises and Customs thereof, and will keep this City harmless, in that which is in me; that I will also keep the Queen's Peace in my own person; that I will know no Gatherings nor Conspiracies made against the Queen's Peace, but I will warn the Mayor thereof, or hinder it to my power; and that all these

points and articles I will well and truly keep, according to the Laws and Customs of this City, to my power.

Once he agreed to this the freeman was given a parchment and a wooden casket in which to keep it – in medieval times it is believed that many freemen refused to leave their houses without taking with them – rather like a modern passport – the parchment that confirmed their status as freemen.

Some of the rights granted to freemen are bizarre by any standards – even today a freeman is entitled to herd sheep over London Bridge, he may walk about the city with a drawn sword, can insist on being married in St Paul's Cathedral, is permitted to be drunk and disorderly without fear of arrest and best of all if he is sentenced to hang the execution can only be carried out using a silken rope!

HOW BEDLAM GOT ITS NAME

1250

The grand building that now houses the Imperial War Museum south of the River Thames in Lambeth was once Bethlehem Hospital – the hospital from which we derive the word Bedlam, meaning a state of complete chaos.

The first Bethlehem hospital was built just outside the old city walls near Bishopsgate in 1250. It was then the priory of St Mary of Bethlehem and like all religious houses in Catholic England it had a duty to help the poor and needy.

By the middle of the fourteenth century the records reveal that the priory had been greatly expanded: the new parts of the abbey were specifically designed to house the 'weak of mind', many of whom would have been thrown out of their homes and left destitute.

Early attitudes to the mentally ill were, by modern standards, appalling – if they weren't killed for being possessed by the devil, they were often shackled or kept permanently chained to a wall; they were never washed and often fed, if they were fed at all, like animals; therapy consisted of ducking in freezing water or whipping.

After the Dissolution of the Monasteries, in 1534–41 the whole of the priory buildings of St Mary of Bethlehem became a hospital specifically required to take those who had 'entirely lost their wits and God's great gift of reasoning, the whiche only distinguisheth us from the beast'.

In the late seventeenth century the hospital moved again – this time to open fields just outside Moorgate to the north of the city.

Designed by Robert Hooke (1635–1703), the beautiful new classical building concealed a dreadful regime, with patients packed into insufficient space and no attempt of any kind at hygiene.

By this time a curious shift had taken place in social attitudes and the entertainment-hungry populace of London began to see Bethlehem Royal Hospital as a sort of circus or amusement park. We don't know exactly when it began but by the mid-eighteenth century every weekend hundreds arrived to be shown around the madhouse; it was a visit 'guaranteed to amuse and lift the spirits', said one commentator.

Sadly there is evidence that the warders deliberately worked the patients up before these visits in order to make them behave even more wildly than they would otherwise. The governors were probably pleased as they had no thought that their patients could ever recover and the visitors paid good money to see them.

By now the hospital was known as Bedlam and the word quickly became synonymous with any scene of chaos. Most of the hospital's income came from paying visitors so it was important to put on a good show. It took another century and more – until the late eighteenth and early nineteenth centuries in fact – before more enlightened hospital governors decided to stop all visits of this kind. It's a sad commentary on earlier attitudes to social class and mental illness that the mentally ill ceased to be whipped daily only when George III (1738–1820) became mad and his plight aroused widespread sympathy.

By the early 1810s it was time for the hospital to move once again. Plans had been drawn up for a new hospital on marshland south of the river. The land was cheap and it was even thought that the air, being cleaner, might do the patients some good.

The domed classical building we see today was designed by James Lewis (1750–1820) and finished in 1815. Patients were brought across London from Moorfields in a long sad line of Hackney cabs and under careful guard. And here the patients stayed until 1930 when a new hospital was built at Addington in Surrey. In 1936, having dithered about the fate of the old buildings, it was decided that rather than demolish them they should be used to provide an excellent home for the Imperial War Museum.

A PIECE OF CAMBRIDGESHIRE IN LONDON

1290

The rationalisation of London's boundaries and the counties that border the capital destroyed some wonderfully comic anomalies. Middlesex, for example, was once split in two – Epping Forest which is now in Essex was once in the eastern portion of Middlesex while Uxbridge far away to the west was in the western portion. Between the two parts of Middlesex was a substantial stretch of Hertfordshire!

Most but not all of these anomalies have vanished. One of the most interesting and unusual that remains is centred on Ely Place just off High Holborn and a little above the course of the now covered River Fleet.

It is one of the few places that still embodies the ancient rivalry between the Lord Mayor and the monarch, for within the city boundaries the mayor is in charge and successive monarchs have had to accept this. They, in turn, have made sure that the mayor's jurisdiction is kept rigidly within the bounds of the old city limits. Traditionally the monarch has to ask permission to enter the city, which used to happen every year at a special ceremony at Temple Bar in the Strand.

Ely Place is within the city boundary but is owned by the Crown. Because of this, it is exempt from the authority of the Lord Mayor and is still – even today – a private road with its own gates and a beadle. Even the police may enter this street only with the permission of the beadle.

15

Ely Place has a long and unusual history. Successive Bishops of Ely had their London palace here from 1290 until 1772 when, neglected and almost ruinous, it was demolished. The church of St Ethelreda, which is still here, was completed in about 1291 and is the oldest Roman Catholic pre-Reformation church in London – although church is a rather grand term for what was and is a small private chapel.

The Palace had many famous residents over the years – John of Gaunt lived here from 1381 until his death in 1391 and Henry VIII was an occasional visitor, as was his daughter Elizabeth I.

There is a delightful story of Elizabeth insisting that the Bishop of Ely should rent some part of the palace to her courtier Sir Christopher Hatton, whose name is commemorated in the diamond merchant district of nearby Hatton Garden. The bishop was told he could charge Hatton 'ten pounds a year, ten loads of hay and a rose picked at midsummer'.

Until about 1920 a policeman had to be dispatched from Ely 100 miles away in Cambridgeshire to police the street because officially this is part of Cambridgeshire!

The houses which now surround St Ethelreda's were built at the end of the eighteenth century and until recently Britain's only diamond cleaver carried on his business in one of them.

In his play, *Richard III*, Shakespeare mentions the wonderful strawberries that once grew here in the gardens of the old Palace.

BOARS' HEADS AND FRANKINCENSE

1300

Despite the evils of modernisation which have destroyed much of the ancient physical fabric of London a host of wonderful traditions survive – a number are still with us simply because ancient statutes tie the modern incumbents of various offices into certain duties. These duties can include odd little ceremonies and, rather enchantingly, it is very difficult to abolish ancient ceremonies – if you agree to be elected to certain offices you have to carry the old ceremonies however keen you might be on doing away with them.

The ceremony of the keys at the Tower of London in which the yeoman warder locks the gates and then presents the keys each night to the governor is well known, as is the distribution of Maundy money by the sovereign each year. In this ceremony the monarch is supposed to wash the feet of the poor in memory of Jesus at the Last Supper, but what was good enough for Jesus was eventually not good enough for the British monarch and Elizabeth I, having grown tired of washing feet each year (she always made sure they had been washed before she got near them) started to give money to the poor instead, which is the form in which the custom survives today. The last monarch to actually kiss the feet of the poor was William III. The present Queen merely hands out the specially minted coins to a group of the elderly.

But if these ceremonies are fairly straightforward, there are others that can still amaze anyone coming across them for the first time. One such is the Presentation of the Worshipful Company of Butchers. This involves members of the old Guild of Butchers giving the Lord Mayor a boar's head as payment for land that was once used for 'cleansing the entrails of slaughtered beasts'.

But the oddest of all London ceremonies is perhaps the Royal Epiphany Gifts Service at the Chapel Royal next to St James's Palace. This ceremony has been held every year on 6 January for seven centuries – in other words since 1300 if not earlier. Members of the Royal Household carry gold, frankincense and myrrh into the chapel on behalf of the sovereign.

After the ceremony the myrrh is taken to Nashdom Abbey, the frankincense goes to a nearby church and the gold – temporarily borrowed from the Bank of England – is quickly returned to the vaults under heavy guard. An equivalent monetary sum is then given to various charities. Curiously, no sovereign has attended the ceremony in person since George I.

HOW THE WOMEN BEAT THE LAWYERS

1314

Lawyers have always been hated. Even when we need them most we think of them as arrogant parasites whose trade union – the Law Society – regulates their affairs in such a way as to ensure their fees are always exorbitant. In surveys lawyers are always voted among the worst professionals, only a little behind journalists.

Perhaps one reason for this is the curious history of the legal profession in Britain. The lawyers' history is intimately tied up with their presence in the Inns of Court.

Lawyers arrived on the site they still occupy between Fleet Street and the river in the early fourteenth century when they took a lease on land formerly owned by the Knights Templar, whose order had been proscribed by the Pope in 1314.

The lawyers took the lease on the site because Henry III, who had established a law school at Oxford, did not want a rival lawyers' college in the City of London. The lawyers didn't like this so they retaliated by establishing their Inns (the first buildings were designed as a hotel for lawyers – hence the name 'inn') outside the City boundaries. In other words, in typical lawyer fashion they avoided legislation they didn't like by exploiting a loophole! But there was a price to pay for what turned into a centuries long battle between the lawyers and the City authorities.

On three occasions in the late medieval period the Mayor of London attempted to enter the Inns of Court; each time the lawyers slammed the doors in his face and threatened to fight him and his men if they attempted to break down the gates. The Mayor appealed to the King who was forced to seek legal advice – the result of course was a foregone conclusion and the lawyers advised in their own favour.

The City didn't forget the slight and when a major fire broke out in the Temple they refused to help put it out. Legend has it that the lawyers raided their vast cellars and found enough wine and beer to put the flames out unaided!

Just before the Great War in 1913 the lawyers' sense that they were outside the law was tested when the City coroner tried to enter the Temple to register a death. The gates were slammed in his face and nothing could be done. Today, according to legend, the lawyers refuse to pay council tax or business rates in the normal way – they insist on deciding themselves just how much they will or will not pay.

It took several centuries for the lawyers to persuade the Crown to sell them the land they had leased since the fourteenth century. James I finally gave in but he did so reluctantly – so much so that the lawyers were fearful he would change his mind. To prevent any going back they buried their freehold agreement beneath the altar in the Temple church where it remained until early in the twentieth century.

The person with ultimate control of the lawyers here on the banks of the Thames is the Master of the Temple. In the past, masters thought of themselves as easily the equal if not the superior of the Mayor of London and they took their duties very seriously. One of these duties was looking after the moral welfare of the junior members of the inn. A Victorian master decided that too many young lawyers were bringing women into the inn so he decided to put a stop to it by issuing a directive that all women coming into the Temple must in future sign their names in a ledger together with the name of the lawyer they were visiting.

Imagine the poor master's horror when he discovered a few days after the new rule was in place that hundreds of young women had signed themselves in and put his name down as the lawyer they were visiting!

A STREAM FLOWS AT WESTMINSTER

1360

It's difficult to visualise now but Westminster Abbey once stood on a windswept inhospitable island in the Thames. Not a distinct island midway across the river, but a solid island surrounded by marsh and bisected by streams. The abbey was part of a monastery, deliberately sited here to be well away from the worldly temptations of the city of London but with plenty of fresh water from the Thames and from the streams that separated Thorney Island, as it was then known, from the surrounding land.

You might think that not a scrap of physical evidence of that distant time remains but you'd be wrong – opposite Charles Barry's (1795–1860) splendid Gothic Revival Palace of Westminster, and standing isolated now on a small patch of grass is a stone tower – the Jewel Tower.

Other parts of the old Whitehall Palace survive – most notably Inigo Jones's (1573–1652) Banqueting House of 1620 further up Whitehall. But this is the earliest part of the ancient structure still standing. It has been here since the second half of the fourteenth century, built when the poet Geoffrey Chaucer (1343–1400) was a young man.

Visitors today can see a small exhibition about the history of the palace and the tower, and until recently large rainbow trout lived in the remains of the moat that surrounds the tower. A stream fills the moat before running under the main road and into the Thames. Astonishingly the stream is still running exactly as it ran a thousand years ago to separate this side of Thorney Island from the countryside beyond.

PLANNING FOR CENTURIES AHEAD

1399

When a new building goes up the builders and planners never think of how that building may (or may not) survive into the near future let alone the more distant future, but in the past buildings were put up that were meant – at least when they were built – to last forever. A case in point is Westminster Hall, whose builders came up with an extraordinary idea to ensure that it would last for generations.

The lower parts of the walls of Westminster Hall, which seem now to the casual observer to be part of the Georgian Palace of Westminster, are actually unchanged since this huge building was begun shortly after the Norman Conquest of 1066. The earliest work is dated to the end of the eleventh century and what we see today is the building that was finally completed in 1399.

The hall has one of the greatest architectural treasures of the late Middle Ages – the vast, intricate and magnificent hammer-beam roof. Like any ancient building Westminster Hall has needed to be repaired now and then: parts of the walls were rebuilt or repaired along with the windows in earlier centuries; the roof too has been renewed here and there as the ancient timbers have decayed, and a section had to be replaced after a bomb caused some damage in the 1980s.

The last major period of restoration was in 1913 when several major timbers had to be renewed. But this presented the board of works with a major headache. England's oak woods had long ago been felled and officials simply could not find a plantation with oaks big enough to provide the right sort of timber. Oak trees there were but they were perhaps two or three hundred years old and therefore simply not big enough. What was to be done?

Then someone had the bright idea of checking where the original timbers had come from. It was discovered that at the end of the fourteenth century they had been brought to Westminster from an estate near Wadhurst in Sussex. The estate had been owned at that time – nearly five hundred years earlier – by the Courthorpe family. In 1913 there was a descendant of the original Courthorpe family in Parliament – he was MP for Rye, the beautiful Cinque Port on the south coast.

When he was approached Sir George Courthorpe astonished officials with the following story. He explained that when the original trees had been cut and sold to the king in the fourteenth century, Courthorpe's ancestors had thought that the time would come when the timbers needed repair or renewal so they planted a new stand of oak trees specifically for the purpose. Those trees were now – in 1913 – ready and they were duly cut and used to repair the great roof of Westminster Hall.

THE CURSE OF CENTRE POINT

1417

A curious tale surrounds the land on which the tall tower of Centre Point now stands. This busy area where Tottenham Court Road meets Oxford Street was once part of the area known as Seven Dials, centred on the church of St Giles that still stands a little behind Charing Cross Road. Until the mid-nineteenth century St Giles and Seven Dials was a dense warren of tiny courtyards and alleys where vast numbers of criminals and prostitutes lived and the police dared not go. Tucked away between Covent Garden to the south and Bloomsbury to the north the area is a strange survivor – it miraculously escaped wholesale redevelopment in the 1960s, for example.

A medieval leper hospital existed here amid open fields and well away from the City of London until the first developers came in the seventeenth century. They put up houses for artisans and skilled tradesmen, but within a few decades an area that had seemed a model development to Pepys when he visited it, had degenerated into a dark, overcrowded and fearsome place.

The old road to Oxford (now Oxford Street) runs along what is now the northern extremity of the district. It passes close by the parish church of St Giles, patron saint of lepers. For centuries church officials paid for a last drink at the Resurrection Gate for the condemned who passed the church and pub as they took their journey by cart from Newgate Prison in the east to the gallows at Tyburn (now Marble Arch) in the west.

The Resurrection Gate (rebuilt in the nineteenth century and renamed the Angel Inn) is still next to St Giles's Church and you can follow the route of the old Oxford Road as it winds its way through what were once fields.

St Giles's Church was completed in 1712 after the earlier church began to collapse. The walls of the old church, built in the twelfth century, had been gradually undermined by the huge number of burials. St Giles is one of a relatively small number of London churches that escaped Victorian 'improvements' and bombing in the Second World War.

The great seventeenth-century poet Andrew Marvel (1621–1678) is buried here and the pulpit from which John Wesley (1703–1791), the founder of Methodism, preached can still be seen. The plague of 1665, probably the worst outbreak in the whole history of that terrible disease, began here in St Giles. Here, too, lived London's ballad sellers, including James Catnach from whom we get the phrase catchpenny – meaning designed merely to sell quickly. The area was also famous for doctors and astrologers, trinket makers, bird sellers and pawnbrokers.

By the eighteenth century, when William Hogarth (1697–1764) depicted the area in his famous engraving 'Gin Lane', Seven Dials was a place avoided by anyone with the least pretensions to respectability. It was also pretty much beyond the reach of the authorities. Gin shops were everywhere and poverty and desperation made the inhabitants widely feared. If a criminal from the area was being taken from Newgate to Tyburn extra soldiers were drafted in to guard him because, as likely as not, his friends would mount a rescue operation as he stopped for his last drink at the Resurrection Gate and once he'd been carried off into the Rookeries, as Seven Dials was then known, he would never be found. Even with the presence of armed guards pitched battles still sometimes ensued and numerous condemned men escaped.

The name Seven Dials comes from the place, in the southern part of the district, where seven small streets meet to form a star. The plan is that of Sir Thomas Neale and dates back to 1694. There is still a small market here every weekday – the market has been here for more than a century – and many of the houses in the surrounding streets are basically eighteenth century, though much altered. Charles Dickens (1812–1870) called the area Tom All Alone's in *Bleak House* and something of the atmosphere Dickens must have known still lingers.

The obelisk at the centre of the star where the seven streets meet is a modern replacement, but from here narrow streets from the eighteenth century and one or two earlier houses radiate towards Covent Garden, Charing Cross Road, Shaftesbury Avenue and Long Acre.

Much of the original Rookeries, certainly that area north of St Giles's church, was destroyed in the 1880s to make way for Shaftesbury Avenue and New Oxford Street.

St Giles's Church once faced open fields but now faces into a narrow alleyway, so it's difficult to appreciate what a splendid sight it would have been when first built, as it gazed out across open ground towards Tottenham Lane, but the inside of the church is one of the chief glories of the whole area. For some extraordinary reason it is hardly ever visited either by local people or tourists. It is a quiet, forgotten backwater and therefore the perfect place to stop for a few moments to enjoy that rare thing – a London interior pretty much unchanged in almost 300 years.

But the strangest thing about this area is that businesses very rarely thrive – the shops and other outlets towards the top of Charing Cross Road, particularly around Centre Point, have constantly changed and the rate at which they tend to fail is far higher than the failure rate of comparable businesses elsewhere. Even Centre Point itself was a London scandal for a decade after it was built because it was so ugly that no one wanted to lease office space in it.

Why should the area be so unlucky? Rationalists would dismiss the idea but we know that in 1417 Sir John Oldcastle – the model for Shakespeare's Falstaff – was burned here for heresy on the orders of King Henry V. As the flames rose around him Sir John is said to have cursed the land and surrounding area on which he was burned as well as the executioner, the king and all his descendants. Perhaps the Curse of Falstaff still lingers.

GROPECUNT LANE

1450

We tend to think of the modern world as a place where anything goes – we take a very liberal view of swearing and sexual morality and we imagine that all other ages before ours were characterised by strict prudish morality, a morality typified by the Victorians who are popularly supposed to have covered the legs of their tables as the very idea of any sort of leg on display was shocking to them.

The Victorians may well have been excessively prudish, worthy and hypocritical, but it is completely wrong to imagine that all other earlier epochs were similar – there have been many periods in the past that have taken a far more liberal view of life in general than the modern age.

During Charles II's reign, for example, Nell Gwynn (1651–1687) was adored by Londoners who loathed the king's French wife and this despite the fact that Nell was always referred to as the king's whore. Whore in the seventeenth century seems to have lacked at least some of the harsher overtones that it now has.

Charles II himself cared little for traditional morality – he allowed plays to be written and performed that made the pursuit of pleasure, particularly sexual pleasure, the centre and mainspring of life. Puritan London was scandalised but there was little the religious could do as the plays had the king's sanction.

In medieval London too, sex was far more acceptable in a public context than it is now – anyone who looks at a map of London produced before 1450 will see several street names that are so extraordinary by our standards that they simply would not be allowed today.

Addle Street appears on these earlier maps, for example, and to a medieval Londoner Addle Street mean 'filthy spot'. Or take Fetter Lane, which still exists – in 1450 it meant the street of the dirty beggars.

Other names were dropped after the Reformation as the influence of killjoy Protestants came to dominate public life. Public holidays on saint's days were largely abandoned and many London street names were changed. Shiteburn Lane near Canon Street – so named because of the number of cess pits to be found here – was changed to the far more genteel sounding Sherborne Lane, a name it retains to this day.

But the most extraordinary street of all, that vanished with the arrival of the Reformation and the serious sensibility that seems to have accompanied it, was a small lane that ran north from Cheapside. It was called Gropecunt Lane for the simple reason that it was a famous haunt of prostitutes.

WHY WE SAY SIXES AND SEVENS

1490

Only London would retain something as dotty as a company of
tailors who have had absolutely nothing to do with making
clothes for more than three hundred years.

But like most London guilds, the Merchant Taylors have
long since lost all connection with their original calling. Most
guilds exist – again like the tailors – merely to administer
ancient and sometimes more recent charitable bequests.

The Merchant Taylors – now rather sadly run by grey men
in suits – still has some three hundred members and they
administer a number of charities including alms houses in
south London, a school in north London and a number of
churches. But they have enjoyed – or suffered – a turbulent and
fascinating history. Perhaps most interestingly, the Merchant
Taylors are also responsible for that curious phrase where one
describes a state of chaos or indecision as 'being at sixes and
sevens'.

To find out how this odd phrase came into the language we
need to take a brief look at the early history of the guild.

The Merchant Taylors, who were later joined by the Linen
Armourers, originally made clothes – but most particularly a
medieval jacket called a gambeson. This was a thick padded
jacket – padded because it was worn in battle either under
armour, by the nobility, or on its own by the common soldiers.
As the gambeson fell out of use with the introduction of
firearms and abandonment of swords and pikes, the Merchant

32

Taylors moved on to make tents for the army until sometime in the seventeenth century even this became a pointless exercise.

The company received its charter as early as 1327 and is, as a result, considered one of the twelve great livery companies. These tend to be the most ancient companies and they include the mercers, drapers, fishmongers and goldsmiths. They were livery companies because members of particular guilds wore distinctive clothes (or livery).

In its Royal Charter of 1503, the guild is given its full name – 'The Gild of Merchant Taylors of the Fraternity of St. John Baptist in the City of London.'

Early in their history the guilds were jealous of their status and fought for their place in the order of precedence during any progress of the Lord Mayor across London.

After endless arguments with the Guild of Skinners about who should take sixth place in the order of precedence and who seventh, the Lord Mayor of London issued an order in the late fifteenth century to the effect that the Skinners and Merchant Taylors would alternate in precedence: in odd-numbered years the Merchant Taylors would be sixth in order; in even years the Skinners would take the sixth place and the Merchant Taylors would be seventh. Hence the phrase – to be at sixes and sevens.

The alternating precedence continues to this day.

THE HOUSE THAT SHAKESPEARE KNEW

1501

Few domestic houses in central London can lay claim to as many strange tales as a tall narrow house that stands on the south bank of the Thames looking towards St Paul's Cathedral.

The fact that the house is still standing is a remarkable tale in itself for this elegant narrow building – once part of a terrace – is the last remaining of the many Bankside houses that once lined the river here where Shakespeare's plays were first performed.

The house is still privately owned but when Henry VIII's future wife Catherine arrived from Spain in 1501 she stayed here and two centuries later when Christopher Wren (1632–1723) was building St Paul's he too stayed in the house to supervise the work on his great cathedral directly across the water.

Although it has been altered again and again over the years, the house nevertheless is basically sixteenth century. It stands almost next door to the re-created Globe Theatre and running down one side – sadly now closed to the public – is one of London's narrowest thoroughfares – Cardinal Cap Alley.

For the first few centuries after the house was built this was a poor and dangerous area – apart from the theatres (banished to the south side of the river by the more religious-minded members of the government who thought plays immoral) the area was also famous for its bear-baiting and cock-fighting pits, as well as for the sheer number of its brothels. The murder rate here was probably twice that of the city across the water and there are vague references to respectable citizens simply disappearing in the vicinity of Cardinals Wharf – at least one twentieth-century owner of the house said he would never excavate below the house for fear of what he might find!

ROBBING PETER TO PAY PAUL

1540

Few people today realise that Westminster Abbey is not the name of the great abbey church that stands at Westminster. The official name of the abbey is the Collegiate Church of St Peter at Westminster and it is from this name that the phrase robbing Peter to pay Paul comes. Today the phrase simply means taking money from, as it were, the left hand and giving it to the right or to pay one person at the pointless expense of another person.

The origins of the phrase lie in those decades after the Reformation of the mid-1500s that ended Britain's thousand-year monastic tradition. After Henry VIII's death his son Edward VI (1537–53) continued the work of giving monastic lands and money to his favourites. The new parish churches also competed for endowments and Westminster Abbey (St Peter's) petitioned the king endlessly for funding. So much so that he decided to punish the abbey by taking away the revenues St Peter's had long enjoyed from the Manor of Paddington and giving them to St Paul's, which had always been known as London's cathedral. Thus the Royal church lost out to the London cathedral – and the phrase robbing Peter to pay Paul came into the language.

BURNING HERETICS

1555

The area around London's Smithfield is one of the most remarkable parts of London – Wat Tyler, the leader of the Peasants' Revolt in 1381, was stabbed to death here; the king's jester Rahere bizarrely founded the church of St Bartholomew, which is one of London's most ancient and least altered churches; and just across the square is the Charterhouse, the only medieval monastery that survives in London.

At the Reformation the Chaterhouse buildings were not, to general astonishment, demolished. Instead the Duke of Norfolk came to live here and later, in 1613, the Charterhouse became a home for elderly gentlemen – the Charterhouse Brothers – a role it fulfils to this day.

Most bizarrely, any work carried out in the centre of the square in front of St Bartholomew's Hospital that involves digging down a metre or more invariably cuts through a layer of ash – this is not ash from the Great Fire but rather from the hundreds of burnings of heretics that took place here from 1555 through the reign of Queen Mary. She was hated not so much because she insisted that heretics should be burned but because she would not spare those who were prepared to recant. The tradition Mary overturned was that heretics were spared if they changed their minds – and that applied even if the change of heart occurred at the very last minute.

37

VANISHED DUNGEONS REAPPEAR

1555

Many villages and country towns in England still have their ancient lock-ups – these are small, usually single-roomed buildings, often near the market square or by the side of a back street, that were once used to house those arrested before they could be taken to court and dealt with by local magistrates. They were also used simply to get someone unruly off the streets for the night – a drunk perhaps – and having sobered up the miscreant would then be released the next day.

The City of London had similar though usually larger lock-ups until fairly recent times – but in the City they were and are called compters. The original compter buildings have, like so much of London's history, been swept away but here and there the underground cells of former compters do survive.

Casual passers-by would be astonished to discover that what may well have once been the dungeons of the formerly infamous Wood Street Compter – situated in Mitre Court in the City – can still be seen complete with their chains and fetters. Mitre Court gets its name from the celebrated Mitre Tavern that once stood here – it is mentioned by countless writers and features in Ben Jonson's (1572–1637) play *Bartholomew Fair*.

The compter once housed some seventy prisoners. It was built in 1555 and was under the control of the sheriffs of London. It seems to have been used as a lock-up but also, curiously, as a debtor's prison and even to house the overflow of prisoners when nearby Newgate was full. For centuries all

38

trace of it was assumed to have vanished but early in the twentieth century the former dungeons were rediscovered. One wonders how many other parts of ancient London buildings remain underground and awaiting rediscovery.

The compter was unusual in reflecting precisely the social conditions outside the prison: it had three sections – the best section, the master's side as it was known, was for the wealthy and aristocratic; the knight's side was for those of some means, however small; and the hole was for the common people. The surviving cellars – now part of a nearby wine merchant – may well have been part of the hole, the most feared part of the prison and in which incarceration meant you were very likely to die from typhoid, cholera or some other waterborne disease.

CASH FOR WATERBORNE BODIES

1556

Almost everything about London's watermen is unique to that vanished trade. Until the end of the eighteenth century London's watermen were the equivalent of the modern underground, buses, cabs and overground trains all rolled into one. They wielded enormous power, particularly after the Company of Watermen was created by Parliament in 1556 followed by the grant of a royal patent in 1585. In fact one of the main reasons why London had only one bridge until the end of the eighteenth century was that the watermen were against it – they knew that any new bridge would seriously threaten their livelihoods.

Watermen, like cab drivers today, were carefully licensed. They had to ply their trade from a recognised spot – Whitehall Steps, Bridewell Steps or wherever – and they had to wear a red frock coat while at work.

The tradition was that anyone who wanted to hire a boat would shout 'Oars, oars' from the bottom of one of the many streets and lanes that led down to the river before the Embankment was built.

The boatmen would shout 'Oars! Oars!' in a bid to drum up extra trade but this was eventually forbidden, according to a number of early commentators, when it was realised that those unfamiliar with the watermen's role – particularly visitors to London – thought they were shouting 'Whores! Whores!'

When the watermen were not transporting people across the

river or up and down it they would salvage anything found in the river and theirs was a brisk trade in finding bodies – either suicides or those who'd accidentally drowned or been murdered.

By a curious quirk of history, the origins of which are now entirely obscure, bodies were almost always landed on the south side of the river because the authorities would pay a shilling for a body landed in Southwark whereas only sixpence would be paid for the same body landed on the north bank.

From the City proper down to Vauxhall Gardens the fare would be sixpence but the watermen must have been powerful men – they would regularly row their passengers as far up river as Hampton Court and beyond, but Londoners in a hurry would always choose to travel when the tide was in their favour. Rowing with the tide would speed things up considerably.

By 1700 there were more than ten thousand licensed watermen and such was the nature of their work that if you wanted to travel downstream of London Bridge you had to employ a waterman who was almost prepared to risk his life for the journey.

The reason it was so dangerous was that Old London Bridge had so many stone supports that they created a bottleneck in the river which would rush through the arches at a terrific and highly dangerous pace. Shooting the bridge was so dangerous in fact that passengers never stayed in the boat for that part of the journey. The waterman intending to row people downstream to Greenwich or wherever would approach London Bridge and then land his passengers at the Three Cranes Tavern just upstream of the bridge. The passengers would walk downstream of the bridge while the boatman shot the rapids. If he missed his moment, hesitated for a second too long or simply mistimed his journey under the bridge in any way his boat would be smashed and he would almost certainly drown. But an experienced waterman took pride in the danger and in the fact that he could shoot the bridge without mishap. And having done so he would pick up his passengers again and set off down river.

THE QUEEN'S BOSOM ON SHOW

1597

Detailed descriptions of the London scene before 1600 are relatively rare. Those that exist only occasionally satisfy the modern desire for detail – published descriptions mention noble buildings, grand thoroughfares and monumental edifices, but they rarely describe what it was actually like to walk along the Strand, through the mud and the puddles, when the City wall still existed and the Strand was effectively a suburb where the rich had their riverside palaces.

But if physical, detailed descriptions are lacking we are lucky enough to have a number of wonderful descriptions of meetings with the great and the good.

When the French ambassador Andre Hurhault-Sieur de Maisse met Queen Elizabeth I for the first time in 1597 she had been on the throne for almost forty years, a remarkably long reign in an age of regular outbreaks of the plague and general medical ignorance.

It had taken more than a year for the French ambassador to finally fix a date for the meeting and his sense that this was a momentous and long-awaited event comes through in the detailed report he wrote afterwards.

De Maisse was led along a dark corridor to the audience chamber where the Queen sat alone on a low chair. Others in the room gathered in small groups at some distance from her. The ambassador made a low bow at the door and the Queen rose and came over to him. De Maisse takes up the story:

I kissed the fringe of her robe and she embraced me with both arms. She smiled at me, and began to apologise for not receiving me sooner. She said that the day before she had been very ill.

She was dressed in silver cloth, her dress with slashed sleeves lined with red taffeta. On her head she wore a garland and beneath it a great reddish-coloured wig, with a great number of spangles of gold and silver, and hanging down over her forehead some pearls, but of no great worth.

By this time the Queen was in her sixties. Her cheeks were sunken and her teeth were yellow and broken with many missing from her habit of continually eating sweets – in fact so many teeth were missing that it was difficult at times for De Maisse to understand what she was saying.

De Maisse noticed all this and was therefore doubly astonished to discover that she was actually half naked! He explains with evident astonishment that the Queen's dress was completely open down the front and that her breasts – which she continually handled and moved about – were completely open to view.

He says: 'Her bosom is somewhat wrinkled as well as one can see for the collar that she wears round her neck, but lower down her flesh is exceeding white and delicate, so far as one could see.'

The only explanation one can find at this distance in time is that the Queen, who could never be criticised or contradicted, really believed the stories her poets and painters told her – that she was the eternally youthful Virgin Queen. The creature she read about in the verses presented to her was daily confirmed by her courtiers' behaviour and she clearly believed it all – either that or by this time she was simply losing her marbles!

JOHN STOW'S QUILL PEN

1605

It is hard to believe now but right up till the 1950s and early 1960s the City of London – the famous square mile – still had a substantial residential population. Greed and an obsession with redevelopment has reduced the number of those who actually live in the City to a point at which all the City's remaining churches are effectively redundant. Those that survive are kept for the tourists. They date mostly from the period after the Great Fire when Sir Christopher Wren and others – most notably Nicholas Hawksmoor – rebuilt the city.

Churches that predate the Great Fire in the London area were not that rare until German bombs destroyed them or damaged them so badly that what we see today is largely a pastiche of genuine seventeenth-century or earlier work. There are exceptions, however. The delightfully named St Andrew in the Wardrobe on Ludgate Hill was not bombed and looks today much as it would have looked centuries ago. Likewise St Bartholomew at Smithfield. St Andrew Undershaft in Leadenhall Street – undershaft refers to the shaft or maypole that once stood outside the church – is another church that retains much of its original fabric and among its most interesting features is the monument to the great historian of sixteenth-century London, John Stow. Stow was a tailor and antiquarian who spent years crossing and re-crossing the city in order to complete his monumental *Survey of London*, published, as we have seen, in 1598.

When Stow died in 1605 he was buried at St Andrew Undershaft and, despite the many years since his death, a curious tradition has grown up and survives to this day – Stow's monument shows him sitting with his books and in the act of writing. The monument of marble does not, however, include a stone or marble pen. Instead Stow holds in his hand a real quill pen and every year the Lord Mayor of London replaces the pen with a new quill. It is a ceremony that has taken place for centuries with hardly a break.

LONDON'S ONLY MAN-MADE RIVER

1606

With the growth of international trade, the founding of the South Sea Company and other trading groups, seventeenth-century London had a huge and ever increasing problem: how to get enough clean water for the population; and not just the human population – thousands of horses on which the city relied for transport had also to be watered regularly. The Thames was dirty and the water polluted, which caused regular epidemics.

One of the very earliest attempts to find a solution to the water problems can still be seen in north London.

Along the backs of the houses in one or two streets in Canonbury, the most prestigious and expensive part of Islington, runs a narrow watercourse. To the casual observer it looks like an old canal, but a closer inspection reveals something rather odd – this river is far too narrow to be a canal, but it isn't a river or a stream either. It is in fact one of the last remnants of one of the earliest attempts to bring fresh water to London.

The New River Company started life in 1606 when Acts of Parliament were passed to enable a channel to be dug to bring fresh water to central London from Amwell in Hertfordshire. Londoners were aware that it was unhealthy to throw all their rubbish and sewage into the same river from which they obtained their drinking water (i.e. the Thames) but the practical difficulties of finding a supply other than the Thames

46

had always seemed insurmountable. The New River Company refused to accept defeat. The head of the company – Hugh Myddleton (1560–1631) – began the enormous task of digging the channel which was to become the New River. It was to be ten feet wide by four feet deep. Total length was a little less than forty miles. All the work had to be done by hand and much of it was carried out in the face of fierce opposition from landowners along the route. Halfway through the work Myddleton ran out of money and had to be rescued by King James, who offered financial assistance in return for a share of future profits.

By 1613 the route had been completed and water ran into four newly built reservoirs at Clerkenwell. From here it ran to the city through wooden pipes – pipes which are still occasionally uncovered today during roadworks and re-building. Though the system leaked badly it was to provide water for many in the city for more than two hundred years.

The New River was adapted over the centuries and its flow was increased by additions from various newly dug wells and from the River Lea, but in essence it remained unchanged until 1904 when the New River Company was amalgamated with the Metropolitan Water Board. When the Second World War ended a decision was made to stop using water from the remaining reservoirs at Clerkenwell and though the flow continues to this day it now ends at Stoke Newington. However, a few stretches of the channel much closer to central London have survived, including those quiet backwaters running through Canonbury.

DERRICK'S DEATH CRANE

1610

All over the world wherever ships are unloaded the word derrick simply means a special type of crane that allows objects to be lifted and lowered but also swung horizontally. Few realise that the word and the design of the crane have their origins in one of London's most feared historical figures – a man whose name became a byword for death.

From 1388 until 1783 Londoners who were condemned to death were taken from Newgate Prison in the city in a tumbril – a primitive cart – that rolled through Holborn and on to the old Oxford Road (now Oxford Street) until it reached the western end of that road where today Oxford Street meets the Edgware Road. This place was then known as Tyburn. Throughout this long period Tyburn was chosen as the place of public execution precisely because it was open country. The authorities believed that public hangings acted as a deterrent to the rest of the population so when the hanging days came they wanted the crowds of spectators to be easily accommodated. Tyburn was perfect in this respect and 'Tyburn tree' became a euphemism for the gallows. Until the early seventeenth century the condemned stood in the back of the cart that had brought them to Tyburn until the hangman had the noose round their necks. The cart was then driven away and the victim was left dangling in midair. Death at this time was caused by slow strangulation – it wasn't until the nineteenth century and the introduction of the long drop that death by hanging became more or less instantaneous. The long drop meant that the neck was broken by the force of the victim's own weight rather than the slowly tightening effects of the noose as at Tyburn.

Gruesome stories from Tyburn are legion – relatives of the condemned would often run under the gallows, for example, and hang from the dangling man's legs to make sure he died quickly – but there was one major problem and it took the hangman Thomas Derrick to solve it. The problem was that on hanging days – which were always public holidays – there were usually too many to be hanged easily one at a time. Derrick introduced a gallows that could take up to a dozen or more at a time – the general shape of the new gallows took its inventor's name and, its shape being uncannily like that of the modern derrick crane, the name stuck.

Early references to hanging show how far into the consciousness of the London public the name derrick had penetrated. In 1608 an anonymous commentator wrote of a condemned highwayman: 'He rides his circuit with the Devil, and Derrick must be his host, and Tiburne the inne at which he will lighte. At the gallows, where I leave them, as to the haven at which they must all cast anchor, if Derrick's cables do but hold.'

JOHN DONNE, UNDONE

1631

The author of some of the greatest short poems of the seventeenth century, John Donne (1573–1631), is buried in St Paul's Cathedral where he was dean for a number of years. Donne is the author of many famous lines that have passed into the language – 'no man is an island', for example, and 'ask not for whom the bell tolls; it tolls for thee' – but in addition to writing verse he was a busy public man who sat as an MP in Elizabeth I's last parliament and worked for some time as a lawyer before taking holy orders.

By the time he entered the church he was already in middle age and probably a little embarrassed about his earlier versifying days. His piety certainly seems to have increased and towards the end of his life he commissioned his own monument, a life-size marble statue showing the poet in his shroud and peeping gloomily out from the folds of its hood. He posed for the sculptor in the very shroud that was later used to bury him.

Donne kept the monument itself in his house in the years up to his death and it was said that he sat in front of it every day when he said his prayers. When he died in 1631 it was placed in old St Paul's.

Nearly half a century later, of course, St Paul's burned down destroying pretty much everything within the church with one exception – John Donne's monument. Visitors today can still see the smoke-blackened lower parts of the marble – the only visible evidence of the Great Fire that consumed so much of London in 1666 – but Donne peeps out from his hood unperturbed and even at the last his wit did not desert him. He wrote his own epitaph and the words are still there on the effigy: 'John Donne, Undone.'

A CHURCH THE WRONG WAY ROUND

1631

St Paul's Covent Garden is one of London's quirkiest churches. It was built as part of London's first planned square in 1631. Its architect – he was also the architect of the square and all the houses in it – was the great Inigo Jones, who had studied the work of Palladio in Italy and longed to produce something similar in London.

The idea of a square surrounded on three sides by collonaded walks was met with derision by Londoners but the Duke of Bedford, one of London's richest men and a great enthusiast for all things Italian, pressed ahead anyway.

The houses were built and were immediately popular with London's fashionable elite despite those early misgivings. But the church that Jones was asked to build at the west end of the square is bizarre because it is built the wrong way round.

Problems began when the Duke of Bedford, who seems to have been keen for the houses to be beautifully built, told Jones that he really didn't care much for the idea of a church at all and that therefore it was to be built as cheaply as possible – 'I want it little better than a barn,' he is reputed to have said – but Jones, being proud of his work, decided that he would build magnificently anyway: 'I will build the handsomest barn in England,' he claimed.

The planned design involved having a main entrance into the square – in other words at the east end of the church – but when Archbishop Laud got wind of the plan he was furious and, despite the fact that the church was almost complete, he ordered that the east end of the church be blocked up and that the entrance should be rebuilt at the west end where it remains to this day. The heavy portico at the east end, reminds us that this should originally have been the grand entrance.

It is ironic that the building on which least care was lavished, officially at least, is the only one to survive from Inigo Jones's time. During the years of Covent Garden's fame – which lasted until the end of the seventeenth century – the houses were proudly kept but as the fashionable moved out in the eighteenth century the square became famous for its brothels and gin shops.

This was caused partly by the growth of the vegetable market, which had started in the middle decades of the seventeenth century but had grown enormously a century later. With late-night revellers from the theatres, gin palaces and coffee houses open all night to service the market porters, the area lost its reputation as a genteel district and became the debauched squalid place depicted in Hogarth's 'Morning' from the series *Four Times of the Day*.

Inigo Jones's plan for a piazza made the word fashionable for decades and hundreds of London girls were christened 'Piazza' in the years up to 1650.

POET BURIED STANDING UP

1637

Westminster Abbey has long been the last resting place of the great, the good, the brave – and the poetically inclined. Among the more interesting epitaphs is T.S. Eliot's (1888–1965) splendidly enigmatic:

> The communication of the dead
> Is tongued with fire beyond the language of the living.

The lines come from Eliot's own great poem *Four Quartets*.

But the strangest monument in the abbey seems remarkably unassuming on the face of it – a small stone, moved from the floor of the abbey to a wall in the last century to protect it from wear and tear, reads simply: 'O rare Johnson'. The lines (including the mis-spelled surname – it should be Jonson!) were written by the now forgotten poet Jack Young and they refer to the great Elizabethan and Jacobean playwright Ben Jonson (1572–1637), who is buried in the abbey in a most unusual way.

Jonson, the son of a bricklayer, was extraordinarily lucky as a child to come to the attention of the antiquary William Camden, then a master at Westminster School. Camden paid for Jonson's schooling and in robbing us of a master bricklayer he gave us instead a master playwright.

Jonson's comic masterpieces *Every Man in his Humour*, *Bartholomew Fair*, *Volpone* and *The Alchemist* are unlikely ever to be forgotten and they were hugely popular in his lifetime, but despite his success Jonson was not a good businessman like his contemporary William Shakespeare. Where Shakespeare invested his money in land and property, Jonson seems to have spent his on wild living – in a drunken brawl he killed a fellow poet and only escaped hanging because he was able to plead benefit of clergy. In Elizabethan England, bizarrely, a man who had committed murder but could read Latin was not executed. Instead his thumb would be branded – as was Jonson's – with the letter M.

Towards the end of his life and still living in poverty Jonson is supposed to have discussed his funeral arrangements with the Dean of Westminster. 'I am too poor to be buried in the abbey,' he is reported to have said, 'And no one will lay out my funeral charges. Six feet long by two feet wide is too much for me. Two feet by two feet will do.'

The dean is said to have immediately promised Jonson he could have his tiny area in what was to become known as Poets' Corner, clearly thinking that Jonson intended only to have a small memorial attached to the spot. In fact Jonson was properly buried in the abbey when the time came – he did it by arranging to have himself buried standing bolt upright in his grave where he remains to this day. It was his final joke.

In the 1840s work on the floor of the abbey disturbed the grave and Jonson's leg bones were found standing upright; his skull was intact too and apparently still with red hair attached to it!

Other graves in Westminster Abbey have strange stories attached to them – the poet Byron (1788–1824) was not commemorated here until 1967 because of his disreputable lifestyle (despite the fame of his poetry) and even Shakespeare had to wait until 1740 for a monument to be erected for him. The difficulty for the authorities when they thought of Shakespeare was reconciling themselves to the fact that despite being a commoner with only a relatively rudimentary education he became and remains the greatest writer in the English language – perhaps in any language. The same feeling of unease has fuelled numerous claims over the centuries that other more aristocratic scribblers are responsible for the plays and poems and merely used Shakespeare's name.

A SQUARE OF WONDERS

1641

There are lots of wonderfully odd things about Lincoln's Inn Fields. The name reminds us that this was for centuries open ground where the lawyers from the Inns of Court enjoyed walking, so much that when building began in the 1640s a deputation from the lawyers to the builders persuaded them not to cover the whole site with new houses but instead to leave the central area open, which is just as it remains to this day.

Other oddities about the square include Sir John Soane's (1753–1837) extraordinary house – rarely can a single relatively small house have been so stuffed with antiquities. Special cupboards and sliding display cases of great ingenuity and complexity had to be built at great expense to house Sir John's vast collection in such a small space. The house is now open to the public.

The square was and is also home to the Royal College of Surgeons – in earlier times tumbrils travelled regularly across the square carrying the bodies of the recently executed for dissection at the college. And in the college museum is the skeleton of Jonathan Wilde, the famous highwayman who was also the model for John Gay's (1685–1732) celebrated character Macheath in *The Beggar's Opera*.

The square was the scene of an encounter that typified the reasons for the seventeenth-century Londoner's love of 'pretty, witty' Nell Gwynn, Charles II's favourite mistress. Stories about Nell abound but two of the best concern her time here in

Lincoln's Inn Fields. Travelling here from Covent Garden one summer day she found herself surrounded by a mob that jostled her coach. She quickly realised that the angry crowd thought she was Charles's very unpopular French mistress, Catholic Louise de Keroualle (1649–1734). With great presence of mind Nell straightaway stuck her head out the window and shouted: 'Pray good people be civil, I am the Protestant whore!'

On another occasion she sat in her house in Lincoln's Inn – number 58 – with her son by Charles II playing nearby. The boy was aged about five. Nell was irritated that Charles had so far done nothing for the boy but she knew that direct appeals to him would do nothing. When he arrived to see her he played with his son for a while but the boy then ran off to the other side of the room and wouldn't return. Nelly saw her chance: 'Come here, you little bastard!' she shouted. Charles was horrified. 'Why do you use that terrible name?' he asked. 'Well, you have given him no other,' she replied. Charles promptly made the boy Duke of St Albans with land and an income that his descendants enjoy to this day.

But without question the oddest aspect of Lincoln's Inn Fields is that its dimensions are precisely those of the base of the Great Pyramid at Giza!

THE STONE MONUMENT
THAT WEEPS

1652

Most of the world's superstitious belief systems like nothing better than a bit of physical evidence. If you believe in miracles it's always good to be able to claim that you've actually seen one and in many cases the belief in the miracle will even survive proof positive that it was all nonsense in the first place.

London's oldest church, St Bartholomew the Great, was and still is occasionally the scene of what the more credulous would consider a miraculous occurrence.

The church of St Bartholomew is also something of a bizarre joke since it was built by a court jester. Henry I's fool, who was known as Rahere, had the church built in 1123 and it has never been bombed or burned or substantially rebuilt – a very rare state of affairs in London. There is less of it than there once was certainly, for at the Reformation it was trimmed down to its present size. In medieval times church buildings were constructed out across the present graveyard to nearby Smithfield market. The gateway building that leads into the church precincts was long hidden under plasterwork until early in the twentieth century restorers discovered that it is in fact fine Tudor craftsmanship and it has now been restored.

The flexibility of some medieval careers can be judged by the fact that Rahere went from being Henry I's jester to become prior of St Bartholomew the Great and he is buried here in the sanctuary.

Until recently the Butterworth charity was distributed every Good Friday on a table tomb in the churchyard – money and hot cross buns were handed out to the poor here but we have to go inside the church itself to discover something miraculous.

There is a bust of Edward Cooke on the south wall. Cooke died in 1652 and the words carved in marble beneath his bust ask each passer-by to weep for him. If the passer-by finds he has no tears to spare the inscription suggests he or she should 'stay and see the marble weep'. And it really does happen – partly the position of the monument on the wall and partly the fact that it is marble leads to a phenomenon in which moisture condenses easily and then runs in rivulets down the stone eyes.

STRANGLED HARES FOR
KIDNEY STONES

1658

In earlier centuries the idea of objective truth – in the scientific sense in which we might understand that term today – was largely absent. Medical, scientific and religious experts relied on authority: in other words if the great and the good said something was true then that was accepted for centuries without anyone ever worrying about proof.

A good example is the huge number of strange books of cures and medical preparations published over the centuries. In the late seventeenth century there seems to have been something of a flurry of medical publications emanating from London and all claiming that the cures they detailed for everything from the gout to the plague were published on the best authority – in other words they were the ideas of well-known doctors. No one seems ever to have worried about whether these various cures actually worked, which is astonishing when one reads the ingredients of the cures given for various ailments.

The following is a good example. It's a cure for kidney stones and comes from a book of medical recipes published at the Angel in Cornhill in 1658:

In the month of May distil Cow dung, then take two live Hares, and strangle them in their Blood, then take the one of them, and put it into an earthen vessel or pot, and cover it well with a mortar made of horse dung and hay, and bake it in an Oven with household bread, and let it still in an Oven two or three days, baking anew with anything, until the Hare be baked or dried to powder, then beat it well, and keep it for your use. The other Hare you must flea and take out the guts only, then distil al the rest, and keep this water: then take at the new and full of the Moon, or any other time, three mornings together as much of this powder as will lie on a sixpence, with two spoonfuls of each water, and it will break any stone in the kidneys.

How could this – and dozens of equally unlikely recipes – ever have been written down with any confidence as a genuine cure for kidney stones? Impossible though it is to believe, perhaps it really did work! More likely is that as a number of kidney-stone sufferers managed to pass the stones in their urine anyway – thus becoming cured – this vile mixture or something similar came to be given the credit for those who would have recovered unaided anyway.

WHY TEACHERS HAVE TO BE BETTER THAN THE KING

1660

Despite George Bernard Shaw's foolish quip – 'Those who can do, those who can't teach' – the whole future of each generation depends to a large degree on the skills or otherwise of the teaching profession. Given that undeniable fact it is astonishing that teachers are not held in higher esteem – in the past things were very different and a teacher was absolute ruler in his little kingdom, which may explain why teachers were permitted far greater liberties: children could be flogged until well within living memory and for the least mistake or misdemeanour.

The teaching profession was also a great producer of eccentrics – some would say madmen – and among the maddest was undoubtedly Dr Richard Busby (1606–1695).

A prolific author of Latin texts, he was educated at Westminster School where he was later to become headmaster, a role he filled for an astonishing 58 years, and in all that time his proud boast was that not one boy had passed through the school without being personally flogged by the good and no doubt deeply religious doctor. Christopher Wren was among a number of famous men who felt the master's lash in their early days.

Like all dictators, Busby would accept no argument or criticism – when one of his fellow schoolmasters questioned the doctor's judgment, Busby sent a team of schoolboys with axes to chop down the staircase leading to the rebellious teacher's apartments. The teacher was left with no choice but to recant before being allowed to shin down a rope.

When at last old age had taken its toll and Busby was forced out and replaced by Dr Friend, the following verses were being chanted all over Westminster:

> Ye sons of Westminster who still retain
> Your ancient dread of Busby's awful reign
> Forget at length your fears, your panic end –
> The monarch of the place is now a friend!

Two of the best stories about Busby concern his extraordinary sense of his own importence. On the first occasion he welcomed Charles II to Westminster School but refused to doff his hat to the king – an extremely daring omission which at that sensitive time (so soon after the Restoration) could have had serious repercussions. When he was upbraided by the king, Busby is said to have replied: 'I cannot do it, for the boys would then think there is someone greater than I...'

On another occasion Busby was discussing the role of headmaster with someone who suggested that it was perhaps a role of relatively little importance. Busby would have none of it and replied: 'The fathers of my boys rule the country. The mothers rule the fathers. The boys rule the mothers and I rule the boys.'

A MONARCH ON THE SCRAPHEAP

1660

Any visitor to Westminster Abbey at any time of year will notice something curious – there is always a small bunch of flowers, sometimes dried flowers, in the folded hands of the recumbent statue of Mary, Queen of Scots. It is as if there is a stream of people taking responsibility for their constant renewal and the phenomenon has been noted now for decades.

Similarly the statue of Charles I, the only monarch ever to be executed by Parliament, is often decorated with fresh flowers and wreaths. No one quite knows who puts them there but sympathy for the dead king has been passed down the generations and in some circles he has always been seen as a holy martyr. So his supporters still come at quiet times to lay flowers in his memory.

But if that is odd then odder still is the history of the statue itself, which is more a piece of propaganda than a statue.

Like Napoleon, Charles I was tiny, but a dwarf king was unlikely to impress his subjects so the sculptor first put the mini-king on a horse and then increased his dimensions to a strapping six foot. Because he's on horseback the deception isn't obvious at all.

First erected in Covent Garden in 1633, the statue of Charles that now stands in Trafalgar Square was taken down by the Puritan Parliament after Charles had been executed and sold to the appropriately named Mr Rivett. Rivett, it was assumed, would simply break it up and reuse the scrap metal, but being a shrewd man who sensed that things would not always be as they were then, he tucked it away undamaged and made a small fortune selling metal knick-knacks supposedly made from the statue's metal.

After 1660 and the return of the monarchy in the form of the debauched (and secretly Catholic) Charles II, Rivett made another small fortune by selling the king the statue of his dead father.

The new king had the statue set up at Charing Cross and looking down Whitehall to the spot outside the Banqueting House where Charles was executed and there the statue has remained ever since.

But if it had eyes to see and cared to look a little beyond the Banqueting House the statue would no doubt be very cross indeed, for at the other end of Whitehall, and just outside Westminster Hall, stands another statue – a memorial to Charles I's greatest enemy, Oliver Cromwell.

HOW TO AVOID DEBT IN THE MALL

1661

The phrase 'shopping mall' is either greeted with horror or delight depending on one's attitude to a phenomenon that spread across town centres in America and then the UK like a plague (or a blessing) but the origins of the word mall lie deep in the history of central London, where The Mall and Pall Mall commemorate a game that has vanished as completely as the dodo.

The Mall referred originally to a strange game imported from Italy. The game *pallo a maglio* soon became known in English as 'pall mall'. It was played on a half-mile course laid out by James I and Charles I. The two kings were enthusiastic players and the game involved using sticks rather like hockey sticks to knock a ball along the course.

When the first course was destroyed as houses were put up along The Mall Charles II needed a new course. He built it on the north side of what is now The Mall. The old course became what we now call Pall Mall.

Because the king played the game crowds of wealthy Londoners and courtiers came regularly to watch the matches. The great diarist Samuel Pepys records seeing the king play in 1661.

'While the fashionable strollers watched they meandered up and down talking and enjoying the view across the park.' The area where pall mall was played also had the great advantage that being within the jurisdiction of the court of St James it was

67

not subject to the debtors laws that applied everywhere else. This meant that in addition to fashionable promenaders The Mall attracted those who could not pay their debts. As long as they stayed there they could not be arrested. Soon the word 'mall' came to mean any fashionable place to promenade and loiter whether for conversation, exercise, shopping or debt avoidance!

Technically, even today, you still can't be arrested for debt if you are within the jurisdiction of St James's – but don't rely on it!

THE GOVERNOR OF DUCK ISLAND

1661

Jules Mazarin (1602–1661), one of the most extraordinary French politicians in history, was an Italian Jesuit gambler who effectively ruled France during the minority of Louis XIV from 1643 until his death in 1661. During Mazarin's time the poet Charles de Marquetel de Saint-Evremond (1613–1703) fell out with the French Government and was forced into exile. He chose London, where he hoped to find employment at the court of Charles II. This put Charles in a very difficult position because Saint-Evremond was extremely well connected and popular in London. Charles neither wanted to offend Saint-Evremond nor upset the French Government under Mazarin.

He came up with a perfect if rather strange solution: Charles remembered that the island in the middle of the lake in St James's Park was known as Duck Island so he made Saint-Evremond Governor of Duck Island. This pleased the French poet (who hadn't a clue what it referred to) and his friends and it neatly avoided upsetting the French ambassador, who knew precisely where Duck Island was and what it signified!

Saint-Evremond never returned to France. He remained Governor of Duck Island and died in London in 1703. He was buried in Westminster Abbey.

WHERE TO GET YOUR
COAT OF ARMS

1666

The British are obsessed with social class – it's a truism but one that reverberates through history. In earlier times the rising middle classes tried desperately to find an ancestor or two who would introduce a hint of blue blood to the family. Thomas Hardy's *Tess of the D'Urbervilles* reveals that even a poor country girl could be fooled into thinking that her ancestors were aristocrats and that somehow this meant her whole life should change. Then there was Shakespeare, who made every effort to persuade the College of Arms to accept his family's entitlement to a banner that would proclaim them gentlemen through and through. He failed but the institution to which he applied for his coat of arms still exists in the heart of London.

The vast mystery of family coats of arms, their history, design, conception and meaning, can be traced to an ancient, crooked, but still magnificent building in Queen Victoria Street in the heart of the old City and close to the river.

A miraculous survivor of German bombs, the seventeenth-century College of Arms is home to a bizarre range of officials who can be grouped into the royal heralds and the kings at arms. There are three kings at arms – Garter, Norroy and Clarenceux. The royal heralds are York, Lancaster, Windsor, Chester, Somerset and Richmond. The college also houses the pursuivants – Rouge Dragon, Blue Mantle, Rouge Croix and Portcullis. Each of these titles is given to one man. Bizarrely,

70

the head of the college – the Earl Marshall – is always the Duke of Norfolk. Norfolk is England's premier dukedom but the family has always traditionally been Catholic and at least one had his head lopped off for treachery.

The role, complexity and purpose of the various jobs carried out at the College of Arms would take a whole book to explain but suffice it to say that even today, more than five centuries after the college was established, no one, whether company or individual, is allowed to design and use a coat of arms without the permission of the college and there are strict rules about what exactly can appear on a coat of arms. There are a number of cases where those who broke the rules have been fined heavily for so doing.

Most of the terms used by the college are based on a curious medieval mix of Norman French (still current in elevated circles for a century and more after the Norman invasion), Latin and Middle English.

The College of Arms still has the charters and other documentation that survived the Great Fire of 1666 when the fifteenth-century building on the same site was burned down. All the paperwork was bundled into a boat and taken across the river.

Traditionally – though this is apparently not the case now – jobs in the college were given to important friends of important people, which may explain the long line of eccentrics, drunks and lunatics who have snoozed away the decades in the ancient panelled rooms of this delightful building.

Among the most eccentric was William Oldys (1696–1761), apparently given a job as herald because the Duke of Norfolk had enjoyed reading Oldys's book about Sir Walter Raleigh. Dukes of Norfolk, remember, always get the job of Earl Marshall, whose main role is to organise state occasions – funerals, weddings and coronations. Oldys spent his days and evenings in a local pub but employed a man to carry him back – completely drunk – to the college before midnight. If he was later than that it meant a fine. Oldys is best remembered today for a strange little poem he wrote towards the end of his life:

Busy curious thirsty fly
Drink with me and drink as I.
Freely welcome to my cup
Couldst thou sip and sip it up.
Make the most of life you may
Life is short and wears away.

YEOMAN OF THE MOUTH

1669

One of London's least-known but most beautiful buildings is Morden College just south of Blackheath. Not a college at all in the modern sense, Morden was actually built as a charitable foundation to house Turkey merchants who had fallen on hard times. Turkey merchants had nothing to do with the Christmas bird were merchants who, under a charter of Elizabeth I, began trading with the Near East. One such merchant – Sir John Morden – had grown enormously wealthy from his trading exploits. So much so that he bought the ancient estate of Wricklemarsh near Blackheath in 1669. The estate got its name from the Saxon word 'wirckle', meaning 'babbling', because the ground was crisscrossed by streams.

According to legend Morden's luck ran out in the early 1690s and a flotilla of ships on which his wealth depended failed to arrive from the Levant. He was faced with ruin but just when all hope had been lost, his ships appeared in the Thames Estuary and rather than ruined he found himself richer than ever. He was so grateful for what he saw as divine intervention that he commissioned Christopher Wren to build the college that still bears his name.

The college – with its lovely gardens and wonderful collonaded courtyard – is still home to elderly local people and it is still administered by trustees, something for which Sir John made provision in his will.

But the strangest thing about Morden College is not its survival, wonderful though that is, but rather the tombstone of one of its former inhabitants which is to be found in the grounds.

On his gravestone John Thompson is described as Yeoman of the Mouth. The inscription reads: 'in ye kitchen to king Charles II he served the said king as well during his exile as after restoration unto the time of his death. He served also King James the second and King William the third and being aged was allowed by her majesty Queen Anne to come hither.'

Unless Thompson was making it up it looks as if he served as a food taster for a series of monarchs – something not recorded elsewhere. Monarchs were certainly obsessed with the idea that they might be poisoned so it is perhaps not unlikely that Thompson was indeed 'Yeoman of the Mouth'.

THE CHURCH THAT INSPIRED
A CAKE

1672

St Bride's Church in Fleet Street is a fund of wonderfully odd stories. Its lightning conductor was designed and fitted by the great American republican and inventor Benjamin Franklin (1706–1790) but only after a huge row about whether blunt-ended conductors (seen as American) should be used or British pointed-end conductors.

The church steeple, designed by Christopher Wren, was used by a local baker, Mr Rich, as the inspiration for the bridal cake design that we now take for granted – St Bride's didn't get its name from the cake, the cake design copied the church and Rich became very rich indeed as a result of his new cake which, as we all know, survives to this day.

The remains of seven previous churches have been found during excavations at St Bride's and among more recent monuments are two that are very special indeed. On a wall close to the font there is a small memorial to Virginia Dare, whose claim to fame is that she was the first English child to be born in America. There is also a memorial – an unusually light-hearted one – to the man who built the church. We don't know the name of the author but it begins:

> Clever men like Christopher Wren
> Only occur just now and then.
> No one expects

In perpetuity
Architects of his ingenuity.
No – never a cleverer dipped his pen
Than clever Sir Christopher, Christopher Wren.

HOW THE ROYAL MISTRESS GOT HER WAY

1675

The history of political scandal in Britain is the history of sexual intrigue. What a man won't do for patriotic or even financial reasons he will often do for his mistress and that simple fact explains a very odd historical circumstance concerning one of London's most famous streets.

Pall Mall, that street which runs from St James's Palace to Trafalgar Square, is also one of the most historic in London. Today, the area is almost entirely offices and clubs, but it was once one of London's most fashionable addresses and through the bizarre workings of royal patronage and favour it contains a unique building – Number 79. This is the only building in the whole street where the freehold is not owned by the Crown. And the reason? The original house on the site is long gone, but it was once owned by Charles II's favourite mistress, Nell Gwynn.

When Charles offered to find her a house near his own home – St James's Palace – he discovered that No. 79 was free and he simply gave her a long lease and thought no more about it. However, the gift of the lease did not make Ms Gwynn happy. She refused to move into the house on the grounds, as she apparently put it, that she had 'always conveyed free under the crown and always would'. In other words unless she had the freehold the deal – and probably much besides – was off. Charles knew when he was beaten and arranged to have the freehold given to Nell. When she died, her son the Duke of St Albans inherited the freehold and it was sold later to pay off his debts. Its freehold has been bought and sold ever since and never returned to the Crown.

THE ULTIMATE CELEBRITY STREET

1675

One of the most interesting thoroughfares in London is Buckingham Street – a short street of late seventeenth- and early eighteenth-century houses that runs up from the Embankment towards the Strand and a little to the east of Charing Cross Station.

The houses are modest and one or two have been rebuilt but this short street can lay claim to having housed more celebrities than any other comparable street in London.

When London's first great speculative builder – the first modern developer – Nicholas Barbon (1640–1698) bought the land at the end of the seventeenth century he immediately began building the sort of houses that would appeal to the fashionable. Most were complete by 1675.

Number 10 Buckingham Street was once the home of David Hume (1711–1776), the brilliant Scottish philosopher and father of the Enlightenment. Later on the house was lived in by the famous postimpressionist painter Henri Rousseau (1844–1910). Diarist Samuel Pepys (1633–1703) lived both at number 12 and at number 14. Number 12 was later occupied by Queen Anne's Lord Treasurer Robert Harley (1661–1724), who invited Jonathan Swift (1644–1718) and William Penn (1667–1745) (of Pennsylvania fame) to dine with him. Two painters lived in the house at different times – William Etty (1787–1849) and Clarkson Stanfield (1793–1867). The scientist Humphrey Davy (1778–1829) carried out some of his most important experiments in the cellar! Peg Woffington (1720–1760), a celebrated beauty and one of the greatest eighteenth-century actresses, lived at number 9. The Russian Peter the Great (1672–1725) stayed for a while at number 15, while Henry Fielding (1707–1754), the creator of *Tom Jones*, lived here too, as did – a century later – Charles Dickens (1812–1870). Samuel Taylor Coleridge (1772–1834) lived at number 21. Most bizarrely of all, Napoleon Bonaparte (1769–1821) stayed in a house in the street – exactly which one is disputed – for a short period during 1791.

A QUACK ON TOWER HILL

1680

The court of Charles II was probably the most debauched English court in history. This probably had a great deal to do with Charles's years of exile in France. The French, then as now, were little concerned if their king had a wife and a dozen or more mistresses – France after all was the country where the extraordinary feudal system of *droit de seigneur* held sway in rural districts. This bizarre tradition meant that the local lord of the manor could sleep with any newly wed peasant woman on the first night she was married if he chose to do so. The husband could do nothing but acquiesce.

The rather puritanical English were suspicious of Charles, who was addicted to pleasure and cared almost nothing for affairs of state. He also gathered round him a bizarre group of madmen and eccentrics and none was madder or more eccentric than John Wilmot, Earl of Rochester (1647–1680).

Writing about Rochester half a century later, the great lexicographer Samuel Johnson (1709–1784) wrote: 'In a course of drunken gaiety and gross sensuality, with intervals of study perhaps yet more criminal, with an avowed contempt of decency and order, a total disregard to every moral, and a resolute denial of every religious observation, he lived worthless and useless, and blazed out his youth and health in lavish voluptuousness.'

What Johnson leaves out of the portrait is that Rochester was extremely witty and amusing – qualities the king admired above

81

all others and which may explain why Charles forgave Rochester repeatedly for his rudeness, pranks and dishonesties. On one crackpot escapade Rochester pretended to be one Dr Bendo. He set up his stall on Tower Hill and for weeks sold thousands of quack medicines to the London populace. When he was discovered the authorities were only just able to prevent rioting. On another occasion Rochester – an enormously talented poet – wrote of the king:

> Here sits our good and gracious king
> Whose word no man relies on
> Who never did a gracious thing
> Nor ever said a wise one.

Charles found Rochester so amusing that he even managed to forgive this cutting jibe although it did result in Rochester being banished to his house in the country for some months.

Rochester was very much Charles II's 'all licensed fool' and the bawdiness of his satirical verse was only matched by the sexually explicit nature of the London plays that Charles encouraged. Plays like *The Country Wife* by William Wycherley (1640–1716) were all about sexual intrigue; they were amoral and concerned only with wit, intelligence and the pleasures of sex. The extraordinary fact that they could be produced on the London stage at all was entirely down to the power of the king – after he died such plays were banned for a century and more.

Rochester finally went too far (though he died soon afterwards) when he wrote, again about the king:

> Nor are his high desires above his strength:
> His scepter and his prick are of a length;
> And she may sway the one who plays with th' other,
> And make him little wiser than his brother.

Rochester died aged just 33 in 1680, probably from syphilis. He knew that he was considered beyond the pale but made light of it in 'To the Postboy':

> 'Son of a whore, God damn you, can you tell
> A peerless peer the readiest way to Hell?'
> 'The readiest way, my Lord's by Rochester.'

A PITCHED BATTLE WITH THE LAWYERS

1684

Whatever one thinks about youngsters misbehaving today – whether they are fighting in the streets, getting drunk or stealing cars – we should remember that it was at least as bad, if not far worse, in medieval and later London.

Endless ordinances were issued against London apprentices who regularly fought pitched battles against each other – the problem was exacerbated by the intense rivalry between the various guilds who taught their mysteries (their crafts) to apprentices who signed up for a period of training in medicine, leather work or any of the many other trades on which London depended.

But the London mob, as it was known, was even more fearsome than the unruly apprentices. The mob rose whenever rumour ran through the city that foreigners were up to no good (foreigners were periodically attacked and sometimes even killed) but one of the most bizarre uprisings occurred in 1684 after Nicolas Barbon, the famous property developer, bought the land that is now covered by Red Lion Square a little to the north of Holborn.

Barbon had grown rich building houses for the newly emerging middle classes – tradesmen and sometimes minor aristocrats who needed to live in or near London but wanted a fashionable address. In earlier periods (unlike today) older houses were shunned in favour of modern new houses – a

84

complete reversal of the current situation where period houses invariably command a premium.

Problems arose when the lawyers of nearby Gray's Inn decided that the last thing they wanted was a new housing development on what was then open land to the west of their inn. Thinking the law would invariably side with them, the lawyers of Gray's Inn went to court to block Barbon's development but since, then as now, property was nine-tenths of the law, Barbon won. He won because he had bought the land fair and square.

But the lawyers refused to give up and when Barbon's workmen began digging the foundations of his new houses the lawyers, several hundred of them, ran out brandishing sticks and clubs and the workmen fled. The lawyers then filled in the trenches dug for the new houses and retreated to their Inn.

Refusing to be beaten, Barbon hired several dozen of London's nastiest thugs along with a new batch of workmen. He began work again on the foundations. His heavies hid under tarpaulins in the workmen's carts and when the lawyers rushed out again the toughs jumped out of the wagons and a running fight began that lasted for most of the morning.

The lawyers, being essentially desk johnnies, were no match for the professional toughs and Barbon won the day. The lawyers had to accept defeat and Red Lion Square was built. Only one or two houses – much altered – survive from Barbon's time.

THE FIELD OF THE FORTY STEPS

1687

Stories inevitably outlast the places and people that inspired them; sometimes the stories themselves seem to vanish only to be rediscovered by scholars working in obscure corners of history. In London there are many such stories and one of the most mysterious has its origins on the land behind the site of the British Museum.

This area is now covered over largely by Senate House and other University of London buildings, but when the museum was plain Montague House, the land where the university now stands was open fields that stretched away to the old Mary Le Bon Road and the hills beyond. But the fields by Montague House became legendary after a bizarre duel; a duel that made the fields famous through thousands of penny dreadfuls sold by itinerant ballad sellers all over London.

The duel was probably fought in 1687 by two brothers who were in love with the same girl. The girl sat on a grassy bank and watched the brothers as they fought to the death.

According to the legend no grass grew in the field after the brothers died and ghostly footprints – exactly forty in number – were regularly seen here for decades afterwards.

A MOUSETRAP ON THE HEAD

1690

Until the 1980s there was still a strange little jewellery shop tucked away in a corner of one of the ancient Inns of Court. The shop, known as the Silver Mousetrap, had traded continually from these premises since 1690, but if the survival of a shop that long in London is remarkable then the origin of the shop's name is even more noteworthy.

The name dates back to a time when rich fashionable women would spend a day or two having their hair turned into an extraordinary sculpture. First the hair would be piled as high as possible – perhaps with the addition of artificial hair – and then plaster birds might be added to make it look as if birds were nesting in the hair and perhaps a small carved ship or a tree or simply a mass of artificial flowers. Occasionally a mix of all these things and more would be built into the structure of the hair, which was stiffened with flour, chalk dust or arsenic powder.

The problem with these fabulous creations is that they took so long to make that they had to be slept in for weeks at a time and until the style was changed the hair could not be washed. This led to a serious problem with mice.

Today, when we have a range of sophisticated chemicals to control mice and other pests, it is difficult to imagine what it was like when there were no really effective ways to control mice, rats, bedbugs and fleas – beds were routinely infested with bugs until the twentieth century and houses collapsed when wood-boring insects had done their work for long enough; walls and ceiling voids were commonly filled with mice which people tended to ignore, since the business of trying to remove or kill them was simply impossible. Even if it had been possible to eliminate a particular infestation newcomers would soon move in to take their place.

When a woman of fashion slept with her enormous head of firmly fixed hair mice invariably found their way into it, and even for a population that had learned to put up with the presence of various rodents this was too much.

For a woman embarrassed at the prospect of a mouse popping out of her hair during lunch or supper there was only one solution. A trip to The Silver Mousetrap, where elegant ladylike mousetraps made in silver were available. Having bought two or three of these things the woman of fashion, on retiring for the night, would place them strategically around her head. If the mice came out while she slept they would with any luck be caught in one or other of the traps. Users were warned not to roll about too much in their sleep lest an unwary nose or ear set off one of the traps!

WHEN PRISON MARRIAGES WERE ALL THE RAGE

1696

It is hard to believe now but 15 per cent of all marriages conducted in Britain during most of the late seventeenth and early eighteenth centuries were actually conducted in London's Fleet Prison, or more precisely in what were known as the Rules of the Fleet – an area bounded roughly by Fleet Lane, the Old Bailey, Farringdon Street and Ludgate Hill.

Today almost none of the maze of alleys and courtyards that once existed here survive. But in the eighteenth century the mass of cheap lodging houses within the Rules of the Fleet provided homes for Fleet prisoners who'd been given special privileges.

The Fleet was a debtors' prison but, under the strange rules that dated back to medieval times, debtors who provided suitable security were let out of the prison itself on the understanding that they would not leave the Rules of the Fleet. Here they could live and carry on their jobs and professions until such time as their debts had been paid and they were released. But within the Rules imprisoned clergymen (and there were a surprisingly large number of imprisoned clergymen) were permitted to conduct entirely legal marriages.

The first Fleet marriage of which records survive took place in 1613 but by the late seventeenth century an odd ecclesiastical law meant that there was an explosion in the number of marriages carried out in the Fleet.

In 1696 the law changed so that clergymen who married couples without first declaring the banns were prosecuted – as they were beneficed clergymen they might lose their livings. Clergymen in the Fleet were by definition unbeneficed (i.e. they had no parishes) and could not therefore be prosecuted as the law specifically referred to beneficed clergymen, so anyone who wanted to marry without their parents' permission could do so only at the Fleet.

Couples arrived in their hundreds and then thousands and there was little the authorities could do. Some have argued that the authorities deliberately left this loophole open to reduce the number of illicit relationships.

As well as within the prison itself, Fleet marriages took place in coffee houses, lodging rooms and shops of all kinds (from booksellers to bakers). What's more, it was possible to be married at any time of the day or night, seven days a week throughout the year – the Fleet in early eighteenth-century London had the sort of reputation for marriages that Las Vegas has today.

More than two hundred and fifty thousand couples are recorded as marrying in the Fleet before the rules changed and the prison was demolished – some of the marriages were no doubt forced or fraudulent but many couples' motives were entirely honourable. They were merely attracted by the speed and relative cheapness of a Fleet marriage.

THE BOARD OF THE GREEN CLOTH

1698

After a disastrous fire in 1698 that almost completely destroyed the old Palace of Westminster, the monarch and his courtiers moved away, never to return. The Palace – more a collection of haphazard buildings – had covered all the ground from Westminster Hall, which survived the fire, to well beyond the Banqueting House, the only other major part of the old palace that survived the fire.

In other words the old palace covered much of the road still known as Whitehall today as well as all the land running from it down to the river.

Because it was home to the king and his court this area was treated as rather special in every respect and this has led to one of London's strangest survivals – a government body known as the Board of Green Cloth.

Named after the cloth covering over the table at which it met, the Board of Green Cloth was set up while the court was still at Whitehall and before the fire with the express purpose of licensing pubs, theatres and other places of entertainment within what was known in seventeenth-century England as the Verge of the Court. This meant anywhere within the Palace of Whitehall precincts – and remember taverns could be set up within the precincts of the palace as it was more like a village spread over a wide area than a palace in the sense we understand that term today. But the Verge of the Court also included the area around Whitehall extending well beyond the limits of the palace – but precisely how much of this outside area was defined as being within the Verge of the Court has never really been established.

The strangest thing about the Board of the Green Cloth is that it still exists and if you apply for a licence for a pub or theatre within the area of its ancient jurisdiction you will still, even today, have to prove to the board that you are a fit person to work within the bounds of a court that vanished more than three centuries ago.

PIG FAT AND FACE POWDER

1700

Among the dottiest people who ever lived in London was Lady Lewson, famed throughout the middle decades of the eighteenth century for her bizarre lifestyle.

Records suggest she was born in 1700 or perhaps 1701 in Essex Street just north of the Strand. Mrs Lewson – or Lady Lewson as she was afterwards known – married a rich elderly merchant when she was just nineteen and moved to his house at Clerkenwell, then a quiet village on the edge of London.

Her husband died when she was only twenty-six, but from that time until her death in about 1800, she hardly ever left the house. Every day she made sure all the beds in the house were made up, although no one ever came to stay. She was highly superstitious: in over sixty years she never cleaned a window in the house, fearing they would be broken in the process or that the person cleaning them might be injured. And she refused to allow anything to be moved in any room, believing that it might make her catch cold.

In summer she was sometimes seen reading in her garden in attire which would have been far more appropriate to the fashion of about 1690, with 'ruffs and cuffs and fardingales', and she always wore her hair powdered and piled high on her head over a stiff horsehair frame.

She believed washing was highly dangerous and would lead to some 'dreadful disorder'. Instead she smeared her face and neck with pig's fat, on top of which she applied a liberal quantity of pink powder.

When Lady Lewson died it was the talk of London – her house was opened up to mourners and the curious who found a time capsule unchanged in more than seventy years.

SHORT TEMPER, EXTRAVAGANT HABITS

1705

Wealth and position have always allowed the rich to be madder and more eccentric than the rest of us, but even by the standards of a very eccentric age Charles Mordaunt, Earl of Peterborough (1658–1735), stood head and shoulders over other London eccentrics.

He claimed he had murdered three people and got away with it before he was twenty and whether or not this had more to do with bravado than truth, it is certainly true that he was one of the greatest rakes and libertines of the second half of the seventeenth century; a man of short temper, extravagant habits and utter ruthlessness.

He inherited his title in early middle age but was furious when he discovered that the title came with no money.

He joined the army and it was quickly discovered that he had absolutely no regard whatsoever for his own safety – a fact which made him one of the strangest, and bravest, soldiers in British history.

Stories of his bizarre behaviour and eccentricities are legion, but among the more inexplicable of his actions was the incident that occurred in Covent Garden in the summer of 1682. He leaped from his coach on seeing a man dressed in brightly coloured clothes. Mordaunt chased the poor man down the street, prodding him with his sword until he fell over into the mud. Satisfied, Mordaunt climbed back into his coach and sent

95

the man he'd assaulted a large sum of money the next day.

He spent his youth chasing young unmarried woman and much older married women ('Catch 'em at both ends,' he used to shout) and though rumour had it that he was never particularly successful (largely because he was short and very ugly), what he lacked in charm he made up for in imagination.

Once, in middle age and long after he'd become one of Britain's best-known soldiers, he fell in love with a miller's daughter while walking in the country. To get close to her he visited her father's mill the next day wearing workman's clothing and claiming to be called Richard Copp. He became the miller's apprentice, paying heavily for the privilege. But the miller's daughter took absolutely no notice of him – he then discovered she was engaged to someone else anyway.

For reasons that will never make sense, the Duke of Marlborough – a relative of Mordaunt's – gave him command of the army sent to Spain to take part in the War of the Spanish Succession (1700–1714) – and this despite the fact that Mordaunt had absolutely no qualifications of any kind as a soldier. As luck would have it, he turned out to be a military mastermind.

His first great success came at Barcelona where a long siege by the British had ended in stalemate. The problem was that Mordaunt had only a few thousand men where he probably needed at least 30,000. Racking his brains he decided that he'd better raise the siege – Barcelona's militia, seeing the enemy troops marching away, relaxed their guard and immediately Mordaunt ordered his men to turn round and attack – somehow the city's defences were breached and with just 1,500 men Mordaunt had soon taken the city. Back in England he was immediately hailed as a genius.

Mordaunt's great secret was that he was a maverick – on another occasion he heard that his troops were getting nervous about an impending attack and immediately leaped down from his horse, grabbed a pike and joined them in the ranks, an unheard of act for an aristocratic commander at that time.

He refused to stick to the rules which most commanders accepted. One of these was that the cavalry was always the cavalry and the infantry the infantry – Mordaunt made his cavalry dismount and attack as foot soldiers on one day and the next he'd insist they get back in the saddle to mount a completely different kind of attack.

As he moved across Spain no city seemed able to defend itself against him and legends about his invincibility grew – until he reached Madrid. Here Mordaunt came up with what he thought was a foolproof plan to take the city but his plan was dismissed as hopeless by Archduke Charles of Austria, the claimant to the Spanish throne who was supported by England, Holland and Germany. Monarchs – even stupid monarchs – always get their way and a furious Mordaunt instantly resigned and set off for an extended holiday in Italy.

Meanwhile Mordaunt's replacement – Lord Galway – thought that his military advantage was such that even an idiot could take Madrid. Within a few days of starting his carefully planned offensive he realised that it was not so easy after all – his army of 18,000 men had been utterly defeated and their weapons, baggage, animals and horses taken.

Mordaunt was delighted at the failure of his replacement, but by this time he'd been sent to Vienna by the British Government Vienna bored him and thereafter he found he simply could not stay in one place for long – over the next few years he continually dashed between Madrid, Copenhagen, Vienna and The Hague. The British Government began to suspect that he wanted the Spanish War of Succession to continue indefinitely because it gave him good reason for his continual travel at government expense.

Even in old age he was still rushing around like a lunatic – 'He is the most energetic man who ever lived,' said a friend. Then, in his late sixties and back in London, he married a penniless actress.

As he grew older Mordaunt became ever more eccentric – in old age he could be found doing his own shopping in a market at Parson's Green in West London dressed in his full lord's regalia. He eventually died from eating – it was said – too many grapes.

His wife, a former actress, discovered that Mordaunt had written his autobiography – it ran to more than three densely written volumes but in a fit of pique – or maybe she was just overzealous at tidying up – she threw it on the fire.

BURIED WITH HIS BOOKS

1705

London has always bred eccentrics. There is something in the freedom and anonymity the City provides that allows obscure enthusiasms to develop unhindered by the pressure to conform – the sort of pressure that might far more easily be brought to bear in some remote and isolated village.

Among the less well known of London's oddball characters is William Edward Chamberlayne. Born in 1616 in Gloucestershire he came to London as a young man. He made his fortune and began to devote more and more time to studying the past – his fame as an antiquarian and author (he wrote a number of books about ancient Rome) spread. When he died in 1705 few were surprised to discover a strange request in his will. He ordered that his heirs would not receive a penny if they failed to ensure that he was buried with all his favourite books, each volume carefully preserved in wax before the interment. The wax was designed to protect the books from the ravages of damp six feet under ground and in his will Chamberlayne explains that he is looking forward to continuing to enjoy his books in another life.

Today the memorial stone to this strange but rather endearing man can be seen in the churchyard of Chelsea old church. Sadly the large slab has been so weathered by the elements that it is difficult to decipher now, but enough remains to tell the story of this eccentric bibliophile.

THE CANDLE-STUB SELLER

1707

Very few of London's shops last more than a century, but at least one is far older than that and the story of its origins is both strange and fascinating. Most shops survive by adapting and constantly modernising but Fortnum and Mason has in many ways done just the opposite.

One of the last of London's truly old-fashioned stores, Fortnum's still insists that the staff in its wine shop should wear frock coats.

The shop's origins lie in the friendship between William Fortnum, a footman in the royal household, and Hugh Mason, a shopkeeper. As a footman to Queen Anne, one of Fortnum's jobs was to ensure that the candles in the palace candelabra were regularly replaced. He was allowed the stumps of the old candles and sold these on – candles were very expensive in the eighteenth century and William did a roaring trade with his candle-stump business, though the stumps were mostly sold to the very poor.

Over the years he spent working in the royal household at St James's Palace, William learned just how a big house was run, so when he retired he suggested to his friend John Mason that they set up a shop together supplying the nearby palace and the gentry right across Mayfair and Piccadilly.

The shop, opened near the premises it still occupies today, did so well that the two men quickly expanded the business and bought a big team of horses and carts for deliveries.

By the beginning of the nineteenth century Fortnum and Mason were famous for importing a vast range of wonderfully exotic foods – many never seen before in England – from the East, largely through the East India Company which was expanding rapidly at that time.

Explorers and generals took Fortnum's potted meats and other foods with them and soon the shop's hampers were being sent all over the world – Queen Victoria famously sent a huge Fortnum's vat of beef tea to Florence Nightingale (1820–1910) in the Crimea and the explorer William Parry (1790–1855) set off in search of the North West Passage in 1819 with a casket of more than two hundredweight of Fortnum and Mason cocoa powder!

Sadly Fortnum and Mason's beautiful old shop was rebuilt in the 1920s, but an elaborate clock made in the 1960s and fitted to the Piccadilly front of the store commemorates its Georgian origins. It shows the figures of Mr Fortnum and Mr Mason and when the clock strikes the hour the two figures step out and bow to each other. The figure in the red coat is Fortnum – red being the colour of the dress of footmen of the royal household.

Traditions in the shop also hark back two centuries and more – the man in charge of the bakery, for example, is known even today as the 'Groom of the Pastry'.

ST MARY IN THE ROADWAY

1712

Tourists are often baffled when they visit the Church of St Mary Le Strand. Why on earth, they ask, is this church built right in the middle of the roadway? The answer is that when the church was first built traffic flowed easily around it because the Strand was a mere lane with only light horse and foot traffic going steadily between Charing Cross and Westminster to the west and the City and Ludgate Hill to the east. Indeed so quiet was the street that until the middle decades of the nineteenth century St Mary Le Strand still had a graveyard, but it was so small that every inch of ground down to a depth of eight feet was filled with bodies. Between 1830 and 1840 so many extra bodies were being placed in the ground each week that the church officials ran out of room and rotting bodies and coffins were left piled up above ground. The situation reached crisis point because the Thames had become so polluted by this time that there were repeated cholera outbreaks. Large numbers died – but the old tradition was that people who lived in a specific area or parish had to be buried in their parish church (an absurd situation given London's vast population) so those who lived near St Mary Le Strand had to be buried in its churchyard even though there was no longer any room.

By the late 1840s the government decided that enough was enough and they cleared the graves and widened the road to leave the church as we see it today, but having cleared the ground outside the church the authorities made another extraordinary discovery – in the sealed vaults beneath the church and stretching out under the old graveyard there were hundreds of bodies no one had expected to find. In fact, there were so many that when the vault walls were breached so much gas escaped – gas from centuries of decomposing bodies – that the whole area had to be cordoned off for several weeks to allow the lethal fumes to escape.

Many other strange tales swirl around St Mary Le Strand – the world's first cab rank was set up here in 1625 just in front of the church, for example, and when the present building was erected during Queen Anne's reign there was an extraordinary plan to build a vast monument to her. The planned column was to be the tallest in London at two hundred and fifty feet, but when Anne died in 1714 the idea was quietly shelved.

Perhaps most bizarre of all is the fact that the original church on the site – built in the twelfth century – was stolen stone by stone by Lord Protector Somerset in 1548. Somerset was so keen that his new palace (on the site of the present eighteenth-century Somerset House) should be lavish that he also demolished a chapel at St Paul's and a large part of the priory of St John at Clerkenwell. He needed building materials for his new palace and simply helped himself – even the church was not powerful enough to stop him. But the church had its revenge. In 1551 he fell from grace and was executed on Tower Hill in 1552.

The present church was built for Anglican worship but visitors always remark on the fact that it has the sumptuousness and style of a Roman Catholic church – the explanation for this is that James Gibbs (1682–1754), the architect, was a secret Catholic who before taking up architecture as a profession had trained for the priesthood. When the church commissioned St Mary's they no doubt welcomed the lavish design but had no idea about of the architect's secret allegiances.

DOG LATIN

1715

Nothing better illustrates the British obsession with religion than the decision of the English Parliament in 1689 to ask the Dutch Prince William of Orange (1650–1702) – who couldn't speak a word of English and was eccentric to the point of lunacy – to come to London and become King of England.

The job of monarch had become vacant after James II – favoured with an equally eccentric ancestry – fled the country because Parliament didn't like his obsession with Catholicism. The two men were closely related – they also shared the not overly attractive characteristic of short, thin, rickety legs – and their histories reveal how Parliament's strength and importance had increased since Charles I was beheaded in Whitehall in 1649.

The king's duty now was to behave in ways that suited Parliament not, as in previous centuries, the other way round and so to some extent all that was needed was a compliant king who didn't spend too much money. The fact that William of Orange didn't speak a word of English may well in this respect have been one of his greatest virtues, but it did lead to at least one bizarre circumstance.

The Act of Settlement of 1701, which made it impossible for a Catholic to become King or Queen of England, hit a few problems when the childless Queen Anne died in 1714 so yet another German Prince was invited over, his sole qualification once again being that he could not speak English.

Dog Latin

George's I's Prime Minister Sir Robert Walpole (1676–1745) did not speak a word of German, but protocol demanded that the two men meet regularly to discuss affairs of state. The only way they could do it was to speak to each other in Latin. Both had a smattering of the language but communication was poor – so much so that the two men often left their meetings convinced they had discussed entirely different subjects!

A BANK WITH A WOOLLY MAMMOTH

1717

On the south side of Trafalgar Square close to Admiralty Arch are the London premises of Drummonds Bank, one of the oldest banks in the world. Although Drummonds is now part of the Royal Bank of Scotland it kept its own traditions largely intact until well into the 1970s.

The bank has been here since 1717, but when it started few would have guessed that it would still be in business two centuries later. In fact at the outset it looked as if the bank would barely last a year – the main problem was that Andrew Drummond, who founded the bank, was a Scotsman and the Scots were not at all popular in London in 1717, just two years after the Jacobite Rebellion. The London Scots, including Drummonds, survived an initial period of discrimination only to hit further serious problems in 1745 when another Jacobite Rising led to dozens of prominent English merchants and aristocrats withdrawing their money from Drummonds. However, word got about in London that Drummond was in trouble through no fault of his own and hundreds of Scotsmen who had previously banked elsewhere or did not use a bank at all moved their money to Drummonds as a sign of solidarity. The boost was enough to transform Drummonds and keep them going well into the twentieth century, despite numerous banking crises over the years.

Right up until the 1970s anyone who entered the Admiralty Arch branch would have felt as if they were stepping back at least a century – a longcase clock ticked quietly in the entrance hall, Victorian and earlier furniture stood sedately here and there and the grand central table always offered customers a range of quill pens. These were carefully sharpened each week by a member of staff.

For reasons now lost in the mists of history, Drummonds also once housed a museum of fossils discovered in Trafalgar Square. If you arrived a little early for your meeting with the bank manager it was customary to ask an attendant if it might be possible to look at the museum. You were then led through a door into a room that housed a prehistoric lion, a rhinoceros and a woolly mammoth!

THE CHURCH THAT WENT
TO AMERICA

1724

The early churches of New England and indeed right across America are much admired for the simple elegance of their design, but it is a little-known fact that their design is based almost entirely on the design of London's St Martin in the Fields.

What sounds like a delightfully eccentric name today refers to the fact that when the church was completed in 1724 it stood in agricultural land on the edge of the village of Charing – in other words it really was in the fields rather than in the town.

But the design of St Martin's shocked the citizens of London because however traditional it may now look it was revolutionary in eighteenth-century eyes. Until St Martin's was built it was accepted practice to place the steeple at the east end of the church not the west end, but architect James Gibbs (1682–1754) decided to turn the thing on its head and build the steeple where we see it today. He also built it above an imposing portico that looks like the grand entrance to an ancient temple.

Critics and architects marvelled at the audaciousness of the new church and despite the innate conservatism of churchgoers and the church authorities the new design soon became very popular – so much so that several members of Gibbs's architectural practice were enticed to America by the offer of large sums of money. With the design of St Martin's packed in their saddle bags they moved west as the American settlers moved west, building identical or near identical copies of St Martin's as they went.

THE MEANEST MAN IN SOUTHWARK

1730

Many men and women become obsessed with making and keeping money but few allow their passion for cash to take over their whole lives.

An exception to that rule was John Elwes, who was born in about 1730 into a family of notorious misers. Elwes became so famous for his penny-pinching ways that after his death dozens of books, pamphlets and broadsheets were published detailing his extraordinary career.

The Elwes family had lived in Southwark for generations. They made their money – and they were vastly wealthy – from brewing, yet John Elwes's mother is said to have died from malnutrition.

Although John was by all accounts an exceptionally bright child, he rarely opened a book after leaving school; in fact as the desire to make money grew he gave up everything else, including riding, which had been a passion in his youth.

In his twenties he began to visit his uncle, Sir Harvey Elwes, but he always changed into rags before he reached the house, so terrified was he that his uncle, a famous miser, would be offended at his decent clothes and disinherit him.

Later, when he himself was bitten by the miser's bug, he refused to educate his own sons because he thought it would give them grand ideas about spending money rather than keeping it.

The two men, uncle and nephew, would sit by a fire made with one stick and completely in the dark, sharing a glass of wine until bedtime; they would then creep upstairs, still in the dark, to save the cost of a candle.

When he came into his inheritance John became fanatically stingy. He would walk from one end of London to the other in the heaviest rain rather than part with sixpence for a coach; he ate maggot-infested meat; he would never light a fire to dry his clothes; he wore a wig that had been thrown into a ditch by a beggar, and a coat that had gone green with age – it had belonged to a long-dead ancestor and had been found blocking a hole in the wall of the house. When he rode to London – he was an MP for more than ten years – he would always carry an egg or two in his pocket and sleep in a hedge rather than pay the cost of lodgings, and he always rode his horse on the grass verge instead of on the road for fear that his horse's shoes would wear out too quickly. He owned houses all over London as well as an estate in Suffolk, but took a few pieces of furniture with him each time he travelled about rather than furnish each house.

Yet in spite of this parsimony he rarely collected a gambling debt if it was owed to him by someone he liked, and he was himself a very keen gambler, parting with thousands at a go when the mood took him. He could also be enormously generous and considerate; for example, he once rode sixty miles to help two elderly spinsters threatened by an ecclesiastical court. He died in 1789 at the age of fifty-nine and was buried in the graveyard at Southwark Cathedral. He left more than three-quarters of a million pounds to his two sons.

CASTRATED SINGERS

1735

The German composer George Frederick Handel (1685–1759) was in many ways far more English than German. He lived in London from 1710 until his death in 1759 and he was central to one of the most bizarre traditions in the history of music.

In the early decades of the eighteenth century London had begun to rival the great continual centres of music across Europe. This had a much to do with London's sheer physical size but also its increasingly dominant role as a financial centre, a role it retains to this day. In 1713 the musician Johann Mattheson wrote: 'In these times, whoever wishes to be eminent in music goes to England. In Italy and France there is something to be heard and learned; in England something to be earned.'

Handel clearly appreciated this and his music, from *Zadok the Priest* – still sung at every crowning of a new British monarch – to the celebrated *Water Music* was hugely popular; so much so that he was awarded a pension of £200 a year while still in his thirties.

But central to music in London as elsewhere at this time were the castrati – men who had been castrated in their early teens to ensure that their voices never broke. Thousands of boys from poor backgrounds – mostly Italian – were castrated but only a few made it to the top of the castrati singing profession. Castration alone would not ensure that a great boy soprano voice would turn into a great castrato voice. But in London the castrati

112

who retained their magnificent voices were lionised. Handel wrote mostly for seven world-famous castrati: Bernacchi, Senesino, Nicolini, Carestini, Caffarelli, Conti and Guasagni.

The castrati were idolised wherever they went – women swooned when they heard their extraordinary voices and the singers were famous – rather like modern rock stars – for being temperamental. They were paid vast amounts and behaved appallingly.

Working from his house in Brook Street – the house is now the Handel Museum – the great composer one day received a note from a visiting castrato saying he did not like the piece Handel had written for him. Handel, who was one of the few composers not prepared to put up with temperamental singers (partly because he was so temperamental himself!), sent a note to the singer's lodgings saying, 'You dog! You think you know better than I do what is best for you to sing? If you don't sing it I won't pay you.'

The singer – probably Senesino – changed his mind, sang the piece and was cheered to the rafters.

On another occasion Handel threatened to throw a castrato out of the first-floor window of his house in Brook Street!

Whatever we might think today no one in the eighteenth century thought it was a bad thing to castrate a boy in order to protect and enhance his voice. Hormonal imbalances caused by castration often made a castrato look as well as sound rather odd – Senesino was extremely tall but with a tiny head, for example – but he was still adored by his fans.

But how were boys castrated? Well, if a boy was considered to have potential he was given opium or alcohol and then made to relax in a bath of hot water. The carotid artery in his neck might also be depressed to induce unconsciousness – then the *norcini* – a specialist physician who only carried out this particular operation – would slice through the ducts leading to the boy's testes, preventing him ever reaching puberty.

But what did the voice sound like? Apparently its unique ability to move came from the delicacy of the boy soprano voice combined with the power of adult lungs.

113

Curiously many of the most successful modern pop stars, such as Chris Martin from Coldplay and Tom Chaplin from Keane, use the highest register of their natural tenor voices to create songs that are particularly emotionally intense. The effect is without question reminiscent of the castrato voice.

Astonishingly the practice of castrating boys was not made illegal in Italy until 1870 and our direct knowledge of what the voice sounded like comes from a single sad recording of the last known castrato. Allessandro Moreschi made the wax cylinder recording in London in 1902 a few years before his death. It can still be heard by special request at the British Library in London's Euston Road.

GOING TO KNIGHTSBRIDGE BY BOAT

1736

The Serpentine Lake in Hyde Park is one of London's best-known landmarks. It has an unusual history in that it was originally not a lake at all but a stretch of one of London's many small rivers, each a tributary of the Thames.

Just outside the western wall of the old City of London was the Fleet River, which ran down what is now Farringdon Street through Ludgate Circus and thence into the Thames. Further west, but again running north–south, the Tyburn flowed down what is now Edgware Road on through Victoria and parallel with Vauxhall Bridge Road before reaching the Thames.

The Westbourne flowed from Hampstead Heath down through west London and across Hyde Park, down modern Sloane Street and across Sloane Square before reaching the Thames just to the east of Christopher Wren's magnificent Chelsea Hospital.

It was Charlotte, George II's queen, who decided that Hyde Park needed a great lake. The park itself had been the property of the Crown since Henry VIII took it from the monks of Westminster in 1536 (the monks had in their turn no doubt taken it from someone else) to use as a hunting ground. The public at this time were strictly forbidden to enter the park.

Early in the seventeenth century James I allowed limited access to the park but only for the nobility and aristocracy. Charles I opened the park to the public in 1637 and created

The Ring – the sandy road that allowed the fashionable for the next three centuries to parade and be seen on foot and on horseback and in their carriages.

Queen Charlotte decided the lake would make the park far more attractive so the River Westbourne was dammed and excavations began to produce the splendid stretch of water we see today.

But the first phase of the work left the River Westbourne flowing above ground as a way to control the level in the lake. In 1736 a massive flood led to the Westbourne bursting its banks and the whole of the area south of the Serpentine down through the Albert Gate, through Knightsbridge and Belgravia was under several feet of water for weeks. The Thames watermen made the most of an opportunity and rowed sightseers from Chelsea up to Knightsbridge and beyond. At this time most of the roads around London were impassable to wheeled vehicles for most of the year anyway so the sudden appearance of extra water for boat travel – always the preferred mode of transport for Londoners – made Hyde Park far more popular than it would otherwise have been.

MAD MAYFAIR MARRIAGES

1742

Mayfair was once a rather sleazy area and certainly nothing like the millionaires' quarter it has now become. Something of its less salubrious past can be discovered in Shepherd Market where prostitutes still ply their trade, but more or less exclusively for the well to do.

But Mayfair was also once home to one of London's strangest churches. Until the Marriage Act of 1754, the Mayfair chapel was a continual thorn in the side of the authorities – it was here that the eccentric clergyman the Reverend Alexander Keith conducted marriage ceremonies for anyone who turned up at any time of day or night and absolutely no questions asked.

For the church and secular authorities of the eighteenth century, churchmen just didn't do this sort of thing, but if the clergyman was properly ordained there was very little anyone could do to stop it.

For young runaways and the romantically inclined in an age when marriages were largely a matter of convenience, financial or otherwise, the Mayfair chapel was a godsend.

The authorities hated it because it represented a threat to the financial and dynastic plans they had for their own offspring, but Alexander Keith knew the law and he was perfectly entitled to do what he was doing.

The popularity of the Mayfair chapel can be judged by the fact that in just one year – 1742 – he married no fewer than 700 couples – and all with neither licence nor banns.

Parliament launched several attempts to change the law to make these marriages illegal but they immediately abandoned the attempt when they realised – the Lords particularly – that to do so would be to make many of their own nephews, nieces and grandchildren illegitimate.

Among the most famous marriages conducted at the Mayfair chapel was that between the Duke of Hamilton and Elizabeth Dunning, one of the great beauties of Georgian England. The couple were in such a hurry that an old brass washer had to be used in place of a gold band.

AIR BATHING IN CRAVEN STREET

1757

It's a little-known fact that Benjamin Franklin (1706–1790), one of the four men who signed the American Declaration of Independence, lived for 16 years in a crooked little terraced house in Craven Street, a street that, before the building of the Embankment in the 1860s, ran down to the mud banks of the River Thames.

Craven Street survived the building of the Embankment – which effectively pushed the river back two hundred yards – as well as the building of Charing Cross Station, the German bombs of the Second World War and the obsession with redevelopment in the 1960s. Virtually all the houses in the street are eighteenth century although most have been over-restored to create office space.

No. 36, Franklin's old home, is one of the few to survive with its interior virtually intact – what we see today are the doors, chimneypieces and staircases once used by Franklin himself and it was here that Franklin pursued some of his more eccentric interests.

Franklin was a great friend of Erasmus Darwin (1731–1802), Matthew Boulton (1728–1809) and Josiah Wedgwood (1730–1795), all members of the Lunar Society, a Midlands-based dining club of industrialists and engineers who embraced every new invention of the late eighteenth century – the first great period of the Industrial Revolution.

119

Franklin was passionate about science long before he became passionate about American politics. He was also a noted eccentric and if you had wandered along Craven Street early in the eighteenth century on a summer's day you might easily have seen Franklin sitting in his downstairs drawing-room window completely naked!

He was a great believer in the medical benefits of what was then called 'Air bathing' – a form of recreation to which William Blake (1757–1827) was also partial in the garden of his house across the river in Lambeth.

Franklin was also fascinated by electricity, dentistry, chemistry and optics. Like his friends in the Birmingham factories he believed that science would lead to a better life for mankind. He was also keen on practical experiments. He was part of that group of inventors who organised public demonstrations of electricity by spinning a glass ball against a leather pad to produce a huge build-up of static. As one contemporary put it: 'Franklin is a lightning rod philosopher who goes to the Charterhouse School each week, catches a charity boy, strings him up on silk cords, rubs him with glass and extracts sparks from his nose.'

Franklin's other exploits included swimming in the Thames at Chelsea on his back while paring his nails. He did it just to prove it could be done and he also had a set of wooden false teeth made.

The great radical writer William Cobbett (1763–1835) disliked Franklin, describing him as 'That crafty and lecherous old hypocrite', but he was much loved by his Birmingham industrialist friends.

When his house in Craven Street was being restored in the 1990s a mass of human bones was found buried in the basement – at first the police suspected a serial killer but it turns out that Franklin lodged with William Hewson, a doctor who ran an anatomy school from the Craven Street house. The bones showed evidence of surgery – skulls had been trepanned, for example, and leg bones mended.

But whatever went on in this particular house we know there was a roaring trade in corpses in eighteenth-century London. The 'resurrection men', as those who stole bodies from graveyards were known, would have rowed to the river steps at the bottom of Craven Street before delivering their gruesome cargo – human bones from babies, teenagers, the middle aged and elderly were all found buried here. The other source of at least some of these bones would have been the gallows that then stood just behind the garden wall of No. 30.

While he lived at Craven Street, Franklin complained about the smoky fire in his rooms – the metal damper he invented to solve the problem still exists in the house.

Before the Embankment was built Craven Street ran down to the edge of the Thames and, like the Londoners of old, you can still take a boat from here to the Tower of London or to Greenwich. Famous residents included Henrich Heine (1797–1856), the German poet, and Grinling Gibbons (1648–1721), the great woodcarver. The author James Smith wrote a splendid satirical poem about the lawyers who were his neighbours in the street during the early nineteenth century:

> In Craven Street Strand, ten attorneys find place
> And ten dark coal barges are moored at its base.
> Fly honesty Fly, seek some safer retreat
> For there's craft in the river and craft in the street.

A poetical lawyer responded with the following verse:

> Why should honesty fly to some safer retreat
> From attorneys and barges god rot 'em
> For the lawyers are just at the top of the street
> And the barges are just at the bottom.

Benjamin Franklin's house – the scene of so many of these bizarre tales – is now open to the public having recently been beautifully restored.

THE COCKNEY COURTESAN WITH
A SWEET TOOTH

1760

The huge popularity of marzipan in Victorian England (it was far more popular than it is now) is entirely attributable to a cockney girl who became one of the best-known and most sought-after courtesans in Paris.

Born in Stepney in 1760, Eliza Marchpane grew up in abject poverty – with no schooling and no other way to earn a living her only option was to become a prostitute. She began by working the pubs along the notoriously dangerous Ratcliffe Highway, but she quickly realised that once her looks were gone her income would dry up.

She set off for Paris knowing nothing of the city or the language. How she lived after arriving we do not know but within a few years she was certainly known to the aristocracy – she dined regularly at the houses of the nobility under the assumed title Marquesa de Marchpane. Her cockney French simply made her sound exotic to the Parisian nobility, who admired her good looks and vivacity. In memoirs of the time she is described as extraordinarily attractive and her fame quickly spread far beyond Paris – she became the darling of the aristocracy in Vienna where she is said to have seduced the young Mozart.

Gifts of houses, jewellery and lavish clothing from her admirers had made her rich and when she returned to England in about 1800 she brought with her the recipe for an almond paste she had tasted first in Austria.

Her large house in the West End became a fashionable centre and at every party she gave there were always cakes and other sweets made from almond paste. Eliza ended her days in Brighton where she was for a time the lover of the Prince Regent, whose enormous girth no doubt had more to do with his love of Eliza's almond paste than with any affection he might have felt for her. She died in 1830.

HIGHLAND SOIL IN WESTMINSTER

1760

The British are notoriously eccentric and as a general rule it is probably pretty safe to say that the richer the individual the greater the eccentricity. One of the most eccentric London residents of all time has to be the eighteenth-century Earl of Fife. A staunch Jacobite who hated the repression of the Scots that followed their defeat at Culloden in 1745, he was determined to get the better of the English whenever he could.

But the Earl was in a tricky position – from 1760 on he found that he had to visit London regularly for business reasons and the easiest way to do this, then as now for the very rich, was to buy or build a house. But the Earl's motives were not entirely financial – he hated the idea of being in London at all and by building his own house he could avoid the horror of having to stay in an English hotel run by the hated English.

But even if he built his own house in London it would still be on English soil, which was anathema to the good Earl. His solution was to buy a plot of land on Horse Guards Avenue near Whitehall. He then arranged, at enormous expense, to have a merchant ship filled with Scottish soil and sailed down the coast and up the Thames to Whitehall Steps. From here the soil was carried up Whitehall in a series of carts and dumped on the Earl's new acre of ground. Once the detested English soil had been completely covered with far superior Scottish soil the Earl went ahead and built his new house.

Sadly not a trace of that house remains today; but since we have no evidence that the soil beneath the house was ever removed we must assume that the land here is still as Scottish as it was in 1760.

HOW LONDON GOT ITS PAVEMENTS

1761

Near the top of Whitehall, a hundred yards or so from Trafalgar Square where Nelson looks down from his column towards Westminster Abbey and the Houses of Parliament, there is a little-known alleyway.

Few Londoners ever bother with it, let alone visitors, but it has a history as rich and interesting as many of London's better-known landmarks.

Walking down from Trafalgar Square, Craig's Court is a narrow alley to the left. It runs into a small square or court where the façade of Harrington House, built in 1702 for the Earl of Harrington, still stands, though it has been remodelled over the centuries. The Earl built his house here just a few years after a huge fire destroyed the medieval palace of Whitehall.

Harrington was convinced that Whitehall Palace would be rebuilt, so it must have seemed logical that if his family lived right next to it – overlooking it in fact – they would be perfectly poised to visit the court every day and seek patronage. Patronage meant titles or jobs in the king's gift that entitled the holder to an income, but required little or no work of him. It was a system that, by the beginning of the nineteenth century, was known as Old Corruption, but in the mid-eighteenth century it was just the way things were done.

As it turned out, Harrington was wrong and the palace was never rebuilt, so he sat there in his huge house and with Parliament half a mile away at the other end of Whitehall.

A more curious tale than the history of the house is the history of the alleyway beside it, because this is where London's pavements began.

Until the mid-eighteenth century, London's streets had no pavements at all. In other words there was no physical distinction between that part of the roadway where wheeled vehicles travelled and that part where pedestrians walked. Whenever the cart and carriage drivers wanted to they would drive along the streets as near to the walls of the houses as they liked. This meant that going for a walk was a dangerous business, particularly when you remember that eighteenth-century London had far fewer wide streets than it does today. It also meant that in particularly narrow streets, carriages occasionally got stuck – quite literally – between the houses.

Kerbstones and pavements began to appear after the Speaker of the House of Commons, Mr Speaker Onslow, got stuck in Craig's Court after a visit to Harrington's house.

Parliament had long debated what to do about the narrow, dirty, dangerous streets of London, but they could never reach agreement about who should pay for improvements. Then one day early in the 1760s Onslow drove in his massive, stately carriage up Whitehall and into Craig's Court. At the narrowest part of the alleyway where it opens into the courtyard his carriage got stuck fast between the walls of the houses on either side. If there had been kerbstones and pavements the driver would have been stopped before he got stuck.

After fruitless attempts to extricate the carriage, a red-faced and by all accounts extremely angry Mr Speaker Onslow had to be extricated through a hole cut in the roof of the carriage.

He returned to Parliament on foot and when the next debate on the state of the streets was held he helped vote through a bill that compelled each householder in London to pay for a row of kerbstones in front of his or her house.

More early kerbstones can be seen if you retrace your steps down the narrow alleyway and out into Whitehall. If you cross the street and look at the kerbstones here (roughly in front of the 1930s theatre) you'll see several are marked with an arrow.

The mark was introduced by Elizabeth I to stop people stealing army and navy property and it is still used today. The pavement act of 1762 that made the Harringtons provide kerbstones in Craig's Court also obliged Admiralty officials to provide kerbstones outside their premises at the top of Whitehall. As they were Admiralty kerbstones they had to have the arrowhead mark which one or two retain to this day.

THE WORLD'S OLDEST HATMAKERS

1764

Two-thirds of the way down St James's towards the palace of the same name is a small ancient shop that seems to be out of keeping in its scale and appearance with every other building in the street. These are the premises of Locks, the world's oldest hatmakers, whose records conceal a wealth of odd tales about famous long-vanished Londoners.

Locks have been making hats in this part of London since the seventeenth century. Since 1764 when they moved a few yards along the street, they've been in the shop in St James's Street they currently occupy. Its interiors and fixtures have changed little – creaking timber shelves hold hats of all kinds and the shop still uses an extraordinary device – a conformator – to measure each client's head. The details of the head, including distinguishing lumps and bumps, are then kept on file so that new hats can be made to order even if the customer is on the other side of the world.

Locks have made hats for everyone from Nelson to Charlie Chaplin. Most famously they invented that iconic fashion statement of the late Victorian and early twentieth-century City of London – the bowler.

First made in about 1850, the bowler hat actually started life as a gamekeeper's hat – it was designed for the immensely wealthy Lord Coke of Norfolk whose gamekeepers were occasionally attacked by poachers. The bowler was, it seems, an early form of crash helmet to protect them from attack and presumably from an occasional plummeting pheasant!

How the bowler made the bizarre transition from the broad acres of rural Norfolk to the square mile is still a mystery, but from 1850 until 1950 and beyond it was the one fashion item no City worker would be without.

WHY ACTORS SAY 'BREAK A LEG!'

1766

The theatrical phrase 'break a leg!' – a good-luck wish before a performance – has its origins in a little-known but curiously endearing story from the Theatre Royal in the Haymarket.

When Samuel Foote (1720–1777) took over the running of the theatre in the second half of the eighteenth century he knew he was taking a risk because the theatre, then known as the Little Theatre, did not have a licence – theatre licences could only be granted by the King and the King resolutely refused to grant the Little Theatre a licence because a previous owner had published a number of pamphlets attacking the government and the Crown.

Foote was undaunted and attempted by every means to obtain the necessary royal warrant but all to no avail. He found a way round the problem temporarily by not charging those who came to see his plays. Audiences could get in free but Foote made up for what he failed to take at the door by charging hugely inflated prices for coffee and food during the intervals.

This infuriated the Crown and made it less likely that Foote would ever get the royal seal of approval, but a bizarre turn of events changed all that. The King's brother the Duke of York overheard Foote boasting about his horsemanship and challenged him to ride with him the following morning. Foote agreed but the Duke deliberately brought a horse that had never been ridden. Foot inevitably was thrown and badly injured – he broke a leg and spent weeks recovering. The Duke was stricken with remorse and to make up for what he had done he granted Foote the royal licence for which he had waited so long. It was 1766 and the Little Theatre in the Haymarket became the Theatre Royal, a title it has enjoyed uninterrupted ever since. The phrase 'break a leg' passed into the language – a sign that present disaster can quickly be transformed into future success.

BYRON GETS BURNED

1768

Albemarle Street just off Piccadilly was for more than two centuries the home of one of the world's most extraordinary publishers: John Murray, who came to London in 1768 to seek his fortune.

Born in 1739 he was originally John McMurray but dropped the Mc on coming to London after a number of years' service as a lieutenant in the marines. Murray's first office was in Fleet Street where, quite by chance, he took over No. 32, the site of Wynkyn de Word's printing press established in 1500. But within a few years he had moved to 50 Albemarle Street from which office, among a host of dazzling writers, the firm published David Hume, Byron, Jane Austen, Charles Darwin, Gladstone and Sir Arthur Conan Doyle.

By 2005 – some two hundred and thirty years later – the firm was still being run from this small house at 50 Albemarle Street, making it the oldest independent book publisher in the world. The original fireplaces were still here until the company was finally sold in 2003; the alcoves and odd corners remain in what is still in essence an eighteenth-century house.

Little had changed in more than two centuries by the time the company was sold and, most astonishing of all, the firm was always run by a John Murray – the last was the seventh direct male descendant of the founder.

It was only when the seventh John Murray's two sons (neither incidentally called John) decided they did not want to go into the family business that the firm was reluctantly sold to a huge multinational whose name – for the sake of decency – had probably better not be mentioned.

There are moves to make 50 Albemarle Street into a museum but in the meantime the company's archives – thousands of letters and other documents relating to its history and the host of famous authors it published – are likely to be sold, at the time of writing, for as much as £40 million. Most of the material has never been catalogued or seen.

Everything to do with John Murray is remarkable but most intriguing of all was a meeting that took place in 1824 in an upstairs room in front of a fireplace that is still there. John Murray the second met with the executors of Byron's estate shortly after the poet's death. They held in their hands two manuscript volumes of the great poet's diaries but they were so scandalised by the contents that they decided to throw them on the fire and thus was lost for ever what would have been one of the greatest literary treasures of the Romantic age. Perhaps, too, the publisher was getting his revenge on the poet who would often arrive in the office and while talking to Murray would practise his fencing by lunging at the various books around the room and tearing holes in them with his sword!

MODERN BRIDGE, MEDIEVAL MONEY

1769

Right across London numerous ancient and sometimes very obscure foundations and trusts run and maintain everything from schools to rowing competitions – some of these date back four or five hundred years and they are still administered in the way the original benefactor intended. One of the most delightful of all these ancient funds has had enormously beneficial consequences for Londoners and tourists alike.

For more than a thousand years the only river crossing downstream of Putney was London Bridge. But by the early eighteenth century London Bridge was so crammed with houses and shops that the narrow lane for pedestrians and horse carts that ran across it was a nightmare to negotiate.

Pressure began in Parliament for a new bridge to be provided and in 1750 Westminster Bridge was built, put up despite huge protests from the watermen who had plied their trade on the river since the Dark Ages and whose living was seriously threatened as each new bridge was built.

Westminster Bridge cost a fortune to build – there were regular complaints in Parliament about the money being spent on it – but it would have cost nothing if it had been within the city boundaries. The reason is that over the long centuries that London Bridge had been the only crossing, countless wealthy Londoners had left money in trust for its upkeep. This money had been shrewdly invested in property across the city and elsewhere. When Blackfriars Bridge was built in 1769 the cost was entirely covered by the Bridge House Estates – the fund that had been set up in 1209 to keep London Bridge in good repair. Astonishingly money from that fund is still used to maintain Blackfriars, Tower Bridge, Southwark Bridge and, of course, London Bridge itself.

OBSESSED BY SNUFF

1776

Today drug taking is frowned on by the respectable, but in earlier times there was no stigma at all attached to those who regularly took opium – famous drug-addict authors like Thomas de Quincey (whose *Confessions of an English Opium Eater* was published in 1821), poets such as Samuel Taylor Coleridge and members of the royal family were enthusiastic drug takers and they would have laughed at the idea that taking opium was somehow a bad thing. However, opium was always the drug of choice for the relatively well off – lower down the social scale, the most popular drug of all before cigarettes was snuff. Snuff taking was almost universal in Georgian and Victorian England, but few were as enthusiastic about powdered tobacco as the infamous Margaret Thomson.

When she made her will in the early part of the nineteenth century Mrs Thomson, who lived in Essex Street just off the Strand, stipulated that the beneficiaries of her will would not get a penny if they failed to ensure that her coffin was filled with all the snuff handkerchiefs that were unwashed at the time of her death; she also wanted to be surrounded with freshly ground snuff in her coffin. Six of the greatest snuff takers in the parish were requested to be her pallbearers, and each was asked to wear a snuff-coloured hat. Six girls were instructed to walk behind the hearse, each with a box of snuff which they were to take copiously for their refreshment as they went along.

The priest who officiated at the ceremony was invited to take as much snuff as he desired during the service, and Mrs Thomson left him five guineas on condition that he partook of snuff during and throughout the funeral proceedings. In return for a bequest of snuff, her servants were instructed to walk in front of the funeral procession throwing snuff on the ground and on to the crowd of onlookers. And throughout the long day of the funeral, snuff was to be distributed to all comers from the door of the deceased's house.

COCKNEY MAORI CHIEF

1777

Poverty and a long tradition of seafaring and work on the river – both as dockers and sailors – meant that historically London's East End was always one of the most cosmopolitan districts of the capital.

The East End has also produced a large number of eccentrics and odd characters whose instinct for survival was second to none – becoming eccentric may well have been one way to survive the incredible poverty of an area that was so run down at one time that even the police were careful to avoid certain districts.

One of the most extraordinary characters ever produced by the East End was Joseph Druce. Born in Shadwell in 1777, the son of a labourer who was often out of work, Joseph never went to school but having been a mudlark – a child who searched for copper nails and other flotsam and jetsam below the waterline – he eventually got a job working on the wherries and fishing boats that plied the Thames at that time in large numbers.

Earning a pittance no doubt contributed to Druce's descent into petty crime – this gradually became more serious and in 1791 he was caught red-handed having broken into a house and taken to Newgate Gaol.

At his trial the verdict was a foregone conclusion. He must have expected the death sentence since it was virtually mandatory for everything from pickpocketing to stealing apples – even children were routinely hanged. But the tide was turning

– not towards more lenient sentences necessarily but towards the idea of sending criminals to the distant colonies. Aged just thirteen Druce was sentenced to transportation to New South Wales for life.

In practical terms transportation was a death sentence anyway – if the convict was lucky enough to survive the long sea journey in what were usually unseaworthy vessels, he had a good chance of dying quickly from an unfamiliar disease in the new country.

According to one estimate only 10 per cent of those transported were still alive ten years after reaching Australia.

Druce was one of the lucky ones. He worked on a farm and later became a bush ranger. Before he was twenty he'd become a policeman, but the lure of adventuring proved too much and he took a job on a merchant ship sailing between Australia and New Zealand. In New Zealand he became friendly with a Maori chief who became ill – apparently at death's door, the Maori chief and his family had given up hope, but Druce made a few suggestions about the chief's diet and miraculously he recovered. As a gesture of thanks the Maori chief suggested that Druce marry his daughter, which made Druce the first and only Londoner ever to become a Maori chief!

By 1801 Druce's wife had died and on hearing that his life sentence had been rescinded he was free to return to London, which he did the following year. In 1819 he was provided with a home at the Greenwich Seamen's Hospital where he died the same year.

HOW THE BRISTOL HOTEL
GOT ITS NAME

1778

London still has at least one Bristol Hotel – it is in Berkeley Street, W1 – but during the late eighteenth century the city boasted a profusion of hotels, all called Bristol. Outside London and indeed right across Europe the situation was the same. There were Bristol hotels wherever travellers tended to stop for the night.

The reason has to do with one of London's oddest characters – a man largely forgotten today but in his lifetime a byword for luxury and extravagance.

Born in 1730, Edward Hervey studied at Westminster and Cambridge. Through the influence of his brother, Lord Bristol, he was made Bishop of Cloyne, though as he himself admitted he had absolutely no connection with or interest in Ireland. However, he soon started manoeuvring for the bishopric of Derry, which was worth more money than Cloyne, again using the influence of his brother, and he was successful. When he heard the news he was playing leapfrog with his fellow clergy in the garden at Cloyne Palace and is reported to have shouted: 'I will jump no more, gentlemen. I have surpassed you all, and jumped from Cloyne to Derry!'

He was thirty-nine, married, and earning a reputation as an eccentric largely because he was sympathetic to the local Catholic population which, under English rule, could own virtually nothing nor hold any office of any worth. His outspokenness on the subject almost led to him being impeached for treason, and Walpole, Charles James Fox and most other English parliamentarians thought him mad, bad and dangerous to know.

He got nowhere with his radical views, however, and developed instead his personality. He built three huge houses, his favourite being the size of Blenheim Palace, perched on a cliff top at Lough Foyle. On the death of his brother in 1778 he became Lord Bristol and went to live in London.

His house parties – held in his huge London residence – were legendary; he would often invite the fattest clergy to stay and then, after dinner, make them race round the house against each other. If he invited the clergy wives he always sprinkled flour outside their bedroom doors to see if he could catch them moving about between bedrooms during the night.

In his latter years he rarely visited Ireland and spent most of his time getting drunk in London and travelling extensively in France and Italy, where he spent so lavishly that hotel owners vied with each other to make their hotels more attractive to the great man. Hundreds renamed their hotels after him in order to indicate to other potential customers that the great Lord Bristol had stayed there and dozens retain the name 'Bristol' to this day.

Towards the end of his life he received a 'round robin' criticising him for being absent for so long from his parish, but he sent each signatory an inflated pig's bladder containing a dried pea along with a copy of the following verse:

> Three large bluebottles sat upon three bladders.
> Blow bottle flies, blow; burst, blow bladder burst.
> A new-blown bladder and three blue balls
> Make a great rattle.
> So rattle bladder rattle.

He died in 1803 aged seventy-three.

CHILDREN FOR SALE

1778

The idea that parents are and always have been concerned for the welfare of their children is certainly untrue. Even today in parts of Africa parents sometimes decide that a child is possessed by the devil and that child may, as a result, be killed. So-called honour killings – common across many parts of the Islamic world – mean that a female child who speaks to a person who is not a member of her family will sometimes be killed.

In Britain in earlier centuries – indeed even as recently as the end of the nineteenth century – children were regularly sold by their parents either for sex or into domestic service that amounted to a lifetime of slavery.

Travellers to London were always astonished at the number of prostitutes who swarmed around London's theatres and parks – many reported that at times on a Saturday night there were more prostitutes than potential customers!

But one of the most extraordinary and shocking stories from Victorian London came from the pen of the famous Russian writer Dostoevsky. After visiting London in 1863, he wrote: 'In the Haymarket I saw mothers who had brought their young daughters, girls who were still in their early teens, to be sold to me. Little girls of about twelve seize you by the hand and ask you to go with them.'

143

EIGHTEENTH-CENTURY VIAGRA

1779

Dr James Graham was a genuine doctor, but at a time when all genuine doctors were by modern standards complete frauds – the evidence for this can be seen in the fact that, for example Edinburgh medical textbook of 1750 listed under 'valuable remedies' the following: horse dung, pig skulls, frogspawn, ants' eggs and ground-up human skulls.

But Dr Graham, though interested in medicine, was far more interested in money, which is why when he left his native Edinburgh for London in around 1774 he set up his surgery in the most fashionable part of town – St James.

By 1779 he had realised that an important medical affliction was not at that time being addressed by any medical practitioner. Dr Graham decided that he would corner the market in cures for infertility. He set up his Temple of Health in Pall Mall and took large expensive advertisements in the London newspapers. In these he made outlandish claims for the extraordinary benefits of what he called his 'Celestial Bed'. The idea was that infertile couples would seek out the doctor, ask his advice and then be directed to his own certain cure: the Celestial Bed. Not only would the bed cure infertility – it would also ensure that any children conceived on it were far stronger and more beautiful 'in mental as well as in bodily endowments than the present puny race of Christians'.

The bed could only be rented and couples paid exorbitant sums for the privilege – perhaps as much as £100 per session.

144

Graham claimed that while an infertile couple had sex on his bed he would activate a mechanism that would surround the happy couple with 'celestial fire' and cherishing vapours. He would also pump through glass tubes the very same perfumes used by the Turkish Sultan to guarantee that he could keep up with the demands of his enormous harem.

Despite the bed's mattress being made from the baked tails of sexually rapacious 'English stallions', history does not record the levels of satisfaction enjoyed by Dr Graham's customers, but we do know that within a few years of the advertisements appearing the good doctor vanished from the London scene.

BEAU BRUMMEL'S BLUE NOSE

1794

Beau Brummel (1778–1840), close friend of the Prince Regent and arbiter of fashion in the early part of the nineteenth century, had in his younger days been an officer in the 10th Light Dragoons. When he wasn't soldiering he lived in some splendour in a house in Chesterfield Street in London's Mayfair, where he taught the Prince of Wales to tie his own cravat (the prince never quite mastered the art) and where endless numbers of the fashionable came to be passed fit to be seen in society by the great arbiter of taste.

Brummel had been commissioned into the dragoons by his friend the Prince Regent but despite his fashion sense he was a hopeless incompetent when it came to matters military, for Brummel was one of England's most forgetful soldiers.

His biggest difficulty was that he could never remember the faces of the men in the troop he commanded – it was a chronic problem that led to huge embarrassment and there seemed to be no solution but, then as now, incompetence was no bar to high rank in the British army provided one had the right accent and background, which of course Brummel had.

Then Brummel himself came up with a solution – he noticed that one of the men in his troop had a very blue nose and he ordered that this man should always be in the front rank when the men were assembled. If Brummel then failed to identify his troop of men he would need only to look for that blue nose to know that he was in the right place.

146

All went well until one day at the Horse Guards in Whitehall. Brummel sat immaculately dressed on his splendid horse and was approached by a senior officer who demanded what he thought he was doing.

Brummel stared in blank amazement at the squadron commander.

'You are with the wrong troop,' he was told in no uncertain terms.

Panic-stricken, Brummel stared around and with a sigh of relief spotted the blue nose in the men lined up just in front of him.

'I think, if I may say so, you are mistaken,' he replied. 'I'm not so foolish as to be unable to recognise my own troop.' But what Brummel, who famously spent most of his army career in front of a mirror, did not know was that there had been a troop reorganisation and 'blue nose' had been moved to another troop without his knowledge.

BETTING ON CATS

1795

Bond Street is unusual in that unlike almost every other London district it has never lost its reputation as a fashionable place to shop. It's also unusual in that it is the only street that runs right across Mayfair from Piccadilly to Oxford Street. Despite this, the street is actually two streets – the southern section, which runs as far north as Burlington Gardens, was built in the early 1680s by Sir Thomas Bond, the northern section in the 1720s.

Most of the original seventeenth- and eighteenth-century houses have now gone (Aspreys' shop is an exception) but from the first the street was so popular as a shopping destination that it also became an important place simply to be seen, so much so that it began to rival both the famous pleasure gardens at Ranelagh and Rotten Row.

Among those who regularly promenaded here in the late eighteenth century was the Prince of Wales, later the Prince Regent. The prince was a notorious gambler who would bet on almost anything – he once took a bet on which of two raindrops would be first to run to the bottom of a window – but he was also something of a simpleton who was regularly fleeced by his gambling-mad courtiers.

The politician Charles James Fox (1749–1806), a supporter of American independence, anti-slavery campaigner and Britain's first Foreign Secretary, once got the better of the Prince of Wales in a bizarre bet made while walking down Bond Street one sunny afternoon.

Fox noticed a cat lounging at the side of the street so he suggested to the Prince that each should choose one side of the street and then wager who would see the greatest number of cats during a walk from one end of the street to the other.

Fox was crafty enough to choose the side of the street in full sun rather than the shady side and at the end of their walk he had spotted thirteen cats to the Prince's grand total of none. The baffled prince was forced to hand over the entire contents of his purse.

NELSON'S SECOND-HAND TOMB

1805

Despite suffering almost continually from seasickness – he never became a seasoned sailor – Nelson became the greatest of all British naval heroes. It seems, too, almost as if he knew that it was his duty to die in battle at sea, which is of course precisely what happened.

But Nelson was so concerned that his death should be in keeping with his life that he commissioned his own coffin well in advance. Though it sounds rather ghoulish today this was actually quite common in earlier times. Nelson was very specific about his coffin – he had it made from the salvaged timber of a French ship sunk at the Battle of the Nile in 1798 and left strict instructions about what was to be done in the event of his death.

When he was killed at Trafalgar in 1805 Britain lost its greatest hero and looked around for a suitable way to bury him. Clearly it had to be in St Paul's Cathedral and as he had chosen his own coffin there was no problem there. But what about a sarcophagus?

As they thought about this someone remembered that stored away and forgotten at Windsor Castle was a massive black marble sarcophagus that had lain unused for more than three hundred years.

The sarcophagus had originally been made for Cardinal Wolsey. At the height of his power in 1521 Wolsey sent for the Italian sculptor Rovezzano. He wanted a tomb in keeping with his sense of his own worth. The vast sarcophagus that emerged from the hands of the Italian was extraordinarily impressive but before he had time to use it Wolsey fell out with Henry VIII. His palaces and houses were taken away and Wolsey was disgraced. Henry VIII decided that the black sarcophagus would be perfect for him so it was sent to Windsor to be ready when Henry died. When Henry finally gave up the ghost more than twenty years later Rovezzano's magnificent work seems to have been overlooked and it remained forgotten until those officials hunting around for something suitable for Nelson remembered the tomb's existence.

The really interesting question however is: how could something as big as Wolsey's sarcophagus have been forgotten and overlooked for so long?

THE MOLE THAT KILLED A KING

1806

St James's Square retains just a few of its original early eighteenth-century houses, but this small square has been home at various times to an extraordinary list of the famous and the infamous – Gladstone and Pitt lived here along with half a dozen earls, several dukes and numerous royal mistresses. In fact within a decade of the square being built in 1670 every single house was lived in by someone who had a title or was sleeping with someone with a title.

But what makes the square really interesting is the bizarre statue of William III in the gardens. The statue is only here because the residents got fed up with the fact that the centre of the square was long used as a refuse tip for the householders – at one time it was piled high with 'kitchen rubbish, dead cats, scraps of timber and noxious mountains of refuse'. They wanted something to give the middle a purpose and a statue seemed as good an idea as anything. But that's where the problems began.

The idea of a statue of William was not initially popular so despite their enormous wealth the residents of the square refused to pay for it. Then a merchant offered money in his will but his family contested the will for the next seventy years and it wasn't until 1806 that the statue was finally completed.

Even when the statue was finally made and put on its plinth there was something odd about it – it includes, for example, a small molehill at the feet of the horse on which William is seated. What is the molehill for? The answer is that William is said to have died after falling from his horse. The horse had tripped on a molehill.

William was the Protestant king brought to England from Holland to replace the last Catholic, King James. James's supporters and all Jacobites then and now still toast the little gentleman in velvet – i.e. the mole that built the molehill that killed a king.

WORLD'S FIRST GASLIGHT

1807

Today we take street lighting – at least in cities and towns – for granted and it is hard to imagine what life was like when a dark night really did mean that you couldn't safely go out at all. On such nights there was little to do other than read quietly by the fire if you could afford oil lamps or candles, or go to bed if you were poor. Along the great and fashionable streets of the city there had been attempts to illuminate the dark winter evenings but with varying rates of success. Until recently it was still possible to see what they might have been like as the In and Out club in Piccadilly still kept its flaming flambeaut alight in two iron braziers fitted high up on the gate pillars. But now they too have gone and London knows only its warm summer evenings when light is unnecessary until late in the evening and its electrically lit winter evenings.

The lack of light at night in Victorian and earlier periods meant that some areas of London – notably the East End Docks, the Rookeries of St Giles and the Devil's Acre, a large area of slum housing near Westminster Abbey – could not be policed. Locals knew the streets and alleys in these areas better than anyone and the police would not risk pursuit in the darkness.

But though it is popularly believed that gaslight – the first great revolution in London lighting – did not generally become available until the latter half of the nineteenth century, there was in fact a bizarre and much earlier attempt to bring systematic lighting to London.

154

The year was 1807 and Londoners were eager to do what they could to celebrate the king's birthday. London was full of Germans at this time – Britain had a German king who was surrounded by German courtiers and all things Germanic were fashionable.

A German engineer called Albert Winsor was then living in London and he decided to do his bit by installing posts with lamps on top all along one side of The Mall. He set up a small gas tank and built underground pipes connecting the lighting posts with each other and with his gas tank.

The gas tank was based on an invention of the Scottish engineer William Murdoch – Murdoch built an airtight tank which he filled with coal that was then heated up from the outside. The coal in the tank then released gas which Murdoch allowed to escape through a pipe fitted to his tank. The gas was fed to an appliance that was then ignited. This was the system Winsor employed in The Mall.

Late one gloomy autumn evening he had an assistant release the valve on his tank and another assistant walked along the mall lighting each flaring lamp.

These were not the gas lamps we are familiar with from old films about London – later gas lamps had silken mantles that meant the gas and the light could be angled downwards. Winsor's lights simply flamed up from the top of their posts, but the world's first street lights – which these certainly were – caused a sensation across the capital.

A journalist on the *Pall Mall Gazette* wrote: 'London saw something so strange in the Mall of late that our parents and grandparents having seen it would take to their beds quaking with fear that the end of the world and the general loss of sanity had come. The distinguished Mr Winsor threw light along this royal road in a manner unprecedented and we are left wondering as much at his audacity as at his ingenuity.'

But the oddest thing of all about Winsor's lights were the pipes he made to link them – he tried conventional water pipes but they simply would not stand the pressure. He tried various other solutions and all failed. Then he thought of gun barrels –

they have to withstand enormous pressures from exploding cartridges, he thought, and promptly approached the Woolwich Arsenal from whom he obtained a large number of elderly muskets. He stripped them down and reused the barrels to make his gas pipe.

The experiment worked perfectly. It is perhaps ironic that the street that runs from The Mall through St James's Palace is today one of the last streets in the world still to have traditional mantled gas lamps. They have been there now for more than a century – if you want to see what London looked like at night in Victorian times this is the only place you can still do it.

BIGGEST PRACTICAL JOKER

1809

There's something rather odd about practical jokes – they're not witty and they rely for their humour on other people's discomfort, but for centuries the British have made coming up with spoofs of various kinds something of a national obsession.

One of the greatest of all practical jokes became known as the 'Berners Street Hoax.

It was perpetrated by the writer and serial bankrupt Theodore Hook (1788–1841), who was said to be the most entertaining man in London – he was so entertaining in fact that when he was known to be at his club, the Athenaeum, other members would make a special effort to be there just to listen to him.

The Berners Street Hoax began when Hook laid a wager with a friend that he could make an obscure house in Soho the most famous house in London and he could do it in a month.

The two friends parted and Hook set to work. He paid several of his friends to write letters to hundreds of London tradesmen, politicians, men of the church, celebrities, writers, actors and artists. All the letters were written as if from an obscure house in Berners Street, Soho.

Having posted the letters Hook invited the friend with whom he'd made the bet to sit in the upstairs drawing room of a house opposite the house that was the subject of the bet.

As the day progressed hundreds of tradesmen arrived with various goods; furniture drays arrived carrying beds and wardrobes; a hearse arrived, a clock maker; plumbers and carpenters, tailors and fencing masters.

But then, just when Hook's friend admitted that he had lost the bet, the hoax started to go wrong, because Hook had persuaded his friend to write also to a number of powerful officials – the Archbishop of Canterbury and the Prime Minister to name but two – and when they began to arrive Hook realised that his harmless jest could have serious repercussions.

Half London was in an uproar over the hoax and there was almost a riot. The policed were informed and but for a few high-placed officials who tried to calm the situation, Hook would undoubtedly have been prosecuted for wasting everyone's time. Realising that he had badly miscalculated Hook suddenly vanished and spent the next six months holed up in a friend's house deep in the countryside.

THE DIRTIEST PUB IN LONDON

1809

Many London pubs are far older than they might at first appear. In Bishopsgate, for example, Dirty Dicks dates back to the early eighteenth century despite the fact that the pub looks typically mid-Victorian. The cellars here are original and it was in the pub above them that one of London's most extraordinary and eccentric characters once lived.

The story varies in its details but it seems that Nathaniel Bentley, a local businessman and dandy who ran an alehouse, decided to get married. Everything was prepared and the pub's dining rooms had been laid out with beautiful flowers, cutlery, linen and a huge cake, but on the night before the wedding the bride died. Distraught, Bentley sealed up the room where the table had been laid for the wedding breakfast and never opened it again. He also stopped washing and only changed his clothes when they rotted and fell off him. He allowed his pub to become one of the filthiest houses in London but people flocked to it to see if it really was as bad as they'd been told and Bentley made a fortune – a fortune he never spent because he bought nothing. He lived for nearly forty years, and died finally in 1809. He was a rich man by then. He once said: 'What is the point of washing my hands or anything else for that matter when they will only be dirty again tomorrow?'

The remnants of the old clothes that hung from the ceiling were only cleared out (they fell foul of new health and safety rules) in the 1980s, but the old pub still has a few fake rags here and there to remind us of its decidedly grubby past.

A MISTRESS'S REVENGE

1809

Disputes between lovers always involve emotional excesses and when lovers fall out it adds a new twist to the old saying: all's fair in love and war.

Salisbury Square, just off Fleet Street, once witnessed the conclusion to one of the strangest emotional disputes in the history of England. The problem began when Frederick, Duke of York (the second son of mad George III), began to lose interest in one of his mistresses, one Mrs Mary Anne Clarke. Mrs Clarke was his favourite mistress from 1803 until 1809 but then his enthusiasm began to wane. In short he completely lost interest in her. Mrs Clarke was furious at being unceremoniously dumped, but she would have accepted this meekly enough if the Duke had given her the pension she felt she deserved, together with a house in a fashionable part of London. The Duke for his part thought that he could simply discard her and that would be the end of it, but he had reckoned without the fury of a woman scorned.

When the Duke refused to see her or give her any money Mrs Clarke sat down and wrote her memoirs, in particular her memories of her relationship with the Duke. The notoriety of Mrs Clarke and the public's appetite for scandal meant the publisher was convinced he would have a huge sale and make his fortune, so he printed ten thousand copies – an enormous number for any book at the time. Mrs Clarke then let the Duke know that the book was about to come out. In earlier times he'd

161

have had her head cut off, but even in Georgian England such an idea was unthinkable. The Duke knew when he was beaten. He immediately paid her a pension, bought her a house and bought up all 10,000 copies of the book – these were piled up in Salisbury Square and burned. If one copy survived and were to turn up now it would be worth a fortune!

WHICH SIDE ARE YOU ON?

1811

In eighteenth-century London political party meant more than the side of the House of Commons on which one sat. Particular clubs, for example, were associated with particular factions – Brooks's Club was for the Whigs (who later transformed into the Liberals) and White's for the Tories. But there were other more bizarre ways to indicate one's political allegiance.

At the Theatre Royal in Drury Lane – the present building, put up in 1811, is the fourth on the site – new plays were always attended by the great and the good, but there was a problem. King George III and his son the Prince Regent hated each other and refused to sit in the same room, let alone speak to each other. But they both hated to miss a first night. To get round the problem the King was always directed up one side of the grand foyer and the Prince up the other side. Politicians who arrived at the theatre would make sure that they were seen to go up the right side according to whether they supported the King or the Prince's faction.

The tradition of theatre staff directing theatregoers up 'the King's side' or 'the Prince's side' continues to this day.

NAPOLEON'S SOAP ON SHOW

1816

It's hard to understand now, but despite the fact that he was defeated at Waterloo the Emperor Napoleon was one of the most popular figures in London at the beginning of the nineteenth century – popular in the sense that people were absolutely fascinated by everything to do with him now that he was safely imprisoned on the island of St Helena.

The great bogeyman of Europe who had terrified the British ruling classes (they thought he would encourage the lower orders to get above themselves) was now like a lion in a cage – awe-inspiring but harmless.

Napoleon fever reached a peak in around 1816 when the showman William Bullock bought a vast collection of Napoleon's personal effects – the collection included Napoleon's carriage, his horses, his combs, brushes, wine, spirits and even a small bar of his soap!

Even more extraordinary was the fact that Bullock managed to persuade Napoleon's former carriage driver to accompany the collection. It was all brought to Bullock's new British Museum, which was situated in Piccadilly, and within a few months almost half a million people had queued to see the collection. Bullock made a fortune and the British appetite for sensation was satisfied.

In fact Bullock did so well that he moved his collection of Napoleon artifacts into what he called the Museum Napoleon. But the obsession with the fallen Emperor didn't end there –

a forty square metre replica of the battlefield at Waterloo was created at the Egyptian Hall in Piccadilly with every detail, soldiers, artillery, horses and landmarks included.

HOW TO STOP DEAD CATS FLYING

1819

One of the delights of London is that if you know what you are looking for you will find odd, quirky little places in the busiest thoroughfares and many of these have fascinating and often curious histories. Piccadilly must be one of the most famous streets in the world, but just off it is a row of tiny Georgian shops virtually unchanged since they were completed in 1819.

The shops in question are in the Burlington Arcade and they are here for a most bizarre reason. Visitors often think the Georgian planners who built these little shops were simply building to make a profit. In fact they built the arcade to cover a narrow alley that ran alongside Burlington House, now the home of the Royal Academy but in the early nineteenth century still a private home. The owner of Burlington House was Lord George Cavendish, who had complained for years that while sitting in his garden he was constantly hit on the head by oyster shells, apple cores, old bottles and even an occasional dead cat. These unpleasant items were thrown over the wall between the garden and the lane which then existed at its side. Cavendish decided that a row of shops would put paid to the nuisance and so he had them built and the alleyway vanished forever. Samuel Ware was asked to design the beautiful shop fronts which exist largely unchanged today, and though the shop interiors are tiny the shopkeepers have always sold luxury goods, so what they lack in quantity of stock they more than make up for in quality.

Originally the arcade was a single storey, but an upper level was added in 1906 and above the shops the rooms were let – according to one wag they were let to 'the better sort of courtesan'. The beautiful triple-arch entrance was destroyed for no good reason in 1931 and the new design was much hated. There was also some damage during the war but the arcade remains one of the world's first shopping malls. Instead of security men it still has a beadle who will ask you to leave the arcade if he catches you running or whistling or carrying an open umbrella!

THE GREATEST LEGAL
SCANDAL OF ALL

1819

The law has always been something of a scandalous institution. Lawyers have the best trade union in the sense that entry to the profession is strictly controlled and because lawyers never undercut each other and there is no genuine competition between practitioners, the poor public is always forced to pay very high prices for the advice it receives.

But the scandal of lawyers' costs today – a disgrace that no government dares tackle simply because politicians themselves tend to be drawn from the ranks of the legal profession – is nothing compared with the scandals of the past.

One of the greatest and most extraordinary of all legal humiliations, a scandal that outranks every other London legal dishonour, was known as the Great Jennings case.

Anyone who has read Charles Dickens's great novel of London life *Bleak House* will remember the case of Jarndyce and Jarndyce, which is the central symbol in that novel of social decay and corruption.

The case of Jarndyce and Jarndyce, though bizarre in its tortuousness, impenetrability and sheer longevity, was based on the Great Jennings case which was heard in the Old Hall, Lincoln's Inn. The real case was no less absurd than the story Dickens created to satirise it.

The Great Jennings case started in 1819 when Dickens was only seven and didn't end until 1870, the year in which the great novelist died. But why was the case such a scandal? The answer is that the lawyers involved made no real efforts to conclude it; it was in their interest to keep it going as long as possible only because they were earning fat fees. The case finally ended when the money involved in the case ran out – it had all been used up funding lawyers' fees.

A CLUB FOR MEN NOT ABLE TO SING IN THE BATH

1820

Old pubs tend to survive longer than other buildings in London – with the exception of churches, of course. The Coal Hole in Carting Lane is a case in point. The present building dates back to the early 1800s but the pub commemorates an earlier nearby tavern of the same name.

The pub gets its name from the wharf used by coalmen that stood nearby before the Embankment pushed the river further away. For centuries coal was brought to London by ship from the mines of Northumberland and Durham (which is why in earlier centuries coal was always called sea coal) and the tough city coal heavers who lugged the sacks from the ships uphill to the carters liked to drink in this pub.

During the eighteenth century the pub was hugely popular with actors and theatre managers including the great tragedian Edmund Kean (1787–1833), who started the Wolf Club.

The sole qualification for membership was that the applicant should have been forbidden by his wife to sing in the bath! The Wolf Bar in the present attractive Arts and Crafts interior with its pretty leaded windows commemorates this bizarre drinking club. And when you step out of the pub you can still look down the sloping lane and see the bright river – just as the coal heavers of earlier centuries did.

WOMEN BUYING MEN

1820

We are all familiar with the idea of men paying women for sex – prostitution is, after all, the world's oldest profession – but it is less common for the traffic to operate in the other direction. A bizarre tradition of women buying men did, however, exist in Victorian London though it probably only rarely led to sex.

The story begins with the bizarre development of Kensington Gardens and Hyde Park. To the modern visitor the two areas of open space seem almost indistinguishable, though they are divided by the road that crosses the park from Bayswater Road in the north to Kensington Gore in the south – Kensington Gore takes its name from 'gara', an old English word describing a triangular plot of land which was left when ploughing fields of irregular shape.

Kensington Gardens really began to develop when William III decided he didn't like Whitehall Palace, the traditional home of English monarchs. He retreated to Kensington soon after 1688 and to the palace we see today. The gardens round the palace – including the famous Round Pond and the Broad Walk – were developed by Queen Anne and later by Queen Caroline, wife of George II.

It was Caroline who commissioned the work to dig the Serpentine – before Caroline, this had been a series of small ponds surrounded by marshland and through which the Westbourne River ran. When Caroline died George discovered that she'd stolen more than £26,000 of his money to complete

171

the work. He was apparently furious as he'd been under the impression that the work had kept Caroline occupied for years and at no cost.

But throughout this period Kensington Gardens was a private area open only to royalty and their courtiers. Hyde Park by contrast was open to all and as a result it developed a slightly seedy reputation – prostitutes plied their trade here and robberies were commonplace.

By the beginning of the nineteenth century the rules were relaxed a little and Kensington Gardens was opened to 'the respectably dressed' – the gates were guarded by officials who turned away those who did not look respectable. At that time this meant the poor, who would have easily been identified by their practical, workday clothes.

But the ban on the lower orders meant that servant girls and soldiers from nearby Knightsbridge Barracks could not walk in the park. Instead they walked in Hyde Park and a tradition began that servant girls and others would pay soldiers to escort them – the girls wanted their friends to see them being escorted by a handsome guardsman in full dress uniform and they wanted it so badly they were prepared to pay for it.

A walk in the park with an artilleryman cost nine old pence; a guardsman's company for half an hour would set you back a shilling. If you could only afford a private it would cost sixpence. Such things would never have been allowed in Kensington Gardens.

But even today the distinction between the parks is very real and this is reflected in the way they are policed – the Metropolitan Police still control Hyde Park while the Royal Parks Constabulary look after Kensington Gardens.

TOM AND JERRY IN LONDON

1821

If they think about them at all, most people probably imagine that the famous cartoon characters Tom and Jerry have their origin in the United States and more particularly in the vast film industry of that country.

In fact Tom and Jerry have their origins far earlier and on the other side of the Atlantic. The story starts in 1821 – well within the Georgian era – when London was enjoying a boom in publishing. Books, pamphlets and newspapers were being produced in ever greater numbers as literacy and the appetite for reading material spread through society.

A century earlier books had been largely the preserve of the rich or at least the comparatively well off, but by 1821 the popular press had taken off with a vengeance – in addition to cheap pamphlets and books there were broadsides (single news sheets usually about murders and executions) song sheets, chapbooks and penny dreadfuls.

Among the most innovative of the new publishers was Pierce Egan (1772–1849), a sporting journalist, who began a new series of publications in 1821 entitled *Life in London or the Day and Night Scenes of Jerry Hawthorne Esq and his elegant friend Corinthian Tom, accompanied by Bob Logic, the Oxonian, in their Rambles and Sprees Through the Metropolis.*

The series was so popular that other publishers produced pirated versions of it and within a few months it had been turned into a stage play – the title had changed by now to *Tom and Jerry or Life in London* but it was so popular and tripped so easily off the tongue that it is not difficult to see how it crossed the Atlantic in the head of some entrepreneur emigré and ended up transformed into the cartoon we know today. The basic idea of two characters getting into a series of scrapes remains the same but Egan's loveable human rogues have been transformed, of course, into a cat and a mouse.

A MONUMENT TO A MAN NOBODY LIKED

1824

One of the most curious monuments in London, the Duke of York's column just off The Mall, was built to commemorate Frederick, the second son of George III, a man who did nothing other than run up huge debts. Despite being a member of the royal family and therefore by definition enormously well connected, Frederick's monument could not find a financial backer: George his brother wanted it built but wouldn't pay for it; none of Frederick's wealthy friends would pay so the government decided, without consultation, to dock one day's pay from every soldier in the British army to finance a monument to a man for whom the population had neither respect nor affection.

So some of the poorest subjects in Britain were forced to pay for a monument to one of the richest and most profligate aristocrats in the land. But Frederick had to pay in the end, because from the moment it was completed in 1824 the monument, which cost £25,000, and the figure of the Duke which surmounts it, became the butt of jokes: a favourite for many years was that Frederick's column had to be as high as it is – 124 feet – so that Londoners wouldn't have to put up with the stink of the Duke whose undistinguished statue stands on top; the other highly popular jibe was that the column had to be exceptionally high to protect Frederick from his creditors.

175

ONLY FOR THE ROYAL BIRD KEEPER

1828

Birdcage Walk runs along St James's Park from Buckingham Palace almost to Parliament Square. It's a curious street with the park on one side and the backs of houses on the other.

Casual visitors and tourists who notice the name of the street at all probably imagine that it commemorates the fact that people once kept birds here – perhaps in cages hanging from the elegant windows in the tall old houses that still overlook the park. In fact, Birdcage Walk reminds us that in the days when the Palace of Whitehall stretched far along the River Thames nearby this was the site of the royal aviary.

Built by James I, the aviary was doubled in size by his grandson Charles II. Neither James nor Charles were known for their love of budgerigars – in fact the aviary housed the royal falcons and hawks, birds kept specifically for hunting.

Birdcage Walk was once the focus of a bizarre set of rules. Although it is now a wide, busy road, it was once a route that had to be walked for the simple reason that only the king and the Hereditary Grand Falconer were allowed to drive their carriages along the route. This rule was rigidly adhered to until as recently as 1828 and when the route was opened to lesser mortals the downfall of Empire was predicted.

The houses that line the walk are some of the earliest still standing in central London. They were built right at the beginning of the eighteenth century, but what you see from the walk are actually the backs of the houses. A narrow set of old stone steps lead up past their gardens to the house fronts. Here you will see the best complete group of Queen Anne houses in the capital. Queen's Anne's statue stands against the wall of one of the mellow red-brick houses which still have their fine staircases, sash windows and original doorcases.

WHEN THE DEAD MOVED OUT OF LONDON

1832

Most visitors brave enough to include a graveyard on their London itinerary go to Highgate cemetery to the north of the city, but tucked away by the side of the Grand Union Canal over to the west in what was until recently a fairly poor part of North Kensington, Kensal Green Cemetery is an extraordinary monument to Victorian funeral piety – and even more bizarre funeral rituals.

Until the coming of the canal in the eighteenth century this was a quiet place: there were a few houses at the junction of Harrow Road and Kilburn Lane but the rest was open farmland with an odd isolated inn and London half a day's walk away. But by the early 1800s the small village centred round the junction and its green was expanding. By the 1830s London's church graveyards were filled to bursting and All Soul's Cemetery, as Kensal Green Cemetery was originally known (the land was owned by All Souls College, Oxford), was opened in 1832 to ease the problem.

Within a few years Kensal Rise Cemetery – as it quickly became known – was the fashionable place to be buried. Among the bizarre monuments the cemetery contains are Greek temples, Egyptian halls, gothic fantasies and medieval castles, as well as more ordinary but equally fascinating gravestones and tombs.

The cemetery is full of mature trees and shrubs and gives every indication of being deep in the heart of the countryside –

among the tombs to look out for are those of Sir Anthony Panizzi (1797–1879), who created the famous round Reading Room at the British Library (now part of the British Museum), Charles Babbage (1791–1871) who created the first computer, authors Wilkie Collins (1824–1889), William Makepeace Thackeray (1811–1863) and Anthony Trollope (1815–1882), as well as the greatest of all the Victorian engineers, Isambard Kingdom Brunel (1806–1859).

But Kensal Rise Cemetery has a strange secret – here and there are tombs that reveal an astonishing obsession that gripped Victorian Londoners for several decades. And what was this obsession? It was the fear of being buried alive.

From roughly 1870 until 1900 an idea grew up that doctors were constantly making mistakes when it came to deciding when a person had died. It was said that in many cases death certificates had been issued and the body was being prepared for laying out, when suddenly an eye flickered or the apparent corpse groaned. If a corpse could come back to life at this stage, who was to say that dozens – perhaps hundreds – had not been buried and only then come back to life?

Visitors to Highgate and Kensal Green cemeteries in London even today may see the remnants of a strange invention designed to guard against the risk of being buried on Monday and waking up in one's coffin on Wednesday. A number of tombs were built with a hollow stone column running down into the buried coffin. At the top of the hollow column two or three feet up in the air above the tombstone would be a small bell tower complete with bell.

The idea of the bizarre contraption was that if the deceased happened to wake up after burial he or she would be able to pull vigorously on a chain that ran up the hollow column to the bell, which would ring out, bringing rescuers hotfooting it across the fields.

A number of different coffin alarm systems were created around this time and, indeed, from then until well into the twentieth century, when in a few cases nervous relatives had electric alarms fitted to their relatives' coffins.

Despite all the terror and fears, however, there is no record of anyone buried with an alarm pressing the button or ringing the bell.

THE MAN WHO HAD HIMSELF
STUFFED

1832

In earlier epochs the belief in the resurrection of the body –
central to Christianity – meant that cremation was frowned on
as a means of disposing of the dead. By the eighteenth century,
in England at least, such ideas were being questioned and
among the rationalists of the Enlightenment arguments about
cremation versus burial came to seem absurd. It may well have
been partly why the philosopher Jeremy Bentham (1748–1832),
one of the great political and social thinkers of the later
eighteenth and early nineteenth centuries, came up with a rather
more unusual way of disposing of his own corpse.

Bentham's more than sixty published works cover everything
from the need for political reform to animal welfare,
discussions of the state of the colonies and the evils of swearing.
Most famously, of course, he is associated with the creation of
utilitarianism – the doctrine of the greatest good of the greatest
number. He was also closely involved in the whole idea of a
dissenters' university, which is what the University of London
originally was. Dissenters were not allowed to study at the old
universities so they set up their own. Bentham was considered
wildly eccentric in his day for advocating universal suffrage and
the decriminalisation of homosexuality.

The University of London started life in 1828 when
Bentham was in his eighties and though he took no practical
part in establishing it he is often considered its spiritual father,

largely because of his advocacy of religious tolerance and education for all. Bentham loved the new university so it should come as no surprise that he left the university (later to become University College London) all his manuscripts. But he also left a legacy of surpassing eccentricity. Visitors to the South Cloisters of the main building cannot fail to see the large wooden and glass cabinet that stands in the corridor.

Inside the cabinet is a surprisingly lifelike and life-size Jeremy Bentham, comfortably seated with a stick in his hand and dressed in the very clothes he wore in life. The figure is not a model but the actual preserved remains of the great man. It was Bentham's last joke, if you like, at the expense of those who argued over burial and cremation for superstitious (i.e. religious) reasons.

When Bentham first arrived in his case a few weeks after his death in 1832, the head and face were actually those of Bentham, but the embalming technique used wasn't up to scratch and the head deteriorated badly until a wax replica had to be made. Bentham had left his body to the college on condition that it was preserved in this way and beneath the clothing even today Bentham's skeleton keeps an eye on the academic world he so loved in life.

Legends and extraordinary stories about the preserved philosopher abound – one says that he is wheeled into every university council meeting. At the end of each meeting the minutes record: Jeremy Bentham – present but not voting. Another legend has it that for a decade before he died Bentham carried around the glass eyes he wanted used in his preserved head. When they were finally used in the preserved head they fell out; then the head itself fell off and was found between Bentham's feet. Whatever the truth or otherwise of these and many other stories (including the one about the students found playing football with the head) we do know that in fact the real head is kept in the college vaults.

No one knows precisely why Bentham stipulated in his will that he should be preserved and set up for public display in this way, but it ties in nicely with the philosophy of a man who took a practical view of affairs and who thought it was important to make a contribution to the day-to-day life of the society in which he lived – at the end of his life he probably thought it would be nice to be in some position where he could watch the world go by and it was good to cock a snook at the more religious among his colleagues who were outraged at this refusal to stick to the Christian rules about the dead. No doubt Bentham also thought that if there was anything in the stories about the survival of the soul then his could hover where it had been happiest – in the corridors of the university.

WHY THE NATIONAL GALLERY HAS GIANT PEPPERPOTS

1835

When the National Gallery was built the architect found himself in a tricky position. His brief was to build something long and very narrow, as the access road behind the site (which is still there today) had to remain as it was when the royal stables, or mews, was here.

Not only that but, in a typically English and eccentric fudge, he also had to agree to build his new gallery no higher than the mews buildings it replaced. The idea was that the skyline at this point should look pretty much as it had done since the Middle Ages when the Royal Mews, a little to the north of the Palace of Westminster, was first established. The mews was where the king's animals – particularly his falcons – were 'mewed up'.

The architect of the National Gallery, as good as his word, came up with the design we see today and the oddest echo of the building the gallery replaced can be seen at either end of the present building. If you look carefully at the roof there are what look like two stone pepperpots, one at either end of the structure.

The reason these are here is that the original stables had almost identical decorative pepperpots – the originals were actually part of the ventilation system for the stables. As the heat and smell of the dung of several hundred horses rose it had to be dispersed from the building as quickly as possible – the pepperpots with their open stone latticework allowed just that to happen and the replacement pepperpots on the building have the same open decorative latticework, despite the fact that the horses departed forever nearly two centuries ago.

WORLD'S SMALLEST PRISON

1835

At one time most English towns and villages had lock-ups – small single-celled buildings where local drunks might be kept secure for the night or where thieves or other antisocial individuals could be kept to await the arrival of the magistrate.

At the southeast corner of Trafalgar Square and missed by almost every tourist who comes to this place is a lock-up that is unique even by the standards of these odd little prisons, because the Trafalgar Square lock-up is also Britain's (possibly the world's) smallest police station.

The structure looks like a rather fat lamppost and it is only when one looks closely that one notices the tiny door and window. There is barely room for two people to stand upright inside but it is said that this tiny lock-up had and still has a direct telephone link to Scotland Yard.

Right up until the 1960s the Trafalgar Square lock-up was still in use, but it is by no means the only strange thing about this part of London.

Take the famous lions at the bottom of Nelson's Column, for example. When the column was being built an artist had to be found to design the four huge lions round the base of the column. They are so much bigger than life size that it was feared the final result would be embarrassingly out of proportion unless someone with the right talents was chosen to complete the work.

186

Queen Victoria wanted Edwin Landseer (1862–1873), one of her favourite painters, to carry out the work but Landseer was horrified at the suggestion. He was not a sculptor and had no useful experience to bring to bear. He refused the commission, but the Queen would not give up. After being approached by peers and MPs, Landseer finally agreed but only on condition that he could take as long as he needed and that a dead lion would be sent round to his studio so he could study it before putting pen to paper.

It took several months before a lion died (presumably of natural causes) at London Zoo. It was immediately sent round to Landseer's house where he kept it until it stank so badly the neighbours began to complain. It took more than a year of preparatory drawing (and several more dead lions) before Landseer was finally happy – and the result was the splendid lions we see today.

But a century and more ago nothing seemed quite so straightforward – the drawings were ready but the sculpted lions were not installed until 25 years after they should have been put up. When Landseer died wreaths were draped around the lions' necks as a mark of respect.

Another curious tale concerns the capital at the top of the column on which Nelson's statue stands and the bronze bas-reliefs at the bottom of the column showing Nelson's victories (as well as his yet more famous death). All are made from French cannons captured after the Battle of Trafalgar in 1805.

PERFORMING PIGEONS

1835

We've all heard of flea circuses – though they are rare now – and animals were for centuries a central part of circuses and shows that toured the country. In medieval times and right up until the mid-nineteenth century London, like most parts of Britain, had numerous fairs. London's most famous fair was probably St Bartholomew's but almost all were gradually suppressed by an increasingly puritanical government that saw fairs as a waste of time – the common people who enjoyed fairs (which, like St Bartholemew's, were often held on old saint's days) were seen not as enjoying themselves, but as wasting time that would be better spent at work. But try as the authorities might to suppress the whole idea of the fair they never quite succeeded. Fairs, though far fewer in number, did continue and they offered a spectacle that in many cases we would find extremely offensive today. Deformed animals and humans – like the 'elephant man' John (Joseph) Merrick (1862–1890) – were often exhibited but animal trainers also produced some of the most bizarre entertainments ever seen in London. It is hard to know now if smaller performing animals were badly treated or not but the extraordinary skill of their trainers cannot be doubted. The following comes from Joseph Strutt's *The Sports and Pastimes of the People of England*. It describes a group of birds, probably pigeons, that travelled the country entertaining ordinary people at shows and fairs. They were known as Breslaw's Birds after their trainer. Strutt quotes a contemporary description of the

188

show when it came to London:

The birds formed themselves into ranks like a company of soldiers; small cones of paper bearing some resemblance to grenadiers' caps were put on their heads and diminutive imitations of muskets made with wood were secured under their left wings. Thus equipped they marched to and fro several times; when a single bird was brought forward, supposed to be a deserter, and set between six of the musketeers…who conducted him from the top to the bottom of the table on the middle of which there was a small brass cannon charged with a tiny amount of gunpowder; the deserter was situated in front of the cannon; his guards then divided, three retiring on one side and three on the other, and he was left standing by himself. Another bird was immediately produced and a lighted match being put into one of his claws, he hopped boldly on the other to the tail of the cannon and applying the match discharged the piece. The moment the explosion took place the deserter fell down and lay like a dead bird, but at the command of his tutor he rose again and the cages being brought the feathered soldiers were stripped of their ornament and returned into them in perfect order.

THE TRAIN DISGUISED AS A SHIP

1836

The train was to the nineteenth century what the internet is to our century – the greatest scientific innovation of the age. It transformed Britain from a land of remote villages where people rarely travelled more than a few miles in all their lives to a place where eventually even the relatively poor could afford to travel distances undreamed of by their parents and grandparents.

The huge success of the very earliest railways in the north of England meant that trains quickly spread and, of course, part of the spread took the iron roadway to London. The earliest London service of all was that which ran from the City to Greenwich.

Crowds gathered in those early days to see the extraordinary new invention – a breathing monster that could pull huge loads without the assistance of horses. The new method of transport was very popular with the travelling public, or at least that part of it wealthy enough to indulge in what was seen as a luxury, but much as people admired the technology there were many complaints about the aesthetics of the whole enterprise. The chief complaint was that somehow the engines were rather ugly. Letters were written in great numbers to the railway company asking if they could not brighten up these dismal-looking locomotives. The real problem was that the first generation to experience railways judged them against the brightly coloured mail coaches that still dominated the national transportation system. Since coaches were still on the scene,

190

though declining in numbers, older people looked back to them through the rose-tinted spectacles of nostalgia and hoped that the rather brash trains could be somehow given the glamour and glitter of the older form of transportation.

According to the then editor of the *Railway News*, the London and Greenwich Railway (L&GR) company took the complaints about the appearance of their engines very seriously. They studied the problem and after some time one of their engineers came up with a solution. Because the brick-built viaducts that carried the line into London looked rather like Roman aqueducts an eccentric engineer at the L&GR suggested to Braithwaite and Milner, who made the company's engines, that they should build a locomotive in the style of a Roman galley!

The result was that a year later huge crowds gathered at Cornhill in the City to watch the arrival of a long line of carriages pulled by a very passable imitation of an ancient ship.

When word got out much of the route was regularly lined with spectators eager to see this extraordinary engine, which was – as its inventor had suggested – particularly impressive when viewed from the ground as it passed sedately over one or other of the company's viaducts.

The only thing that spoiled the general effect was the noise and the clouds of dense smoke.

Despite its initial popularity the idea of locomotives imitating ships did not catch on and the London and Greenwich soon reverted to more practical-looking engines.

TRAFALGAR SQUARE –
PERMANENTLY UNFINISHED

1838

Present-day Trafalgar Square is built on the site where Henry VIII and earlier kings once kept their birds of prey and their horses. The site was first built on when Chaucer was Clerk of the King's Works in the 1380s and Richard II needed somewhere close to the rambling Palace of Whitehall for the royal hawks. Gradually the word mews was used not just for hawks and falcons but for other animals kept either for royal use or entertainment. The royal mews lasted well beyond the destruction by fire of the Palace of Westminster but the area in which the mews stood gradually became a warren of small dirty lanes where 'thieves and vagabonds abound', but by the time the area (by then known as the Bermudas) was cleared completely to allow for the building of the present square the word 'mews' had passed into the language and meant any narrow alleyway where horses were kept. Today in Belgravia and Mayfair the narrow back lanes behind grand house are still often called mews, for here the servants lived in small cottages or above the stables where their employers' horses were kept.

Like most building projects in London, Trafalgar Square was the subject of endless disputes and arguments – the plans for the National Gallery (completed in 1838) were derided by many who thought the proposed building an architectural disaster.

But unlike most projects, which are eventually built and completed, however greatly modified during the planning process, Trafalgar Square has never been completed and remains unfinished to this day.

The unfinished bit is the empty plinth in the northwest corner – this has been empty ever since the square was first built and though in recent years some bizarre sculptures have been placed on the unused plinth (including an upside-down see-through version of the plinth itself!) there are still no plans to erect a permanent statue here.

THE MYSTERIOUS CROSSING SWEEPER

1840

It's easy to forget that London's streets were, until comparatively recently, completely uncared for. In Victorian times
many streets were cobbled, or were made from wooden sets
(blocks of wood packed tightly with their end-grain uppermost
to reduce wear) but elsewhere they were entirely unmade. In
poorer districts the population would still throw their slops into
the street just as their medieval ancestors did. And of course
everywhere was the dung left by thousands of horses. But the
mess in the streets had one great advantage – it produced jobs
for hundreds if not thousands of London's poorest citizens.
These were the crossing sweepers. Perhaps the most famous
crossing sweeper – a trade that vanished with the coming of the
motor car – was Jo in Charles Dickens's novel *Bleak House*. Jo
was Dickens's attempt to show how damaging it was to society
as a whole to allow children to live the sort of life Jo lives.
Illiterate, half-dressed even in winter and forced to sleep in the
streets, Jo earns a few pennies each day by sweeping a path
through the horse manure from one side of a London street to
another. Many destitute men, women and children were forced
to do this work simply because they had nothing else, but one
of the most remarkable stories of a crossing sweeper concerns a
real-life sweeper called Brutus Billy or Charles McGhee.

Nothing is known of McGhee's history, but he was an elderly
black man who had probably come to England from the West

Indies. For many years in the early nineteenth century he swept a path across Fleet Street where it meets Ludgate Hill near a wealthy linen draper's shop in Fleet Street. The shop was owned by Robert Waithman who later became MP for the City of London. From the window above the shop the draper's daughter watched the old crossing sweeper and on cold days she arranged for someone to take him a bowl of hot soup and some bread. When McGhee died some years later it was discovered that he had left all his savings – some £700, which was an extraordinary sum in Victorian times – to the draper's daughter.

A BRIDGE FROM LONDON TO BRISTOL

1845

The Clifton Suspension Bridge is one of the wonders of nineteenth-century engineering, but one of the strangest things about it – a fact that is almost forgotten today – is that it started life in central London.

The story begins with the decision by the Earl of Hungerford to build a fruit and vegetable market to rival the one at Covent Garden. Hungerford market began life in 1692 on the site now occupied by Charing Cross Station but it never came to rival Covent Garden, the more famous market down the road. An attempt to improve things – by bringing customers in from south of the river – came when Isambard Kingdom Brunel built Hungerford Suspension Bridge in 1845.

Hungerford market finally disappeared when the railway company bought the land and built Charing Cross Station, but they too needed a bridge over the river and it would have to carry trains.

Before the current walkways were built, the railway company sold the old suspension bridge to the city of Bristol and then built their new railway bridge – in the strict legal sense there are still two bridges here, which may explain why on some maps the existing bridge is referred to as Hungerford Bridge while others insist on calling it Charing Cross Bridge. The reason is that the London public had got used to being able to cross the bridge and the railway company's plan would have deprived them of their old crossing because the new bridge would have been used by trains only. The railway company was forced by public pressure to build its railway bridge with a pedestrian footbridge alongside, which is why today the railway bridge into Charing Cross Station is the only railway bridge in London that also has a pedestrian footbridge. The pedestrian footbridge is Hungerford Bridge, while the railway bridge alongside is Charing Cross Bridge.

WHY THE JOCKEYS ATE TAPEWORMS

1845

One of the most expensive and fashionable parts of London is Notting Hill. Until the 1850s, however, Notting Hill was an area mostly of poor cottages, remote farms, brick kilns and gravel pits. It first became fashionable, not when the grand houses we see today were built but a decade or so earlier when one of London's long-forgotten racecourses attracted the rich and the fashionable from right across London and beyond.

An article in the *Sporting Magazine* for 1837 describes the wonders of the new racecourse:

> Making the cours aristocratique of Routine (alias Rotten) Row, you pass out at Cumberland Gate, and then trot on to Bayswater. Thence you arrive at the Kensington Gravel Pits, and descending where on the left stands the terrace of Notting Hill, find opposite the large wooden gates of a recent structure. Entering these, I was by no means prepared for what opened upon me. Here, without figure of speech, was the most perfect racecourse that I had ever seen. Conceive, almost within the bills of mortality, an enclosure some two miles and a half in circuit, commanding from its centre a view as spacious and enchanting as that from Richmond Hill, and where almost the only thing that you can not see is London. Around this, on the extreme circle, next to the lofty fence by which

it is protected is constructed, or rather laid out – for the leaps are natural fences – the steeplechase course of two miles and a quarter. Within this, divided by a slight trench, and from the space appropriated to carriages and equestrians by strong and handsome posts all the way round, is the race-course, less probably than a furlong in circuit. Then comes the enclosure for those who ride or drive as aforesaid; and lastly, the middle, occupied by a hill, from which every yard of the running is commanded, besides miles of country on every side beyond it, and exclusively reserved for foot people. I could hardly credit what I saw. Here was, almost at our doors, a racing emporium more extensive and attractive than Ascot or Epsom, with ten times the accommodation of either, and where carriages are charged for admission at three-fourths less. This great national undertaking is the sole result of individual enterprise, being effected by the industry and liberality of a gentleman by the name of Whyte. This is an enterprise which must prosper; it is without a competitor, and it is open to the fertilization of many sources of profit. As a site for horse exercise, can any riding-house compare with it? For females, it is without the danger or exposure of the parks; as a training-ground for the turf or the field it cannot be exceeded; and its character cannot be better summed up than by describing it as a necessary of London life, of the absolute need of which we were not aware until the possession of it taught us its permanent value.

But if the racecourse was one of the wonders of Georgian London, the jockeys were even more astonishing. Such was the pressure to win at all costs that tactics were used that would be completely unacceptable today. A jockey's weight, then as now, was vital and a practice arose among the jockeys at the Notting Hill Hippodrome that seems grotesque now but was apparently perfectly accepted at the time. When a jockey wanted to lose weight he deliberately infected himself with tapeworms so that regardless of how much he ate or drank he lost weight. This was vital before a big race that might earn a successful jockey a small fortune. After the race, or when it was no longer necessary to be stick-thin, the jockey would take a powerful emetic to purge himself of the tapeworms, though without modern medicines this can only ever have been partially successful.

Despite its popularity Notting Hill Racecourse did not survive long. The pressure for building land in those far off unregulated days was such that it was quickly buried beneath bricks and mortar.

The *Sporting Magazine* takes up the story:

After four years of a very chequered and struggling career, its last public meeting was held in June, 1841. At this date the land along its southern and eastern sides was beginning to be in demand for building purposes, and so pieces were sliced off to form those streets and thoroughfares which lie to the north of Westbourne Grove and south of the Great Western Railway. A large portion of the riding ground, however, was still kept laid down in turf – rather of a coarse kind, it must be owned; and some hedges were preserved, over which dashing young ladies would ride their chargers as lately as the year 1852. But in the course of the next five or six years the green sward, and the green trees, and the green hedges were all swept away.

KEEPING THE RICH OUT OF THE POOR SEATS

1850

Very soon after the railway system began to spread across England, the Victorian obsession with class began to rear its ugly head – carriages were quickly designated first, second or third class and they were used according to whether a particular traveller was at the top of the social pile (i.e. did absolutely no work at all), solidly middle class, or rough working class. But the railway owners prided themselves on the fact that their first-class carriages attracted only the very well-to-do and the aristocracy. Refinements to the service were always aimed at first-class passengers and at the groups who could be assumed to enjoy travelling in some style. After all, this is where the greatest profits were to be made. And it is easy to imagine the railway owners lamenting the fact that it was necessary, merely to keep the wheels of commerce in motion, also to provide third-class coaches, or wagons as they might better be described.

Third class made little in the way of profit for the railway company owners but factory owners who might have a share or two in railway stock wanted cheap transport for their staff. Imagine then the horror of the railway directors when they heard rumours that the well-to-do were, in increasing numbers, buying third-class tickets for some of the busiest and potentially most profitable routes. The problem was particularly acute in and around London.

One director simply could not believe that this was happening so he spent several weeks travelling each day on trains across and around the capital. He discovered that a significant proportion of those who, judging by their dress, should have known better were happily asleep or reading their newspapers in carriages made to carry only those lesser mortals who dug the roads, or cleaned the sewers. Those behaving badly included landowners, gentleman farmers and even, God help us, the odd baronet.

In short, first class had invaded third, an event that hinted at the worst kind of revolutionary fervour and, worse, meant a loss of funds for the railway directors and shareholders. This situation could not be allowed to continue, but the solution was hard to find. Booking-office clerks could hardly be asked to refuse to issue third-class tickets to anyone who seemed able to afford first class.

The director reported the situation to his fellow directors: 'I discovered that there were certain persons in superior positions who were base enough to travel third class and in order to bring these offenders to a proper sense of their position and to swell the revenues of the company, I recommend that we introduce what might best be termed special inconveniences.'

Special inconveniences turned out to be 'soot bag men'.

Thus on a bright spring morning in 1850 began one of the most extraordinary journeys in railway history. A team of four chimney sweeps had been specially hired. Each was assigned a third-class carriage that was believed to harbour individuals who did not belong to the working classes.

The decision about which carriages needed 'special inconveniences' was based on observations made by a senior porter who watched to see if anyone well turned out entered a third-class carriage. He then kept a note and reported his findings to the sweeps.

As soon as the train set off on its journey from Euston the sweeps went into action. They entered the third-class carriages and immediately unfolded several of their recently used sacks and began to shake them out, thus covering everyone in the carriage with a layer of grime and dirt. The working men, of course, took little or no notice since their work obliged them to wear rough and dirty clothes anyway. But the well dressed were horrified. But what could they do – if they complained to the management they would be told to travel first class since third-class passengers were used to dust and dirt and the railway company could do nothing about it.

The ruse worked and the numbers of passengers travelling first class rose, and as time passed fewer of the middle classes risked a confrontation with the soot-bag men.

According to an early edition of the *Railway Times* other rail companies found it more convenient to make sure that sheep or even pigs travelled regularly in their third-class carriages.

STAYING IN THE LIMELIGHT

1850

In the nineteenth century the passion for theatrical extravaganza reached such dizzying heights that real bears and lions were brought on stage for certain plays; in the West End for drama set in hotels real waiters from nearby hotels were sometimes engaged (a few people in the audience could always be relied on to recognise the waiters who were thought to add to the reality of the scene); real trains were driven across the stage; and special effects of dazzling complexity (though entirely mechanical) were used to create various illusions – one of the most bizarre was the use of the limelight men.

These were men employed to heat manganese dioxide in a sealed bag to produce oxygen; at the appropriate time the oxygen was mixed with hydrogen from another bag to produce an extraordinary incandescent light – colours varied from yellow to red and a skilled limelight man could produce the whole range of colours by judicious mixing.

If various coloured lights had to be produced at the same time dozens of limelight men had to be employed in the wings, since one man could produce only one light at a time. Then there were the extraordinary pulleys and wires, sliding backdrops, trapdoors, painted boards and sheets that became ever more complex and intricate as the years passed, but nothing could compare with the Standard Theatre in London's East End. Here, from 1850 on, the theatre re-created Derby day and Ascot races using real horses.

As many as fifty horses and riders were kept waiting in a special marshalling yard to the side of the stage but outside the building at the back. When the principal players in the drama started watching a race a door was opened at the side of the stage but out of sight of the audience. The massive door led to a ramp which ran down to the marshalling yard. At a given signal the horses were galloped round the back of the theatre so they had time to pick up speed before racing up the ramp on to the stage and across it at full speed, to the astonishment of the audience. At the other side of the stage from the entrance ramp there was another large door and another ramp that allowed the horses to gallop off the stage down the ramp and back into the yard where they slowed up. They might then gallop around the back of the theatre again to hurtle back on to the stage two or three times before the play came to an end.

THE SCANDAL OF A HORSE
IN CHURCH

1852

When the Duke of Wellington died in 1852 plans were immediately put in hand to erect a suitable monument in St Paul's Cathedral to a man perceived as the greatest military genius in British history. The monument was commissioned from the sculptor Alfred Stevens (1817–1875). He was offered £14,000 – a huge sum at the time – but Stevens was a man of extravagant vision, so much so that almost all the money was found to have disappeared within a few years and it hadn't even paid for the materials, let alone the work required.

One of the problems was that, with no thought of cost, Stevens simply continually ordered the most expensive materials he could get his hands on. He also decided to build on a colossal scale and by the time the authorities realised what was going on it was too late.

Officials at St Paul's were so horrified that they washed their hands of the whole business and immediately called in the services of the notoriously parsimonious (and bizarrely named) Acton Smee Ayrton, who was the government's Official Surveyor of Works.

Ayrton, who was not known for his diplomacy, went straight to the High Court and obtained an injunction that threatened Stevens with imprisonment if he did not complete Wellington's monument within thirty days. The task was, of course, impossible. When the deadline passed bailiffs were sent in to

206

Stevens's studio where they took everything – paint brushes, easels, chisels and other artistic paraphernalia. The sum raised from the sale of Stevens's equipment was derisory but the pettiness of Ayrton's actions roused the fury of the whole of Britain's artistic community. They petitioned Parliament and the Queen, and Stevens was soon back at work – but shaken by the disaster that had befallen him, he died soon after returning to St Paul's and still the monument remained unfinished.

Incredibly, it took another thirty years for the artist John Tweed (1869–1933) to complete the monument – it was Tweed who made the bronze figure of Wellington on his horse, Copenhagen, atop the spectacular marble base that Stevens had made all those years ago.

Further difficulties arose when there were protests from religious zealots at the idea of a horse in a church and works stopped again – in fact it was only in 1912, some sixty years after Wellington had died, that his extraordinary monument was finally completed.

But Stevens had the last laugh – after the monument was completed someone noticed that the figure representing calumny at the base of the monument bore a striking resemblance to the man who had sent the bailiffs in to remove possessions – Ayrton's only memorial is this deeply unattractive sculpture.

WHY BIG BEN ISN'T BIG BEN AT ALL

1852

Big Ben is one of London's oddest buildings and the story of how it came to be built is typical of the eccentric way in which things tend to get done in London. Like the rest of the Palace of Westminster, it was built by Charles Barry (1795–1860) and Augustus Pugin (1812–1852) after a nationwide competition to find a new design for the seat of government after the disastrous fire of 1834.

The late Georgian passion for Gothic gave the Barry design a head start and after duly winning the competition, he began building the clock tower we see today, but when it was first built it wasn't known as Big Ben at all – the name Big Ben refers to the huge bell on which the hours are struck.

All the statistics to do with St Stephen's Tower (as Big Ben is really known) and its great clock are astonishing: the tower is nearly three hundred and twenty feet high; it took almost nineteen years from laying the first foundation stone to getting the clock going, largely because no one could agree about who should make it.

The job was first offered to Benjamin Vulliamy, the Queen's clockmaker, who was based in Pall Mall. His design was attacked as absurd and incompetent by another clockmaker, J. Dent, and after a huge fight with letters banging to and fro and *Times* leaders thundering out various opinions, the commissioners charged with organising the work gave in and launched a competition to design and build the new clock.

The contract finally went to Dent amid much acrimony, in 1852. Two years later the unique clock – twenty three feet diameter – was ready, but there was nowhere to put it because wrangles over the building of the tower had delayed construction.

While all this was being sorted out, an east London company cast a great sixteen-ton bell, but during tests using a thirteen-hundredweight clapper the bell cracked. It then had to be melted down and recast, this time by the Whitechapel Bell foundry. It took sixteen horses the best part of a day to haul the gigantic bell to Parliament Square. It was then hoisted into position at the top of the tower, which was completed just in time.

When the clock began to run it was discovered that the two and a half ton hands were so heavy that the mechanism could not move them. They were redesigned in a lighter metal but now crashed down past the three each time they reached 12. Remade for a third time in hollow copper, they worked and they have kept time accurately ever since.

There are two theories about the origins of the name 'Big Ben': around the time the clock was due to be completed, the prizefighter and publican Ben Caunt went sixty rounds with the best bare-knuckle boxer in the country, Nat Langham. The bout was declared a draw but it made both men national heroes. Ben Caunt was a huge man and one story has it that the great bell was named after him. The other story attributes the name to Benjamin Hall, the chief commissioner of works, who was addressing the House on the subject of a name for the new bell tower when, to great laughter, someone shouted 'Call it Big Ben!'

Perhaps the most remarkable thing about the clock is that even by the standards of today's atomic timepieces it is wonderfully accurate. When the commissioners launched their competition to design it they stipulated that it must be accurate to within one second an hour – most clock makers at the time agreed that this was impossible but that's how accurate the clock still is today. If it does get slightly out of time, a tiny coin, kept especially for the purpose, is placed on the huge pendulum and the weight of the coin is enough to adjust the clock by a fraction of a second.

TRAINS ONLY FOR THE DEAD

1854

Just outside Waterloo Station between what was once York Street (it was recently renamed Leake Street) and the Westminster Bridge Road is a curious reddish building with a grey-stone arched entranceway. This is the former entrance to one of London's most extraordinary railway stations.

The current building dates from the early twentieth century but it replaced a station building opened on the same site in 1854. The station was the London terminus for the Necropolis Railway – a railway devoted entirely to the dead.

To find out how this bizarre situation came about we have to remember that by the mid-nineteenth century London's churchyards were full to overflowing. Bodies were stamped down into graves already too full and in many cases just a few inches of soil covered the decaying corpses. The result was appallingly insanitary conditions and frequent outbreaks of disease.

To ease the problems London's churchyards were closed and building began on a number of out-of-town cemeteries – Kensal Green and, more famously, Highgate. South of London, Brookwood Cemetery was opened some 25 miles from London, but the great difficulty was how to get corpse, coffin and mourners there. The solution was the Necropolis Railway.

Funeral trains ran from what was really a private station attached to the main line. Once out of the station the funeral trains joined the main line until they reached Brookwood. Here they reversed into the grounds of the cemetery. Until 1902 when the station was rebuilt following the complete rebuilding of the rest of Waterloo Station, Necropolis trains ran every day if there was a booking. After 1900, for some inexplicable reason, trains ceased to run on Sundays and a few years later they were running no more than twice a week. In 1941 the station was bombed (the façade survived) and the funeral trains were never revived after the war.

In the late 1940s the track from London to Brookwood was taken up but the station and track survived in the grounds of Brookwood Cemetery for a little longer. There were two stations in the cemetery – the north station served Nonconformists and the south station served the Anglican dead. The north station was demolished in the early 1960s but the south station survived until a fire in 1972. Today, the remains of the station platforms can still be seen at Brookwood – the only reminder of the thousands of dead who took their last journey on the Necropolis railway.

FREE LOVE IN VICTORIAN CLAPTON

1859

In the first centuries of the Christian era there were dozens if not hundreds of odd little sects and heretical groups that broke away from the ancient Jewish tradition (as did Jesus himself) and claimed that their leader was the messiah. Christos is merely the Greek rendering of the Hebrew word messiah.

Many of these early sects were ruthlessly suppressed as what was considered 'orthodox' belief came to be enforced by one particular group – the Christians. This, of course, later split into the Roman Catholic strand of Christianity and the Orthodox strand. But there were also many Gnostic (meaning secret knowledge) Christian sects whose beliefs were considered heretical.

One gnostic sect believed that Judas was the one true disciple on the grounds that he was the only one who helped Christ slough off his mortal body. The existence of this gnostic strand of early Christianity was confirmed spectacularly when in 2004 scholars discovered a previously unknown gospel from the late third century – this was the Gospel of Judas Iscariot.

In later centuries, Christianity was split and riven by other sects, the Rosicrucians, Muggletonians, Ranters and Peculiar People among others. Most spectacular of all, of course, was the major split that occurred at the Reformation.

But a little church in north London which still stands today was once home to a Christian sect that was bizarre even by the standards of early gnostic and other apocalyptic sects.

212

The church, whose architecture hardly betrays its bizarre origins, was once the home of the Agapemonites, a sect that – like the American Mormons – has its origins in one man's desire to legitimise a promiscuous sex life.

The story begins with Henry James Prince who, while a student at St David's theological college in Wales, set up the Lampeter Brethren in 1836. Ordained at the age of 28, Prince made himself head of the brethren whose main aim seems to have been what in the 1960s would have been termed free love.

By 1859 Prince had married a wealthy woman who then conveniently died. He also resigned from the Church of England and set up the Agapemonites using money he'd inherited from his wife. Prince was apparently a remarkably charismatic man and within a few years his new church – 'agapemone' is Greek for abode of love – was attracting numerous followers. Women seem to have been particularly keen to join. All new members pooled their wealth and lived communally under the rule of Prince.

A wealthy London businessman gave Prince a huge donation and agreed to become the great man's butler, but when Prince helped himself to Louisa Nottidge's fortune her family sued him and won – the Agapemonites had to pay the money back.

Despite an occasional setback the Agapemonites were now wealthy enough to build the church that still stands in the Clapton district of Hackney. The building was known as the Ark of the Covenant and it cost £16,000 to build.

By the 1890s the church was attracting people from across the world, though in relatively small numbers. They came to listen to Prince tell them that he was John the Baptist come back to earth. By the end of the century he was telling his congregation that he was no longer John the Baptist but had become the Incarnation of the Holy Ghost.

Prince's right-hand man was John Hugh Smyth Piggot, a parson who had studied at the London College of Divinity in Highbury. He met Prince in Ireland in the mid-1880s and was a member of the Salvation Army for a while.

The two men seemed to have spent most of their time

persuading the female members of their congregation that the way to salvation was via the bedroom. But there was an occasional explanation of the sect's more general theological ideas – the Testimony, for example, was published in the 1890s. It is astonishing it ever convinced anyone given that it is full of precisely the same sort of predictions and pronouncements that characterise pretty much every other oddball sect from the Mormons to the Jehovah's Witnesses.

The Testimony says that the world is about to end and that members of the church must be celibate unless called upon by the church itself to sacrifice their celibacy in pursuit of a higher truth.

Prince insisted that as the Lord's anointed he must travel in style – he had a coach and four and whenever he thundered through the London streets his coach was accompanied by a full complement of foxhounds.

He told his followers that as a spirit he could not die so it must have come as a shock when he dropped dead in 1899.

What really astonished his followers, however, was the fact that Prince had condemned every other church member who had died – he had said that any member who died only did so because he had not lived properly according to the rules of the Agapemonites. As he, by implication, was supremely aware of how a good Agapemonite should live he would never die, but die he did.

Prince was buried upright (another Agapemonite idea) and Piggot took over as leader. Piggot clearly thought that Prince had undersold himself when he declared that he was John the Baptist (and later the Holy Ghost) so on 7 September 1902 he told his congregation something even more remarkable. His exact words were recorded for posterity:

Christ suffered for sin and it was promised for them that waited for him He would appear a second time with salvation to man from death and judgement. Brother Prince was sent before his Lord's face to prepare the way for the second coming of him who suffered for sin, to prepare the way for the restoration of all things.

His testimony was true and the word of the holy ghost in him was perfect and I who speak to you tonight – I am that Lord Jesus Christ who died and rose again and ascended into heaven. I am that Lord Jesus Christ come again in my own body to save those who come to me from death and judgment.

Yes, I am he that liveth and behold I am alive for ever more. I am come again for the second time as the bridegroom of the church and the judge of all men, for the father has committed all judgment unto me because I am the son of man. And you – each one of you – must be judged by me.

By the following Sunday word of this astonishing sermon had leaked out and a crowd of more than six thousand gathered outside the Ark of the Covenant. Police were called to keep order and the mood grew ugly. In earlier times, of course, anyone claiming to be Jesus would have been burned at the stake. The Edwardians of north London were cross but not that cross – they confined themselves to jeering Piggot when he arrived in his coach and four.

In the event the police failed to keep order and the crowd surged into the church, where Piggot duly repeated his claim to be Jesus.

Piggot's coach was bombarded with sticks, stones and bricks as he travelled home and such was the scandal surrounding his outrageous claims that the sect was forced to move to a remote location in Somerset. Here a young woman called Ruth Preece joined the sect and became Piggot's second wife.

Life was strict in the Somerset Abode of Love – the women members of the sect were known as helps (they did all the work) who might graduate to be ornamentals, entitled to be waited on by the helps. About thirty of the youngest and most attractive members of the sect became Piggot's concubines. Piggot sat on a gilded throne and everyone had to call him master.

Ruth Preece eventually became spiritual bride in chief but seems to have got on well with the first Mrs Piggot.

215

In 1909 it became known to the church authorities that Piggot's concubines had given birth and a consistory court was instituted to try Piggot in *absentia*. He was defrocked on 9 March.

By this time more than one hundred women were living at the Abode of Love with Piggot. As he grew older all sorts of potions were tried in an attempt to keep him young and vigorous; all failed. He died in 1927 and the sect was taken over by Douglas Hamilton. The sect began to decline and by the 1940s only a dozen or so members were left. Piggot's two sons served in the forces; his daughter vanished abroad. Hamilton died in 1942.

By 1950 the tiny group of remaining sect members were still convinced that Piggot would return to them. He did not and the last of the Agapemonites – Ruth Preece – survived into the 1960s. The Ark of the Covenant in Clapton still stands but is now a Catholic church. Piggot's bizarre sect has gone forever.

MR CRAPPER'S BOTTOM SLAPPER

1860

A strange London story that turns out not to be true is that the word 'crap' – in the vulgar lavatorial sense – comes from the pioneer of the flushing lavatory, Thomas Crapper (1837–1910).

But even if that is not true there remain some wonderful tales about Crapper, who walked penniless to London in 1850 aged fourteen and became apprenticed to a master plumber in Chelsea. A decade later he had set up on his own and his company soon became the most famous sanitary-ware manufacturer in the world – a manufacturer that was still in existence in the early 1960s.

Crapper was a brilliant engineer who revolutionised the way we go to the loo. Before Crapper, London lavatories relied on turning a simple tap on to flush the loo, but the problem with this system was that people forgot to turn the tap off and water was left running (sometimes intentionally) all the time. A trickle of water did not make for a particularly hygienic flushing system. The result was a chronic loss of pressure in London's water system and badly flushing loos.

Crapper's flushing lavatory was brilliant because it was automatic, saved water and was propelled by enough force to flush properly. Instead of the loo with a simple running tap he invented the system we use today – a small tank filled automatically with no risk of overflow and using only relatively small amounts of water. The tank also produced enough pressure to flush the loo properly in one go.

So convinced was he of the brilliance of his various designs that he invited a bemused public into the works every now and then to see how a particular loo and cistern combination could flush away a dozen apples or several potatoes. Visits became one of the highlights of Saturday afternoons in Chelsea!

Crapper also invented the disconnecting trap – a device fitted in each soil pipe just below ground that prevented the smell of the drains coming back up into the house.

Crapper seems to have been almost the only Victorian not to have been squeamish and permanently embarrassed by matters lavatorial, but on one famous occasion in the early days of his success he put his loos and cisterns in the window of his shop in Chelsea and several lady passers-by fainted with shock!

Not all Crapper's inventions were warmly greeted, however. He invented a loo that used a complicated system of pistons attached to the loo seat to flush the loo automatically. Having used the loo the user stood up and the loo seat automatically rose up – the rising movement automatically activating the flushing mechanism. However, it was discovered that within a few months of being fitted the loo seat began to stick – this meant that the unsuspecting user would begin to stand up only to find that the loo seat stuck until enough pressure had built up from the system to unstick it. The loo seat would then fly up at speed, hitting the user painfully on the bottom. The invention became known as the bottom slapper and was eventually discontinued.

Thomas Crapper died in 1910 but the firm he founded was still being run by his descendants in 1963, when it was finally sold to a rival company. Crapper was never honoured despite the fact that his flushing loo probably did far more to improve the health and happiness of humans worldwide than any number of politicians, businessmen, army generals and celebrities put together.

LAST OF THE GREAT LONDON COURTESANS

1861

English prostitutes probably suffered most in the nineteenth century, which not only criminalised them but also patronised them. Earlier centuries accepted the role of the honest whore with more equanimity. In the nineteenth century only one sort of prostitute could live within the vague bounds of respectability – the sort who slept with kings and princes. If the king insisted that his mistress be allowed to accompany him to country houses, the theatre and other social engagements then everyone had to be polite to her. Lower down the social scale a mistress would be completely ostracised in a society that expected respectable women to be so delicate that it was as much as they could do to lie on a sofa all day complaining about headaches.

But in the thick of all this hypocrisy we can still espy the mighty creature that is Catherine Walters (1839–1920), tales of whose extraordinary exploits filled the air of Victorian and Edwardian London. Mrs Walters – whose nickname was 'Skittles' – is also proof that the power of personality can overcome almost any obstacle.

She was known as Skittles for reasons no one can now discover – it may have been that she started work as a prostitute in Skittle Alley, Liverpool, but she was a great beauty in her youth as well as being the last in a line of professional courtesans stretching back to Nell Gwynn and beyond.

219

What is most remarkable about Skittles is that she lived through an age that was probably the most moralistic – even if hypocritically so – in British history. The Victorian obsession with purity and chastity except within marriage combined with the absolute rule of respectability meant that any middle- or working-class woman suspected of sexual irregularity (as the Victorian newspapers might have put it) would be shunned by everyone, but as always there was one rule for the majority and an entirely different rule for the elite.

Because Mrs Walters was the paid mistress of a number of members of the aristocracy and royalty she had to be received into society if her various partners insisted on it. But even without aristocratic patronage the decidedly eccentric Skittles would have survived anyway. She was in many respects immune to the rules that applied to most people simply because she didn't give a fig about them. She was the mistress of the Duke of Devonshire and the Marquis of Hartington among others and insisted on the finest clothes and carriages – finer even it was said than the wives of her lovers. Stories about her are legion. She loved horses and hunting and once when out with the Quorn in Leicestershire she had kept up with the leaders of the field until the fox was caught. The master of hounds ventured to compliment her on the fine flushed colour of her cheeks. 'That's nothing,' she replied. 'You should see the colour of my ruddy arse!'

She reached the height of her fame in 1861 when any rumour that she might be driving in the park on a Sunday would lead to huge crowds assembling to catch a glimpse of her.

She lived for many years at No. 15 South Street, Mayfair – the house is still there – and in old age was pushed in her wheelchair through Hyde Park by none other than Lord Kitchener.

HOW TO MAKE A LIVING SELLING DOG POO

1861

Poverty in earlier centuries pushed tens of thousands of Londoners into very peculiar occupations – peculiar at least by modern standards. There was a huge market for live birds, for example, and this market was met by hundreds of live-bird sellers who might walk twenty miles out of London to catch a dozen or so birds before walking the twenty miles back again. They would then repeat this journey three or four times a week.

Or take the mudlarks who scoured the river foreshore at low tide. They went barefoot whatever the weather, searching for copper nails from the ships, for old bottles – anything in fact that they might be able to sell.

The toshers, on the other hand, were men who risked their lives searching for valuables in London's vast, unmapped warren of sewers. Toshers tended to be from the same few families and they handed down their knowledge of the sewer network from generation to generation, but even generations of experience couldn't always protect them and many died when sudden rainfall flooded the system or the lamps and candles they carried were blown out or they were overcome by gas.

But perhaps the strangest job of all was that of the pure finder – a job that existed, perhaps could only have existed, in Victorian London.

A pure finder was someone who spent his days searching for dog faeces to sell to leather tanners, particularly to those

221

tanners engaged in producing leather for the bookbinding trade.

Henry Mayhew's extraordinary book *London Labour and the London Poor* charts the lives of a number of pure finders. Mayhew explains that in the 1830s and 1840s only women seem to have been involved in the trade and they were known as 'bunters'. By the 1850s, when Mayhew carried out his research, men, women and children were working as pure finders. Pure finders sold the dog faeces they collected for roughly ten old pence a bucketful. The tanners – mostly based in Bermondsey (where thirty tanneries are recorded in the 1860s) – preferred the dry sort of faeces as it contained more alkaline and it was the alkaline that worked its magic on the leather.

Curiously, Mayhew and others recorded that many of the pure finders were well-educated men and women who had fallen on hard times. His description of the trade is hugely evocative:

> The pure-finder is often found in the open streets, as dogs wander where they like. The pure-finders always carry a handle basket, generally with a cover, to hide the contents, and have their right hand covered with a black leather glove; many of them, however, dispense with the glove, as they say it is much easier to wash their hands than to keep the glove fit for use. The women generally have a large pocket for the reception of such rags as they may chance to fall in with, but they pick up those only of the very best quality, and will not go out of their way to search even for them. Thus equipped they may be seen pursuing their avocation in almost every street in and about London, excepting such streets as are now cleansed by the street orderlies, of whom the pure-finders grievously complain, as being an unwarrantable interference with the privileges of their class.
>
> The pure collected is used by leather-dressers and tanners, and more especially by those engaged in the

manufacture of morocco and kid leather from the skins of old and young goats, of which skins great numbers are imported, and of the roans and lambskins which are the sham morocco and kids of the slop leather trade, and are used by the better class of shoemakers, book binders, and glovers, for the inferior requirements of their business. Pure is also used by tanners, as is pigeons' dung, for the tanning of the thinner kinds of leather, such as calf-skins, for which purpose it is placed in pits with an admixture of lime and bark.

In the manufacture of moroccos and roans the pure is rubbed by the hands of the workman into the skin he is dressing. This is done to purify the leather, I was told by an intelligent leatherdresser, and from that term the word pure has originated. The dung has astringent as well as highly alkaline, or, to use the expression of my informant, scouring, qualities. When the pure has been rubbed into the flesh and grain of the skin (the flesh being originally the interior, and the grain the exterior part of the cuticle), and the skin, thus purified, has been hung up to be dried, the dung removes, as it were, all such moisture as, if allowed to remain, would tend to make the leather unsound or imperfectly dressed. This imperfect dressing, moreover, gives a disagreeable smell to the leather and leather-buyers often use both nose and tongue in making their purchases...

UNGODLY TRAVEL DENOUNCED

1863

In a pamphlet published in London midway through Queen Victoria's reign, various so-called experts denounced the new fashion for railway travel. It was ungodly, ungentlemanly and un-Christian according to many of those who contributed to the pamphlet.

One short contribution sums up the general tenor of the whole: it was written Dr Walter Lewis, the medical officer of the London Post Office. He wrote that his views and scientific conclusions on railway travel were based entirely on observations of the health of the travelling public. He was determined to give the impression that his views were based strictly on science yet to the modern traveller his views seem bizarre in the extreme.

Dr Lewis wrote:

Railway travel has little, if any, injurious effect on healthy, strong, well-built persons, such as are typically to be found among the London populace, but provided that the amount be not excessive, and if passengers ensure that they take moderate care of themselves; but persons who take to habitual railway travelling after the age of twenty five or thirty are more easily and dangerously affected than those who begin earlier, and that the more advanced in age a traveller is, the more easily is he affected by this sort of locomotion.

Weak, tall loosely-knit persons, and those suffering under various affections, more especially of the head, heart, and lungs, are very unsuited for habitual railway travelling. They may also find the extreme motion induces delusions of a most unwholesome sort and may even inflame the passions.

WHERE IS THE CENTRE OF LONDON?

1865

One of the oddest things about London is that most people have no idea where it begins – or more precisely where its centre actually is. Many think that the statue of Eros in Piccadilly Circus marks the centre point; others are convinced that Buckingham Palace marks the spot, or St Paul's Cathedral.

In fact – and for the strangest reason – the centre of London is located at a spot just behind the equestrian statue of Charles I at the southern edge of Trafalgar Square. If you look carefully there is a brass plate in the roadway that marks the precise spot.

But what adds to the oddity of this is that strictly speaking – and despite modern rearrangements to suit the traffic – the brass plate set in the ground here is not in Trafalgar Square at all. It is Charing Cross. The Charing Cross we see today – which is outside the Charing Cross railway hotel just a few hundred yards away – was put up in 1865 as a publicity stunt to attract attention to the new railway terminus.

The medieval Charing Cross from which the area gets its name was actually at the top of Whitehall where the brass plaque is now.

But why choose this exact spot to define the centre of London? The answer has to do with the bizarre growth of the capital – to the east of the plaque is the City of London; to the south Westminster.

Edward the Confessor (1003–1066) made a vow to go on a the pilgrimage to Rome, but domestic unrest made this impossible and he sought absolution from his vow by promising to build a huge church. He chose Thorney Island for his church – a small area of high ground above the surrounding marsh of the Thames. This area – we now call it Westminster – already had a small monastery, but Edward enlarged it considerably and added Westminster Abbey, the church we see today. The new church was complete by 1065.

The merchants of the City had no intention of moving to what was then a windswept and remote location so they stayed put, but when the legislators at Westminster Hall wanted to hear news of the commercial goings on of the City they came to the halfway point – Charing Cross – and the City merchants wanting to know more of affairs of state also came to this spot.

The brass plaque marks the exact halfway point between the old city and the new seat of government and is therefore the centre point, as it were, of both Londons.

With the growth of the civil service in the nineteenth and twentieth centuries the brass plaque helped solve a more practical problem too: where London weighting was paid to public officials there had to be a decision about the area of London within which the extra rate of pay would be calculated. It was decided that anyone working within a six-mile radius of the brass plaque at Charing Cross would be entitled to the extra payment.

MAD ABOUT FOOTWARMERS

1867

It's no longer acceptable for the general public to treat the staff of particular companies badly just because they are paying for the service those companies provide. But that wasn't always the case and customers in the past could get away with treating shop and railway staff – to take just two examples – as they pleased simply because they were paying.

Some customers were so unreasonable in their behaviour that stories about them have become legendary. Among railwaymen and railway historians the tale of the woman and the footwarmer has been handed down from generation to generation.

The carriages of high-speed trains that ran between major cities in the great age of steam were warmed during the winter season by excess steam, an innovation that overnight reduced the need – at least on some journeys – for vast numbers of greatcoats and capes, hats, gloves and scarves.

The steam heating innovation was a clever one because the steam used to heat the carriages was recycled steam that had already been used to drive the engine. The system was to force the steam along pipes from end to end of the train with connections going into each compartment of the carriages.

Most people loved the new system, which also dispensed with the need for cumbersome and inefficient footwarmers, but a few diehards petitioned for it to be abandoned.

Among the latter was a famously eccentric old lady who, prior to taking her seat in a train shortly to leave King's Cross in London, asked, in a tone that suggested she had no intention of being refused, to be provided with a footwarmer. Since footwarmers were no longer available she was told, as politely as possible, that this would not be possible but that she could comfort herself with the knowledge that the carriages were now heated in a far more efficient way by steam.

According to the policeman who was soon called to the scene, she at once assumed an extremely militant attitude, and railed against the new method, apparently for no conceivable reason other than that it was a departure from a practice she had grown accustomed to, and that she could not bear such newfangled notions.

She demonstrated the full depths of her anger by using an umbrella to poke and swipe at the poor old railwayman who'd originally come along to see if he could help her, which was a bit unfair as he couldn't have supplied her with a footwarmer even if he'd wanted to, since none was available.

With the aid of the policeman who calmed her down, the patient railwayman at last persuaded the old lady to at least try sitting for a few moments in one of the steam-heated compartments. She entered, with misgiving writ large on her countenance, and immediately declared that the atmosphere was unbearable, and that she knew beforehand that it would be so.

'But, how can that be,' said the railwayman, 'when the engine is not yet attached to the train, and the steam pipe, which you're welcome to touch, is stone cold?'

Her only answer was to shout at both the railwayman and the attendant policeman:

'Get away with you both. I will in future travel on a line where they will not both boil me and make me make a fool of myself.'

THE HOUSES THAT EXIST BUT AREN'T THERE

1868

An elegant stuccoed street in Paddington hides one of the oddest pairs of houses in the world. The passer-by would hardly notice that numbers 23 and 24 Leinster Gardens have permanently darkened windows, nor that the front doors have a curiously solid feel to them. But look closely and you quickly realise that these are not actually houses at all.

The story starts in the 1860s when the world's first underground railway was being constructed. The Metropolitan line – which was opened in 1868 – was built on the cut and cover principle. This meant that to build a tunnel you first had to dig a huge trench. Once this was done the circular supports (to make the tunnel) were fitted and the whole then covered with earth again. When the line between Bayswater and Paddington was being built it became necessary to demolish two houses in what was then a recently built and highly prestigious row of terraced houses.

Numerous railway acts tended to ride roughshod over the rights of tenants and landlords in the mid-Victorian era so the railway company simply compulsorily purchased two houses in the path of their tunnel and knocked them down. But the householders on either side refused to be beaten by a mere Act of Parliament – they managed to force through a condition that when the tunnel had been built and covered over, the facades at least of the two demolished houses should be reinstated. And that is precisely what happened. What look like a pair of rather grand houses are actually only walls about five feet thick.

If you retrace your steps from Leinster Gardens to Porchester Road, which runs parallel to Leinster Gardens, you come to a long wall. Look over this and you will see the backs of 23 and 24 Leinster Gardens – a high, blank brick wall held up by steel girders. Below the wall is the tunnel entrance. But this is only a short stretch of exposed railway and it could have been covered over. The reason it is still open to the skies is that the first underground railway trains were steam driven and though they were specially adapted to reduce steam and smoke emissions in the tunnels (which would have been very unhealthy for passengers) they did have to release large amounts of coal exhaust fumes now and then. The spot behind the fake houses was established as an acceptable place for those early drivers to vent their engines!

ISLAMIC SEWAGE CENTRE

1868

Many of London's strangest tales concern buildings put up for the oddest reasons – either the fashion of the time or as a result of the eccentricity of architect or owner. But there are a number of buildings put up in odd styles to hide their real purpose.

The Abbey Mills pumping station is a good example. This dotty-looking building with its Moorish domes and towers, looks like something from Asia or the Middle East – in fact it was built in Victorian times (during a period of enthusiasm for all things Islamic) to disguise, of all things, a sewage works!

The interior is even more bizarre as it looks exactly like an Eastern Orthodox Church.

The architect was Joseph Bazalgette (1819–1891), the man who rescued London from drowning in its own sewage by building the embankments along the Thames and their massive sewers that were designed to carry London's waste miles downstream and away from the bulk of the populace.

Balzalgette's embankment also provided a perfect place to build tunnels for the Circle and District lines as well – later on – as masses of communications wires and pipes.

The embankment sewer scheme had been proposed after Parliament found it increasingly difficult to meet at all in summer because of the stench from the river – at times it was so bad that huge sheets of canvas soaked in vinegar had to be hung behind the windows of the palace of Westminster. Without them the Parliamentarians were unable to stay in the chamber long enough to make any decisions. Bazalgette came up with the answer. But the embankment was only part of the solution and Bazalgette was given responsibility for the whole of London's main drainage system. Hence Abbey Mills pumping station.

Completed in 1868, it had to be made to look like something – anything – other than a sewage pumping station because the Victorians couldn't bear the idea of anyone going to the lavatory and would not have taken kindly to a large building clearly designed with sewage in mind. But with a Moorish palace in their midst they could kid themselves that it had nothing to do with bodily functions of any kind.

WHERE SPHAIRISTIKE STARTED

1869

Lawn tennis (as opposed to what is now known as real tennis) began in England; not in the sports field or even on a piece of ground we would today recognise as a tennis court. It actually started in the gardens of a now vanished house on the southern side of Berkeley Square. The badly designed modern building we see today is on the site of Landsdowne House, an eighteenth-century mansion designed by the great Robert Adam (1728–1792) and completed in 1762.

It was here in 1774 that the scientist Joseph Priestley (1733–1804) discovered oxygen and, almost a century later, in 1869, the world's first game of tennis was played. It came about almost by chance. A Major Winfield came to London to visit the third Lord Lansdown (the house had been built for his ancestor William Petty, first Lord Lansdown). Winfield told Lansdown that he'd been thinking about a new game that four people could play on a small patch of grass. He called his new game Sphairistike.

Lansdown invited A. J. Balfour (1848–1930), the future Prime Minister, and another friend to play the game the next day. It was a success and within a few years Sphairistike was being played all over the country.

The name Sphairistike was quickly dropped (which is not that surprising!) and it was Arthur Balfour who coined the name the sport retains to this day: lawn tennis.

A ROAR ON THE EMBANKMENT

1870

The Thames has always dominated life in London – the City's huge wealth was built on trade via the river and for centuries most people travelled across London by water as the roads were almost always either cluttered or deep in mud or both.

London was in constant danger of flooding too and even today, with the Thames Barrier in place, rising sea levels could threaten the city again.

The real problem with flooding when the embankment walls were built was that, despite the great height of the embankment walls, they had the effect of narrowing the river and increasing its depth. Add to that the fact that nothing could control the great surges that began far out at sea and then drove remorselessly upriver. When heavy rain in winter coincided with a big spring tide the embankment was often breached in numerous places, causing tens of thousands of pounds of damage to property, not to mention disruption to transport and people's lives generally.

There was, however, a bizarre and rather primitive early warning system that is still partially in use today.

Anyone who has ever leaned over the embankment to gaze out along the river will probably have noticed that well below the parapet and fixed at regular intervals into the stonework there are lions' heads with mooring rings hanging from their mouths. Visitors often wonder why on earth so many mooring positions should be required so far below the top of the wall –

the passengers of any boat tying up at any of these rings could not possibly disembark.

The solution to this mystery is tied up with the early warning system for flooding that existed in London before the Thames Barrier was built.

Every policeman whose beat happens to take him along the embankment on either side of the river was formerly instructed to keep an eye on the lions' heads, because if the water level reaches the heads flooding is a serious and imminent danger. The rule used to be that once the water reached the heads all Underground stations were closed and London was put on red alert.

THE BRIDGE THAT COULD FALL DOWN

1873

Albert Bridge – never referred to as The Albert Bridge – looks like just any other bridge over the Thames. It's rather pretty certainly, but nothing out of the ordinary until, that is, you look a little closer.

Built by R. M. Ordish in 1873 Albert Bridge is in fact highly unusual. It has three spans and what's known in engineering circles as a straight-link suspension system. Each half of the bridge is supported by wrought iron bars attached to the top of the two highly ornamental towers. Meanwhile the side girders along the parapets are suspended, making the bridge an odd mix of cantilever and suspension.

What makes it even odder is that there is still a small hexagonal toll house on the south side of the bridge – in fact, this is a very rare survival indeed as it is the only bridge toll house left anywhere in London. But the strangest thing about Albert Bridge is neither its method of construction nor its toll house – it's the sign, put here when the bridge was first built, which says that soldiers must not march in step when crossing the bridge. To the casual passer-by the sign has always been completely mystifying – but there is method in what looks like madness. The reason soldiers are not allowed to march in step over the bridge is that the rhythm set up by their synchronised movements might cause structural damage to the bridge. At worst it might collapse.

The difficulty is that older suspension bridges pick up and then massively amplify synchronised movement – a phenomenon to which Albert Bridge is particularly prone.

THE HOUSE WHERE TIME STOOD STILL

1874

There is a common misconception that London is still a wonderful place to find eighteenth- and early nineteenth-century architecture despite the deadly work of redevelopers and German bombs, but actually the majority of eighteenth-century houses are only eighteenth century in outward appearance. Only a few rare examples are listed in such a way as to prevent their interiors being destroyed, even if their facades have to be left unchanged. This means that thousands of modern houses and office blocks have eighteenth-century fronts. This even happened – back in the 1960s – to houses of great architectural merit – like Schomberg House in Pall Mall, a beautiful seventeenth-century house that developers were allowed to destroy so long as they kept the façade. Great houses and churches often survive with their interiors but the least likely to survive of all are the interiors of the houses of the middle and working classes.

Linley Sambourne House is an extraordinary exception to that rule. Named after the cartoonist who lived here from 1874 to 1910, it is a perfect example of a solidly middle-class household of the mid-Victorian period. When Sambourne and his young wife moved into the house, which had been built only four years earlier, they decorated in the then fashionable aesthetic style – characterised by heavy velvet drapes, William Morris wallpapers, ornate Turkey carpets and a vast clutter of china ornaments.

Sambourne earned his living as a cartoonist, mostly for *Punch* magazine, for almost half a century. Most of his drawings were completed in this house and numerous examples of his work can be seen, along with his photographs – like many artists of the time he was fascinated by this still relatively new art form.

The house remained substantially unchanged through the twentieth century through extraordinary good luck. The Sambournes' son Roy inherited the house and left it unchanged, probably because he never married. When he in turn died he left the house to his elder sister Maud. She too was passionate about preserving it intact, largely because – as she said herself – she'd been so happy there as a child. Her daughter Anne then used the house until at a party in 1957 Anne proposed that she and her friends, including the future Poet Laureate John Betjeman (1906–1984), should found the Victorian Society to preserve the house and its contents and to work for the preservation of other similar examples of Victorian taste. The Victorian style was then hugely unpopular – how unpopular can be judged by the fact that sometime in the mid-1950s George Frederick Watts' famous painting 'Hope', now one of the most popular works in the collection of pictures at Tate Britain, was used to block up an old fireplace in a house in Battersea!

WORLD'S FIRST PHONE CALL

1876

Dover Street, which runs north of Piccadilly, is on the face of it rather unexceptional. A few eighteenth-century houses remain, but mostly their interiors are hopelessly and completely modernised. The Arts Club is here at number 40, it is true, and club members over the years have included such luminaries as the painter Dante Gabriel Rossetti (1828–1882), George du Maurier (1834–1896) – grandfather of Daphne – and of course Charles Dickens (who seems to crop up everywhere in London) but Dover Street's real claim to fame is that it was here in 1876 that the world's first telephone call was made.

Alexander Graham Bell was born in Scotland in 1847, the son of an actor who was also at various times an orator and professor of elocution. With a naturally scientific mind and a deaf mother Bell became fascinated by how sound works – he used to speak in a low voice, keeping his mouth close to his mother's head, convinced that she would feel the vibrations of his voice.

The Bell family eventually emigrated to America and it was here that Alexander Graham made a small mistake that was to change his life – while reading a book on sound written by a German author Bell mistook a line and thought, mistakenly, that the author was arguing that sound could be transmitted by wire.

Bell became convinced this was possible. By 1876 he had found a way to do it and he quickly became the sensation of the age – he travelled the world demonstrating his new device and it was here at Brown's Hotel in Dover Street that his telephone, as it came to be known, was first successfully demonstrated.

A NEEDLE BY THE RIVER

1878

Londoners have never allowed the truth to get in the way of a good story, which is why Cleopatra's Needle – that ancient Egyptian monument on London's Embankment – has always retained a name that has nothing to do with reality.

But then everything about Cleopatra's Needle is bizarre. Like most Egyptian artifacts its history is uncertain, but the most likely date for it is around 1500 BC. It was almost certainly commissioned by Thothmes III, whose name appears on the stone. By the year 23 BC it had been moved by Caesar to a position near Cleopatra's Palace, but that is as far as any connection with the great empress goes.

After that it vanishes from history until early in the nineteenth century when it was presented by the local Egyptian ruler as a gift to King George IV. It arrived in London in 1878 after a long campaign to raise enough money to cover the cost of transporting it.

The cost was enormous because the stone is incredibly heavy – 160 tons – and a special case had to be made to move it without damaging it.

Once the obelisk arrived in England there was more trouble – a row immediately started about where it should be put up.

The forecourt of the British Museum was suggested initially; then Kensington Gardens, followed by Greenwich Park, but a site in Parliament Square near the House of Commons was finally decided on. To convince the doubters – of whom there were many – a wooden replica was first built and erected in the square so that Londoners' reaction could be judged. Then disaster struck – the underground railway company whose line ran under the square was convinced that the obelisk would crash through into their tunnel. This argument was seen as compelling and Parliament Square was rejected. After lengthy further debate the obelisk was moved to its present position by the Thames – appropriate enough, given that it was first built to stand by the edge of the Nile and it now stands, as it has for over a century, on the banks of another great river.

If its journey to England was eccentric the pillar's final placing was even more so. The ancient tradition of burying a child's shoe or a coin beneath a new building for good luck was here taken to ridiculous lengths. Among the objects buried beneath the obelisk – and they are still there – are: a model of the hydraulic equipment used to raise the obelisk; a two-foot rule; a child's feeding bottle and some toys; a tin of hairpins, some tobacco, a portrait of Queen Victoria, a map of London and a collection of newspapers; a set of coins, several empty jars; copies of the Bible; a translation of the hieroglyphics on the stone; a copy of *Whitaker's Almanack*; some rope; photographs of women and some.

The obelisk is a great survivor, however. Having come through the ravages of more than three thousand years it still bears the marks of bomb damage from the Second World War, and Londoners who grew fond of this oddity in their midst soon came up with a rhyme about it that is somehow both affectionate and dismissive:

> This monument as some supposes
> Was put up in the time of Moses
> It passed in time to the Greeks and Turks
> But was put up here by the Board of Works.

WHY SALUTING IS VULGAR

1879

The fact that in the modern world members of the royal family are regularly mocked and their every action and statement scrutinised would astonish any earlier epoch. By the same token the deference shown the royal family in Victorian times seems incomprehensible today. Whatever they did, however badly they behaved, they were treated with the utmost respect.

This may explain why, following the death of Prince Albert (1819–1861) from typhoid (caused it appears by the terrible drains at Windsor), almost every clock made in Britain for the next forty years was cased in black slate or black marble; statues and monuments to the great man popped up everywhere, often paid for after collections among people who really could not afford to pay; other state inspired monuments were erected at vast expense – most famously the great Albert Memorial folly in Kensington Gardens – and streets, stations, pubs and warehouses were named after Albert.

Among all this adulation one statue has always baffled visitors to London. It's the statue of Albert, in the full dress of a field marshall, at Holborn Circus. Albert was hardly the most warlike or militarily competent of royal consorts – he was actually a rather talented composer – but there he is on horseback in his uniform. But instead of saluting as one might expect he is shown doffing his hat.

What on earth is going on? The answer is that saluting is a modern and some would say rather vulgar business. Until well into the Victorian era officers saluted by doffing their hats, which is why Albert is doing just that on this statue.

A HOUSEFUL OF ANIMALS

1880

William Buckland (1784–1856) was Dean of Westminster, a fanatical animal collector and one of the strangest characters ever to grace the streets of the metropolis.

He had a wide circle of friends, which is why tales of his bizarre behaviour spread far and wide. His house in London was always crammed with thousands of natural history specimens, some dead, some alive; some he slept with, others were kept till they died and then eaten or left to rot.

To prove the efficacy of bird droppings as fertiliser William once used great quantities of it to write the word 'guano' on the lawn at his Oxford college. When the summer came and the grass had grown well the letters could be clearly seen. At his house you were almost certain to be offered roast hedgehog or a slice of grilled crocodile steak – and if you partook, the chances are that one or both came from an animal that had roamed Buckland's house and garden a little earlier as a pet!

Travelling to London on his horse one dark wintry night William got lost, but trusting to his extraordinary sense of taste he simply dismounted, picked up a handful of earth, tasted it, shouted 'Uxbridge!' and went on his way.

William's friend Edward Harcourt, Archbishop of York, was, like Buckland himself, a great collector of curiosities and had managed to obtain what was believed to be the shrunken, mummified heart of Louis XIV. He kept it in a snuff box in his London house and rashly showed it to William. 'I have eaten many things,' William is reported to have said, 'but never the heart of a king.' He then popped it into his mouth and swallowed it whole.

Frank Buckland (1826–80), William's son, was if anything an even more eccentric Londoner than his father. He was a naturalist and collector of animals of every description; he also helped found the Society for the Acclimatisation of Animals in the United Kingdom, which introduced all sorts of exotic creatures into Britain in an attempt, it was said, to widen the roast-beef diet of the British. Many of these introductions proved less than useful – like the grey squirrel which, a century after its introduction, has all but eradicated the native red squirrel from England.

At the Acclimatisation Society's annual dinner likely items on the menu would be dormice on toast followed by boiled sea slug, roast kangaroo and grilled parrot; at its first dinner in 1862 the meal included trepang – 'Much like a horse's hoof,' said Frank.

Throughout his life Frank dined regularly on rhinoceros, elephant and giraffe: he had friends at the zoological gardens who would contact him when an animal died and was once given a whole batch of giraffes that had died in an accident.

At school, Buckland was notorious for wandering round with his pockets full of live snakes, frogs and mice, and he was often found wading into the school pond to retrieve a specimen he had left in the water to rot so that he could more easily remove the flesh from the skeleton. He kept a live owl, a buzzard, a magpie and a racoon in his room, and the descendants of a white rat that escaped from his pocket were still to be seen generations later. He also kept a monkey, a chameleon and numerous snakes.

Away from the classroom he spent much of his spare time cooking mice and eating them; when a master discovered what he was up to he didn't ban it, but simply told Buckland he should share his roast mice with the other boys.

Buckland would swap eels and trout for various pieces of the anatomy of patients who had died in the local hospital. He was once heard to mutter while gazing admiringly at a fellow pupil's head: 'What wouldn't I give for that fellow's skull!' Unlike most pupils who used their pocket money to buy sweets and chocolate, Buckland would pay his fellow pupils sixpence each if they would then let him bleed them.

By the time he got to university, where he narrowly missed a scholarship, he had a small menagerie in a specially constructed zoo outside his rooms; here he kept snakes, a monkey, a chameleon, an eagle, a jackal and a bear which he named Tiglath-Pileser after an Assyrian king; it was known as Tig for short. His eagle once escaped and was discovered perched in the college chapel.

Buckland rarely expressed an interest in any subject other than natural history, and said of politics that when he couldn't understand a parliamentary bill he always translated it into Latin, in which language it apparently made more sense.

When entertaining fellow undergraduates his normal dress was a bright-blue coat and a big red hat with tassels. Dressed like this he loved to leap up every few seconds and blow loudly through an enormous wooden horn.

When he left Oxford Buckland decided to become a surgeon in London, but first, like most young men of his background at the time, he left for an extended period of study abroad. With his scientific interests Germany must have seemed a natural choice for Buckland, whose eccentric habits did not meet with universal approval. During one journey he was threatened with eviction from a coach after it was discovered that he had twelve live tree frogs hidden in his pockets; their deafening croaking, of which Buckland was oblivious, infuriated the other passengers who were kept awake for hours. He also tried to bring home a large quantity of big red slugs, but while he was asleep they escaped and he woke to find that one of them was making its way precariously across the bald head of the sleeping passenger opposite. Rather than face a scene Buckland left the slugs where they were and leaped off the coach.

Back in London at a big garden party Buckland turned up with his bear, Tig, in tow. He had dressed it in a scholar's cap

249

and gown and proceeded to introduce it to the assembled glitterati, including Florence Nightingale, several princes and Napoleon I's nephew (their reaction is not recorded). Tig eventually ended up in London Zoo after being caught trying to rob a sweet shop.

At work at St George's Hospital in London, Buckland had become a member of the Royal College of Surgeons in 1851, but he resigned a year later for reasons never fully explained. His time at the hospital did, however, produce a number of amusing incidents. He dined out for many years, for example, on the tale of the poor woman with a bad cough who had come to him regularly every week and each time asked for larger and larger quantities of a certain cough mixture. Eventually he became suspicious and, following her, discovered that she had been making the mixture into tarts and selling them outside the hospital.

Buckland was nineteen when his father was made Dean of Westminster; while he was living with him in the abbey precincts his eagle escaped and was found sitting on one of Hawksmoor's magnificent towers. The bird was captured by Buckland using a live chicken on a very long pole.

Once when travelling with his monkey, Jacko, in a bag, Buckland was about to buy a railway ticket at King's Cross; just as he was handing his money over, Jacko popped his head out of the bag, at which the stationmaster insisted that the monkey would have to be paid for, too. After a long fruitless argument, an extremely exasperated Buckland pulled his pet tortoise out of a pocket and asked what fare he would have to pay for that. 'No charge for them, Sir, them be insects,' came the stationmaster's reply. This same monkey accompanied Buckland everywhere during his time in the Life Guards. He dressed it as a troop corporal major, but when he discovered that it had been ripping the buttons off his coat he had it demoted to private and dressed it accordingly.

In spite of the fact that his house was already filled with animals, both stuffed and living, Buckland continued to haunt the dock areas of London in search of specimens; although he was adding continually to his collection, he never threw anything away.

In 1850 he married Hannah Papps, a coachman's daughter. Luckily for Buckland she seemed to enjoy his mania for collecting animals as much as he did – at least there is no evidence that she objected to the hordes of monkeys one observer once saw sitting round the Buckland fire: 'They did terrible damage and bit everyone, but he loved them dearly,' he commented. But rats could also be seen running everywhere, over desks and tables and around the mongoose and donkey that also had the run of the place. Having so many animals frequently led to minor disasters – for example, when two antagonistic animals met on the stairs and began a terrible fight. Also, Mrs Buckland had reared a South African Red River hog boar from infancy. It was an enormous beast, and at dinner one evening it crept into the dining-room and wedged itself under a guest's chair; then, alarmed by a sudden noise, it got up and ran out of the room but with the guest still in his chair on the pig's back!

Visitors frequently bumped into extraordinary animals in the most unlikely places: one woman tripped over a hippo at a turn on the staircase. The hippo was destined for the pot, but the woman had been frightened out of her wits – though Buckland merely told her that a hippo was a rare and valuable animal. 'They don't grow on trees, you know,' he is reported to have said. When his animals grew old or died Buckland usually ate them anyway, but he abhorred cruelty. He had eaten many things in his time, but pronounced mole 'poo' and bluebottle 'worse'.

A keen historian, he once went through nearly 3,000 coffins in the vaults of St Martin in the Fields looking for the body of John Hunter, an eighteenth-century surgeon whom he admired enormously. Almost the last coffin contained the right man, who was reburied with great ceremony and given a proper memorial.

Buckland was appointed Her Majesty's Inspector of Fisheries, and in this capacity was responsible for making sure

251

that migratory fish were able to get up Britain's rivers. While helping construct a salmon ladder on the Thames he put up a sign for the benefit of any salmon stuck in the weir below the as yet unbuilt ladder: 'No road at present over the weir,' it read. 'Go downstream, take the first turning to the right and you will find good travelling water upstream and no jumping required.'

His appointment as fisheries inspector had a lot to do with his wide-ranging knowledge of natural history, and a major part of his work involved travelling the country in search of spawning salmon and trout. So enthusiastic was he that he claimed he had hatched some 30,000 salmon in his own kitchen sink during his career. And if he had odd things in the sink you could always be sure that he would have even more extraordinary creatures, including humans, in the house. Dwarves, giants, rat- and bird-catchers were all invited, for Buckland delighted in everything that added to his sense of human diversity.

A giant Irishman who visited him wrote his name on the ceiling of the drawing-room; when a spring-cleaning session led to its being obliterated, Buckland was furious.

On one occasion he was sent to Ireland to inspect a salmon fishery, and decided he wanted to know what it was like to be a salmon; so he undressed and lowered himself into the fastest part of the salmon race. 'How on earth do they do it?' he was heard to mumble. It was at about this time that he began to grow oysters; he also opened a fish museum at St Martin's Court in Leicester Square and took over the editorship of a journal called *Land and Water*. Energetic and highly artistic, he next began to make magnificently accurate plaster casts of fish. He once bought a huge fresh sunfish at Billingsgate, threw it down into his kitchen and made a plaster cast of it. He then found that the cast, which of course was rigid, was so big he couldn't get it out of the kitchen again.

Often he had so many specimens in various stages of decomposition that the whole house stank unendurably, but he never seemed to notice, probably because he was intrigued by the processes of decay. In 1866 he wrote: 'I do not think rats will eat putrid meat...I have lately discovered in my London cellar the body of an eagle which I had forgotten and which was rather high. I know there are rats in my cellar because I will not allow them to be killed as I consider they do me good service in eating the bits thrown away in the dustbin. But these rats had not touched the eagle...'

For Buckland, however, it was sometimes difficult to avoid eating his specimens even when he really didn't want to, and good-looking ones were always in particular danger. 'Directly I am out of the way,' he wrote, 'if they look good to eat they are cooked by my housekeeper; if they stink they are buried. What am I to do? I have to keep a sharp lookout in my house...' Nevertheless, towards the end of his life his interest in the culinary quality of all sorts of animals intensified. He tried a porpoise's head but thought it tasted like lamp wick, and in *Land and Water* he once offered readers otter steaks; all they had to do was write to him and he would send a steak by return.

Buckland had his own remedies for a number of ailments; for example, he never wore a coat because it caused colds and flu, and if he couldn't sleep he sat up all night eating raw onions. But apart from what may now seem his greatest eccentricities, Buckland actually did a great deal to improve our treatment of animals: he campaigned for many years for humane methods of slaughter in abattoirs, and he disliked intensely the indiscriminate slaughter of animals for sport. Moreover, he was said to have had infinite patience with animals and humans, and he was certainly unfailingly generous; he often rescued down-and-outs and former friends who had become ill or had fallen on hard times. He believed, too, that inanimate things had feelings, and planned to write a book on the spitefulness of objects: if a lamp didn't burn properly he said it was sulky; and he punished his luggage once by thrashing it.

But some of his vaguely scientific ideas are still difficult to swallow. He suggested fattening fish, for example, by hanging a horse's leg or half a sheep from a branch overhanging the water. Maggots would breed on the rotting flesh, he said, and fall continually into the water where they would be eaten by the fish.

Understandably, he is most remembered for being eccentric: children used to gather outside his London house to see the extraordinary collection of freaks who went continually in and out, and on one occasion Buckland arrived home to find all his servants standing in the street because two badgers had got out of their box and were running amok in the house. Another time a guest spotted one of Buckland's boots apparently moving independently around the sitting-room – a mongoose had got inside it and was running around trying to get out.

At night Buckland often went cockroach hunting – he would dash into the kitchen in his nightshirt holding aloft a syringe filled with benzine and then try to inject any fleeing insect he could catch up with.

A visitor was once horrified to come across Buckland in the kitchen dissecting a large, far-from-fresh animal, and in between cuts he was helping himself to huge spoonfuls from a giant cauldron of stew.

He hated boots and usually went around barefoot; once, on a train, his boots so irritated him that he kicked them off and they flew out of the window. Nothing daunted he walked to his hotel in his socks. Five feet 'and a half' tall, and almost as broad, he was described variously by his contemporaries as 'sentimental, gushing, wild and sensational, and impetuous'. He never took care of his own health, always travelling hatless and coatless however cold the weather. He died at the age of 54, and wrote in his will, 'God is so good, so very good to the little fishes that I do not believe he would let their inspector suffer shipwreck.'

PAYING FOR LAND WITH NAILS

1881

The Law Courts in the Strand were built after a competition to find a suitable design. The architect, G. E. Street (1824–1881), won with the Gothic Revival building we see today but the process of implenting the design was dogged by delays caused by some very bizarre architectural requests.

At the outset Street stipulated that standard bricks would be no good for his building, so more than 30 million odd-sized bricks had to be produced at huge cost. The next difficulty was that bricklayers from Germany had to be brought over to complete the work as all London's bricklayers boycotted the work after a row. Street became so concerned about progress on the building that his health declined and he died before the last brick was laid.

But the strangest thing about the law courts is that each year, in a ceremony dating back to the early twelfth century, officials from the Corporation of London come here to pay rent for a piece of ground in Shropshire, owned by the Crown but leased by the Corporation.

The rent is paid in kind: it consists of a billhook and a scythe. Another small patch of ground on Chancery Lane and also owned by the Crown is paid for annually at the law courts in a slightly different way. For this second patch of ground the Corporation of London hands over the princcly sum of six horse shoes and sixty nails!

THE TRAIN STATION THAT FELL
ON A THEATRE

1882

Craven Street, a narrow thoroughfare that runs down the side
of Charing Cross Station, is a reminder, albeit a ghostly one, of
how very different this area was before the coming of the
embankment and the railway. For Craven Street is one of the
last of the narrow streets that ran down to the river and up
which coal and other goods were brought by wagon from the
ships and barges that once plied their trade along the Thames.

Halfway along Craven Street there is a narrow alley known
as Craven Passage and in the shadow of the bridge above that
carries trains into Charing Cross Station is the Ship and
Shovel. When the Ship and Shovel was first built the river was
only a few yards away – a small round window still exists on the
river side of the pub. This was built to allow the carters and
dockers who unloaded the ships to keep an eye on the river and
any approaching vessels. But Craven Street has other claims to
fame – we've already seen how Benjamin Franklin lived and
worked here. The street's other great claim to fame is that
Charles Dickens's unforgettable account in *A Christmas Carol*,
of Marley's ghost materialising out of a door knocker was based
on a knocker here in Craven Street.

But the most extraordinary thing about Craven Street is the
curiously shaped theatre at the end nearest the Embankment.
Crammed into a narrow space, it is difficult to understand why
anyone would want to build a theatre here at all – the answer

256

has nothing to do with an enthusiasm for the arts and a great deal to do with the oddities of London's history.

The builder was theatre manager Sefton Parry (1832–1887). He bought the plot of land having discovered that the railway company that owned the bridge into Charing Cross was planning to extend the platforms.

The existing platforms were high up above the level of the ground on which Mr Parry had his eye but he calculated that they would need more ground anyway in order to build supports for the new platforms up above. He then calculated that he would get an even better price from the railway company if he built a business on the plot of land – that way he'd get paid for the land and receive compensation for the business that would have to shut down. He decided to build a theatre.

By 1882 the theatre was complete. A year or so later, as he'd predicted, the railway company approached him and offered a large sum of money for the land. Sefton Parry unfortunately overplayed his hand and turned the offer down. He asked for a much larger sum and the railway declined. Parry was convinced they would eventually have to come to terms but he reckoned without the extraordinary ingenuity of the engineers employed by the railway company.

Instead of buying new land on which to place the new supports needed for the new platforms, the railway company designed its new platforms in such a way that they could be propped up by existing supports. The platforms ended up immediately above the theatre but since they did not actually touch the theatre and they had no supports on Parry's land there was nothing he could do.

All went well until 1905 when it became clear that the engineers who'd built the new platforms more than twenty years earlier had been overzealous in trying to save their bosses' money. The overburdened supports gave way one night after a workman accidentally cut through what should have been only one of a number of fail-safe supports and nearly half the station collapsed on to the roof of the theatre. The theatre was demolished and five people were killed, but despite being built for no good dramatic reason Parry's enterprise had done well. The railway company had to pay huge sums in compensation and the Playhouse Theatre was rebuilt. It remains one of London's best-known and most popular theatres even today.

BISMARCK DRUNK ON THE EMBANKMENT

1885

Ever since London's river embankment was completed in the 1880s the authorities have been irritated by the fact that it attracts down-and-outs. With benches set at intervals along its length the Embankment was bound to prove a magnet for the homeless then as now, and among the more illustrious tramps to have slept here are George Orwell (1903–1950), who later described life on the road in his unforgettable book *Down and Out in Paris and London*.

That an old Etonian like Orwell should end up destitute on the Embankment is strange enough, but how few people are aware that the greatest German statesman of the nineteenth century, Otto Edward Leopold von Bismarck (1815–1898), also slept on a bench on the Embankment?

Bismarck became Chancellor of Germany in 1871 and in 1885 he visited England. As part of the elaborate itinerary organised for his visit, Bismarck was taken – for reasons that have never really become clear – to the long-vanished brewery owned by Barclays in Southwark.

Other dignities and celebrities had been taken to the brewery on many occasions and at the end of such visits the visitor was always asked if he or she would like to try the company's strongest beer. Bismarck was delighted at the idea and was presented with a half-gallon tankard filled to the brim. He should have taken a sip and handed it back but instead,

259

assuming it was all for him, he drank the whole lot. Perhaps in a spirit of waggishness one of the brewery staff then told the Chancellor that very few men had managed to drink two of the half-gallon flagons. German honour was clearly at stake so Bismarck immediately insisted that the half-gallon flagon be refilled and he proceeded to drink that as well.

Astonishingly he managed to stay on his feet and even to walk in a fairly straight line back to his carriage – the brewery staff apparently applauded him out of the building – which then crossed the river and headed back towards Westminster along the Embankment.

Before they reached Westminster Bridge the Chancellor shouted for the carriage to stop. He looked out of the window, saw the benches by the side of the river and told his assistant that he intended to sleep off the effects of his huge intake of beer. He staggered away to the nearest bench having left instructions that he was to be woken in exactly one hour. His coach, along with the coaches filled with Foreign Office officials, waited patiently at the kerbside while the most famous German statesman in history fell fast asleep on his bench. Exactly one hour later and none the worse apparently for his ordeal he set off for the Foreign Office and some decidedly ticklish discussions about international diplomacy.

ROYAL SCULPTOR WORKS FROM GAOL

1886

There are two bizarre tales about the statue of Queen Anne that stands in front of the entrance to St Paul's Cathedral. It's not the original statue that was completed in 1712 because by the end of the nineteenth century the original was so worn by time, pigeon droppings, coal smog and vandalism that the authorities decided to commission a new statue.

Public sculpture was far more in demand in Victorian England than it is now and many artists whose names mean nothing today were virtually household names a century and more ago.

When a new statue of Queen Anne was needed the City approached the celebrated sculptor Richard Claude Belt. He promised to complete the work in the year it was commissioned – 1886 – but then it all went disastrously wrong. Like many artists Belt was talented but a bit of a reprobate. He was constantly running up debts and getting into scrapes, and about the time he accepted the commission for the new statue of Queen Anne he got into a particularly bad scrape and was imprisoned for fraud. He'd spent the first part of the money advanced for the statue. The city authorities had no intention of throwing that money away by commissioning another artist to start all over again but they couldn't just get Belt released. The answer was to get special permission to deliver stone and tools to Belt's cell!

261

And that's exactly what happened, with the result that we can confidently say that the St Paul's statue of Queen Anne is the only public work of art completed by a convicted prisoner while he was actually in prison.

Belt's statue was threatened with demolition a few years later when Queen Victoria celebrated her Diamond Jubilee in 1897. The authorities thought that Anne should be removed to make it easier for the royal coach to sweep up to the front of St Paul's so they went ahead with plans to at least move if not simply do away with Belt's statue, but when the Queen heard of the plan she was furious. She is reported to have said: 'If you remove the statue of Queen Anne for me, who is to say that a statue of me will not be removed to accommodate some future monarch after I am dead?' She was no doubt horrified at the thought that the Prince of Wales, the son she loathed and blamed for her husband's death, would become king and then have his revenge on her by getting rid of the dozens of public statues of her that had gone up all over the country during her long reign.

A BICYCLE DRIVEN BY NODDING

1889

Modern inventions can often seem weird but that is often simply because they are made for very specific uses that baffle most of us – the particle accelerator is a good example. But the number and variety of our modern inventions is as nothing to the creative fervour of our Victorian ancestors.

Hugely imaginative and convinced that technology could solve every problem, the Victorians came up with dozens of gadgets that, in a more evolved form, are still with us today – the telephone and the vacuum cleaner to name but two. They also invented the bicycle of course, but not content with the basic bicycle they tried to come up with modifications and improvements that were sometimes taken to absurd lengths.

Anton Oleszkiewicz, who was said to be far more English than the English despite his Russian surname, was convinced that the velocipede, as the bicycle was then known, could be vastly improved if the cyclist's every movement – and not just the movement of his or her legs – could be used to power the machine.

And so it was that in the autumn of 1889 he announced to the world from his London home that his Winged Messenger or New Improved Driving Mechanism for cycles would change cycling for ever.

His new device consisted of a complex series of levers and springs that ran from the back wheel of the bicycle via the saddle and all parts of the frame to an elaborate, all-encompassing leather harness that was fixed around the cyclist's upper body. One cyclist who tried it out took half an hour to strap himself in; once that was done he then had to attach himself to the first of the levers – a long steel rod that ran from a position on the harness at the front of the chest down to a horizontal rod that was hinged, sprung-loaded and fitted to a chain wheel just below the saddle.

To ride this extraordinary new bicycle the rider, having strapped himself in, was advised to ride in the normal way until he had attained 'a stately speed'. According to the instructions he was then to begin throwing his upper body backwards and forwards 'rhythmically and with as much violence as possible'. Each violent movement was – in theory – transmitted down the chest rod into the hinged lever and on to the small chain wheel above the back wheel. An extra chain ran from this wheel down to the main chain wheel in the centre of the cycle's rear wheel.

Oleszkiewicz organised a trial day in London's Hyde Park and passers-by were no doubt astonished to see a group of cyclists apparently suffering from epileptic fits as they whizzed along by the Serpentine. The experiment was not a success, however, as two cyclists fell off the back of their machines, several suffered extreme motion sickness and none could discern any increase in their speed. Nothing daunted, Oleszkiewicz went on to try his hand at man-powered flying machines.

BETTING ON A GOLF BALL

1889

The clubs of St James's are the last bastion of old-fashioned British elitism. You won't find a name plate on the front door of any London club for that would be rather vulgar and might attract the wrong sort; Brooks's doesn't even have a number.

All the members of the Carlton Club, Brooks's and White's are establishment figures – politicians, bishops, members of the aristocracy. Every member will have been educated at an expensive public school in Britain and their general attitudes have probably changed little since the days of empire.

But if London clubs are reactionary today they were far more so in former times. In its day the now vanished Almack's Assembly Rooms (essentially a club) was far more exclusive than any club still with us. Almack's at one time or other refused to admit both the Duke of Wellington (appallingly badly dressed) and the Prince Regent (arriving too late in the evening). Almack's rules were laid down by a committee of half a dozen aristocratic women – an extremely odd arrangement given that most clubs fought tooth and nail well into the second half of the twentieth century to avoid having to admit women at all.

Brooks's and White's were famous in earlier times for their bizarre obsession with strange bets. At Brooks's someone once took bets on whether or not a waiter at a nearby club had been to Eton and was the son of a bishop. The bets were taken and it turned out that the waiter had indeed been to Eton and was indeed a bishop's son.

It is said that when a man collapsed on the steps of White's the members immediately started betting on whether he would survive or not; even more bizarrely a member in the late 1880s took bets on whether or not he could hit a golf ball all the way from the Royal Exchange to the club's front door. The members took bets on whether it could be done in fewer than one thousand hits. The member who took the wager achieved the feat in a little over two hundred and seventy hits.

VIOLINIST HIT BY FISH

1890

It's now quite common in London to see geese flying overhead or swans; even, occasionally, a rarity such as a cormorant. Along the Thames right into the heart of the city herons now stalk the shallows and various wildlife bodies tell us that owls roost in Parliament Square while kestrels hover above the Commercial Road.

In the nineteenth century things were very different, as pollution caused by millions of coal fires – not to mention heavy industry – meant there was far less wildlife than today.

But having said that, London's bigger parks have always provided a haven for wildlife, which is why reports of ducks wandering across Kensington High Street with their ducklings coming along behind were always quite common.

Far less common was the bizarre wildlife encounter in Kensington reported in a Victorian newspaper.

Miss Charlotte Wadham, a young and attractive violinist, was walking home one autumn evening after what the delightfully old-fashioned newspaper reporter described as 'a musical engagement involving the celebrated Mr Bach'. She was halfway up Kensington Church Street when she was struck by what she later described to the newspaper as 'a terrific blow to the side of the head'. In fact the bump was so hard that she was knocked unconscious for a few moments.

One of the witnesses who helped the injured woman into a local house where brandy was administered (much, appar-

267

ently, to the delight of Miss Wadham) described an extraordinary circumstance that almost certainly accounted for the knockout blow. When the witness had run up to the prostrate Miss Wadham he spotted a large fish lying on the pavement nearby. Being a fisherman he knew that this was not the sort of fish one buys at a fishmonger. It was in fact a roach, a common British freshwater fish, but completely inedible. The witness told the newspaper that at first he could not understand how the fish came to be lying in the street, but in helping the injured woman to her feet he noticed something very odd indeed. The woman's head and the shoulder of her coat were dusted here and there with fish scales. The scales were without question from the dead roach found at the scene.

When the newspaper reporter compiled his report on the incident he quoted a professor of zoology who stated that Miss Wadham was almost certainly felled by a roach dropped by a passing bird, possibly a heron or cormorant.

Miss Wadham's violin, much to her relief, was unharmed.

WHY EROS IS ALL WRONG

1893

Londoners often take absolutely no notice of correct terminology. Just because something has an official name doesn't mean it won't end up with a nickname (often an irreverent nickname) – Cleopatra's Needle, for example, has nothing to do with Cleopatra at all but calling it Cleopatra's Needle added an air of romance and the name stuck.

The statue of Eros in Piccadilly is rather similar given that it has absolutely nothing to do with Eros at all. In fact everything about this small, world-famous statue in the centre of Piccadilly is odd. For a start it is made from aluminium, one of the worst metals to withstand the British climate. Then its cupid-style bow is all wrong – bows of this type were strung on the opposite side. As if that were not enough the statue is also facing the wrong way.

The story of this most bizarre statue begins with a fountain built at public expense in memory of one of London's great philanthropists – the seventh Earl of Shaftesbury, after whom Shaftesbury Avenue is named. Shaftesbury spent much of his life and fortune trying to clothe, feed and educate the poor.

The money for the fountain was quickly raised and then some bright spark suggested it should have a statue on top. The money for the statue came pouring in and Alfred Gilbert (1854–1934) was commissioned to design it. Gilbert chose to portray the angel of Christian charity, which is what the statue actually is, but the telltale bow made Londoner's immediately christen it Eros, the god of Love.

269

The statue was designed to aim its arrow up Shaftesbury Avenue (with which Shaftesbury had been most closely associated) and although it has faced in a number of different directions over the years it has never, ever faced the right way. No one knows why.

The statue was put up and the fountains turned on in 1893 but the basin into which the water fell was too small and the force of water too great – passers-by were soaked and the fountain had to be redesigned almost immediately.

Alfred Gilbert, though now largely forgotten, was hugely influential in the 1880s, but he was as eccentric and bohemian as the statue he designed. He argued about every stage of the work, hated the final result (particularly the fountain on which his sculpture stood) and told the people who'd commissioned him to make the statue that they should take it down, melt it 'and make it into pence to give the unfortunate people who nightly find a resting place on the Thames Embankment to the everlasting shame and disgrace of the greatest metropolis of the world'.

Often short of a penny himself, Gilbert accepted every commission offered to him but hardly ever completed them, simply because he had taken on too much. He eventually had to flee the country or risk being imprisoned for debt.

For the first half-century of its life Eros became an unofficial market place – every day throughout the season flower girls gathered here to sell their wares. They were never removed and were in fact much loved – but after the war, for reasons no one has ever quite been able to fathom, they never returned and the statue is now simply a place where every tourist must have his or her photograph taken.

A RIVER FLYING THROUGH THE AIR

1895

Sloane Square Station now finds itself in one of London's smartest districts. It lies at one end of what was London's first bus route – buses ran from Sloane Square up Sloane Street to Knightsbridge and back again a distance of less than a mile – but the tube station is nothing out of the ordinary. Built at the end of the nineteenth century as part of the District line, it has always served the wealthy residents of Eaton Square and Belgravia. Like so many pioneering railway builders, the men behind the District line were used to overcoming geological and political difficulties, but they were almost stumped by the difficulties surrounding the building of Sloane Square Station.

When the engineers started work they discovered that a river ran across the path of their proposed railway.

The long-hidden River Westbourne rises to the northwest of Hyde Park (hence Westbourne Terrace) and originally flowed through Hyde Park, enabling eighteenth-century engineers to build the Serpentine. But where the water flows out of the Knightsbridge end of the Serpentine it once continued down towards Sloane Square and on to the Thames.

The railway engineers who built Sloane Square Station were temporarily baffled. Eventually they came up with the solution that still makes Sloane Square one of the strangest stations on the whole underground network.

The engineers built a huge round pipe more than five feet in diameter to carry the River Westbourne over the platforms and

271

railway lines – anyone who gets off at the station today need only look up to see the massive pipe still in position and the river still runs through it.

Intriguingly it is believed that there may even be a few fish still swimming in the pipe – descendants of the roach, perch and gudgeon that once gathered in the shallows when this was a clean sparkling stream running through open country.

AN OFFICE FIT FOR THE GODS

1895

Number Two Temple Place, just behind the Embankment near Waterloo Bridge, is one of the most extraordinarily luxurious offices in London. It was built in Portland stone in 1895 by the fabulously wealthy American millionaire William Waldorf Astor (1848–1919).

Astor employed John Loughborough Pearson (1817–1897) as his architect but was absolutely rigid in his insistence that certain types of wood and marble be used and that only the finest craftsmen should be employed for every detail of the work. Virtually every part of the interior – from the ebony columns to the marble and stonework and even the window grilles – was handmade. The cost was astronomical, certainly tens of millions in today's terms.

Astor even had a gilded copper model of the *Santa Maria* – the ship in which Columbus discovered America – fixed to a weather vane on the roof and in the courtyard there are two cherubs each holding a telephone receiver to its ear!

All the expense and effort was not designed to produce a fabulous home but an office for just one man!

CROMWELL RELEGATED TO 'THE PIT'

1895

London has many odd statues and monuments, including the recently erected and rather endearing monument in Park Lane to all the animals that have died in human conflicts – the horses and ponies of the First World War, the glow worms used to read maps by and pigeons used to carry messages.

But the animals' monument is a recent arrival on the London statue scene. The statue of Oliver Cromwell (1599–1658) outside Westminster Hall has been there considerably longer and the tale of just how it ended up there is wonderfully odd.

When the idea of a statue to Cromwell was first mooted in 1895 the idea was put forward by the Liberal government led by Lord Rosebery (1847–1929). But in 1895 Rosebery was able to hang on to power only because he was supported in most matters by the Irish Members of Parliament. With their votes the Liberals' tiny majority in the house was turned into a working majority. The Liberals tried to force a bill through Parliament agreeing funds for the Cromwell statue but all the Irish MPs voted against. The bill was defeated and the Irish were so upset at what the Liberals had tried to do that they stopped voting with them. An election was held and the Tories won – and all because Rosebery had been unwise enough to push a point about a statue!

When the statue idea reared its head again some years later those politicians in favour of it being erected told the Irish that it was to be placed in an area known as 'the Pit' – this is the area of lawn well below the walls of Westminster Hall. Considerably lower than the modern street level this is the original level of all the land in this area. The Irish were delighted that the man who had committed countless atrocities in Ireland should be consigned to the Pit and they voted in favour. Cromwell has been in the Pit ever since.

THE WORLD'S ULTIMATE
MILITARY MADMAN

1897

London was once described as a hotbed of eccentricity. Much of this reputation undoubtedly stems from the presence since the Middle Ages of large numbers of lawyers, whose success has always been in direct proportion to their ability to baffle and bamboozle the public.

Military men have also been famously strange, but among the very strangest has to be Lieutenant Colonel Alfred Daniel Wintle, who spent much of his life in London chasing his superiors through the corridors of the Ministry of Defence.

Wintle was born in 1897 in Russia where his father was employed as a diplomat. In spite of his Russian birth, or perhaps because of it, Wintle always claimed that he got down on his knees every night before he went to bed and thanked God for making him an Englishman and a Londoner: being an Englishman was, he said, 'the highest responsibility as well as the greatest honour'.

He was besotted by the idea of Englishness and utterly biased against every other nation, but his European upbringing meant that he spoke German and French 'at all times of the day' and was steeped in the culture of western and central Europe.

During his first stay in England with an aunt in Clapham, south London, when he was about ten, he developed the great loves of his life: horses, cricket, vegetable marrows, country railway stations and umbrellas. The gift of an umbrella from a famous London maker when he was twelve made him feel he was 'on the way to becoming a complete English gentleman – it was the apple of my eye'. In fact he was so fond of this umbrella that he slept with it and always left a note in it when he rolled it up which said: 'This umbrella has been stolen from A. D. Wintle.'

Wintle believed that knowledge of the uses of umbrellas and a proper regard for them was the true mark of a gentleman; umbrellas also lay at the heart of the difference between an Englishman and a Frenchman or a German. 'The Frenchman gets up in the morning,' explained Wintle, 'and consults his barometer. If there is to be no rain he leaves his umbrella at home, sallies forth and gets a drenching.' The Englishman, by contrast, is too stupid to understand all these barometers and things so he always takes his umbrella with him. But it doesn't end there, for whatever the circumstances 'no Englishman ever unfurls his umbrella, which means he gets wet'.

As soon as the First World War started Wintle joined up. On his first day in the trenches the soldier standing next to him was killed. Wintle was so terrified that he stood stock still and then saluted. 'That did the trick,' he said later, 'and within thirty seconds I had again become an English man of action.' A few months later he narrowly missed being killed himself when a shell blew him off his horse. He lost his left eye and most of his left hand, but he was apparently more concerned about the welfare of his horse and relieved to hear that it was unharmed. When the armistice was signed he noted in his diary: 'I declare private war on Germany.' And from that day on he always said that he knew the Germans were merely lying low, and that the First and Second World Wars were parts one and two of the same war; something with which many historians later came to agree.

As part of his campaign to convince officialdom that the war really wasn't over at all, he returned to London and spent every day for months at a time lobbying Whitehall officials until they could stand it no more and he was posted from central London to Ireland. Disappointed, he nonetheless enjoyed numerous compensations, such as the chance to ride virtually every day.

'It is impossible to be unhappy on the back of a horse,' he wrote, adding that, 'all time spent out of the saddle is wasted.'

Back in London recovering in St Thomas's Hospital during the 1930s after breaking his leg in a fall, Wintle met Boy (Cedric) Mays, who was to become a lifelong friend. Mays was dangerously ill with mastoiditis and diphtheria in a ward just down the corridor from Wintle. He was not expected to live, but Wintle heard of the young soldier's plight and visited him. His first words to Mays were: 'What's all this nonsense about dying? You know it is an offence for a Royal Dragoon to die in bed. And when you get up, get your hair cut!' Astonishingly it worked, and Mays recovered. He later said that after Wintle's order he had been afraid to die.

By 1938 Wintle was working in military intelligence in the heart of Whitehall and driving everyone to distraction with his odd habits and obsessions. He said he couldn't remain silent in the face of what he saw as his superiors' incompetence. 'Our slowness during the year gained at Munich was appalling,' he claimed, 'and if our leaders had been deliberate traitors they could not have played Germany's game better.' He just could not believe that there were military men and government ministers who still insisted there would be no war.

Once he was proved right and the Second World War began, Wintle made strenuous efforts to see active service, even though by this time he was well into middle age. He went to see his MP and presented himself at medical boards disguising the fact that he only had one eye; but it did no good. He then attempted to get to France by impersonating a senior officer and trying to steal an aeroplane. This led to a court martial after Commodore Boyle, the man Wintle had tried to impersonate, decided to prosecute. Before the trial date was set, however, Wintle visited Boyle in his Ministry of Defence office, waved his gun at him, and told him that he ought to be shot for doing so little. Next morning Wintle was arrested and taken to the Tower of London.

By now the authorities were thoroughly embarrassed by the whole affair and offered Wintle a way out. To their horror he insisted on a trial, which he thought would be great fun. He was found guilty of assault and given a severe reprimand. Back in the saddle he went to North Africa and then, because of his fluency in French and German, he was sent to work undercover in Nazi-occupied France.

At the end of the war Wintle retired and began his last great battle. This time it was on behalf of his sister, Marjorie. She had looked after a certain Kitty Wells, a wealthy elderly relative of Wintle's, for more than twenty years. When Kitty Wells died it was found that she had left her considerable fortune to her solicitor, Frederick Nye. The will was hugely complex and Wintle believed it had been drawn up by Nye – the main beneficiary – deliberately to cheat Kitty Wells, who would not have been able to understand it when she signed it.

At first Wintle simply wrote to Nye to express his concern. Nye didn't reply. Undaunted, Wintle began his campaign against the solicitor. He printed gross libels about Nye in the local papers. Still no response. Wintle then kidnapped Nye and took him to a hotel room, removed his trousers, photographed him wearing a paper dunce's hat, and then turned him out (still trouserless) into the streets.

This was too much. Wintle was arrested, but then that was exactly what he had wanted. He was found guilty of assault and sent to prison, where he was by all accounts enormously popular among guards and inmates. He himself enjoyed the experience enormously. When he was released from Wormwood Scrubs six months later, he again went on the attack. Assisted by Cedric Mays, whom he had brought back to life all those years ago, he took Nye to court. The case bankrupted Wintle but he merely observed that though he was now a pauper he was at least an English pauper.

But Nye had not reckoned with Wintle's determination. With Mays' help, Wintle appealed to the House of Lords, spent three days presenting his own case and – to the astonishment of everyone – he won. The Lords argued that if they found it impossible to understand the will, it was fair to assume that when Kitty Wells was persuaded to sign it, she could not have understood it either. This was the first time a layman had represented himself and won his case in the Lords.

Wintle had once said that he'd like Schubert's *Serenade* played by the Royal Dragoons at his funeral, and Mays had said he would arrange it. But when Wintle died in 1966, the Dragoons were serving overseas. Nothing daunted, and in a spirit that Wintle would have applauded, Mays fortified himself with the greater part of a bottle of whisky, went into the nave of Canterbury Cathedral, stood to attention, and sang the whole thing on his own.

WOMAN ON A GRAVEYARD MISSION

1897

In the second half of the nineteenth century the British became obsessed with death – furniture became heavier and darker as the century wore on and the cult of death was promoted almost single-handedly by Victoria's refusal to get over Albert's demise. In tandem with this a number of eccentric authors spent years studying and writing about the most obscure aspects of death – and in London death did indeed have an obscure and fascinating history.

In medieval London most churches adopted the same system for burials. Compared to later ideas about burial – particularly in the eighteenth and nineteenth centuries before cremation became acceptable – the medieval system was a good one. Londoners were buried in their parish churchyard but without coffins and without headstones. Generations of gravediggers gradually buried their fellow parishioners before being buried themselves, and the burials moved slowly across from one side of the graveyard to the other. By the time the graveyard was full it was time to go back to the beginning where the first or earliest burial had taken place. The ground was then dug up again for the latest corpses and any bones would be carefully moved into a special section of the church called the charnel house. Because no coffins were used a body would decay completely within ten years   as the gravedigger in *Hamlet* says, a corpse 'will last you some eight or nine year'.

But as the centuries passed gravestones became popular and

the habit of moving old bones to the charnel house fell out of fashion. Instead, graves were dug deeper with corpses placed one on top of the other to fit them all in. Parish populations grew and the number of burials increased dramatically – so much so that churchyard overcrowding became a serious problem and a serious threat to health. This became much worse when coffins began to be used because the coffins made the bodies last longer. Disturbing old graves became unacceptable unless they were the graves of the poor.

In other parts of the world by the early nineteenth century similar problems had already been dealt with – cremation was encouraged and huge out-of-town cemeteries established. It took several serious outbreaks of cholera and typhoid in London before the authorities finally agreed that city churchyards must be closed to all new burials.

With this history very much in mind the London world of books then produced one of the maddest authors in the history of publishing. Mrs Basil Holmes spent most of her adult life trying to track down and record in great detail every burial ground (and burial!) in London – not an easy task given that in the mid-1800s there were more than five hundred graveyards in central London alone.

The indefatigable Mrs Holmes eventually finished her monumental *London Burial Grounds* in 1897. In part its publication is testimony to the Victorian obsession with detail, but despite her efforts and a lifetime's devotion to her research the book has never been republished.

WOOD BARK UNDER THE DISTRICT LINE

1900

When the District line was built beneath the Embankment two of Britain's most powerful lobbying groups – MPs and the legal profession – were not happy. Other landowners had been forced to accept that the new railway would pass under their land because the might of the railway was such that individual objections were always overruled. They had been similarly overruled in earlier decades as the main overground railways opened up even the most remote parts of the country.

But the members of the Inns of Court, from whose ranks MPs, ministers and ultimately members of the House of Lords tend to come, put their collective foot down.

They told the railway engineers that they would not allow trains to run nor tunnels to be dug beneath Parliament Square or beneath the Inns of Court unless extra precautions were taken to ensure that there was no noise and no vibration once the trains began to run.

The railway company knew it was up against some of the most powerful vested interests in the country so they agreed to include a thick layer of finely chopped tree bark immediately beneath the railway track running through the tunnels, but only along those sections running through Parliament Square and through the Temple. Even today if you take the District line you will notice that somehow the train runs smoother and more quietly under the MPs and the lawyers.

A REAL TRAIN IN THE THEATRE

1904

The Coliseum at the bottom of St Martin's Lane near Trafalgar Square is arguably London's strangest theatre. Why, for example, is it called the Coliseum and not the Colosseum, which would be the correct spelling? Numerous odd stories explain the discrepancy but the best is that the builder of the Coliseum, Sir Oswald Stoll (1866–1942), was such a terrifying personality that when he scribbled the name he wanted for his new theatre on the back of an envelope, his staff, who realised it was a misspelling, were too terrified to tell him and so the name stuck.

Another story says that Stoll deliberately chose an odd spelling to make his theatre unique. In later life when he was challenged about the misspelling he always insisted that he knew what he was doing and chose the eccentric spelling so that no one would confuse his wonderful new building with 'that mouldly old ruin in Rome'.

Apart from its odd name the Coliseum is odd in other ways – it is London's largest theatre and was deliberately built to be bigger than its nearest rival, the Theatre Royal at Drury Lane, which Stoll thought a rather inferior piece of work.

The Coliseum was also revolutionary in design: it had a lift that astonished playgoers because it took them to their boxes and to the circle and upper circle; it had a revolving stage – the first ever seen in London – and it had a roof garden and three restaurants.

The Coliseum also had its own post box and its own railway, the latter designed to take VIPs from the door to their seats!

284

BEING NICE TO ALLAH

1905

There is a popular idea that trying to save old buildings – our built heritage to use the current jargon – is somehow a modern phenomenon. In fact for centuries the public has rallied to save much-loved old buildings faced with destruction by corrupt or uncaring officialdom. The unforgivable destruction of London's last Jacobean mansion – the celebrated Northumberland House at Charing Cross – is a case in point. This extraordinary building, largely unaltered since its completion in 1610, was threatened with demolition in 1886 to build, of all things, a road. Despite protests from tens of thousands of Londoners and any number of historical societies the house was pulled down and a dull road – what else could a road be? – was created in its place. But this act of municipal vandalism was only one in a huge number of similar decisions that culminated in wholesale destruction – particularly in the City – in the 1960s when the last few remaining medieval and renaissance buildings were destroyed by Corporation of London officials.

When Northumberland House was demolished another beautiful and rare medieval survival was also faced with destruction – this was Wych Alley, an area of medieval houses on the site of what is now the Aldwych. Wych Alley lasted a little longer than Northumberland House, lasting in fact until 1905.

It was a narrow thoroughfare of early timber-framed buildings swept away by the largely forgotten architect G. L.

Gomme who – like so many London planners – thought it would be a great idea to create a new road. Mr Gomme's new road cut through from Holborn to the north down to the Strand. The result was Kingsway with the crescent-shaped development of Aldwych at the southern, Strand end.

Bush House was to be the centrepiece building of the new Aldwych and it was originally intended as a huge trade centre. An American architect, Harvey Corbett, turned Gomme's dreadful idea into a reality by designing the lumpy buildings we see today – but if the buildings are leaden and undistinguished they do have one virtue. In a bizarre act of eccentricity they are officially and permanently unfinished.

Unlike many modern Americans, Corbett was rather a fan of Islam and he took to heart an ancient Persian adage which states that 'Perfection is an attribute of Allah; it is therefore blasphemous for man to assume he has created something perfect'. With this idea in mind Corbett left the decorative top of one of the building's distinctive columns unfinished. If you walk today through the western colonnade from the Strand look carefully at the tops of the columns – one is quite clearly and deliberately unfinished.

Leaving it like this meant that Corbett could always claim that his building was incomplete and therefore not blasphemous. Modern commentators are inclined to remark that even if he had finished the building no one could have accused Corbett of blasphemy as the building is a very long way indeed from perfection anyway.

COWS IN THE PARK

1905

Despite the best efforts of developers, London's parks have survived the centuries pretty well. Occasionally roads have sliced through some of them – Park Lane, for example, really was a lane before being turned into a six-lane highway for no good reason. The oldest and most interesting of the parks – St James's – was originally established as a hunting ground so kings and courtiers could hunt deer from the nearby palaces of St James and Westminster.

The point of the hunting grounds was not that they should be big enough to give the deer a sporting chance, but that they should be small enough to guarantee a kill. One of the strangest stories associated with St James's has nothing to do with hunting or indeed with royalty. It concerns the small café that still stands near the lake.

The story begins in 1905 when London's planners decided to build the grand semi-circular Admiralty Arch at the Trafalgar Square end of The Mall. The arch was designed to take up only a small area of what had been open space, but there was a problem. Two elderly women had walked to this corner every day for as long as anyone could remember accompanied by three cows. Having arrived at the edge of the park they tethered their cows and set up stall – for a penny a glass passers-by could enjoy a drink of milk, fresh and still warm from the cow. It was a treat much enjoyed by Londoners and visitors alike and the two women made a very good living.

But their place of business was in the way of the new arch and the authorities were not going to let them stand in the way of progress.

They were told to remove themselves forthwith, but word leaked to the press and the public rebelled *en masse* – questions were raised in the House of Commons and the Lords and articles by the great and the good appeared in newspapers saying that it was an outrage to remove one of the most delightful traditions associated with the park. But what clinched it for the two elderly dairymaids was that Edward VII remembered drinking at the ladies' corner and he too thought it was an outrage that they should disappear.

The difficulty was that though the ladies claimed an ancient right to sell milk in the park they had no paperwork to prove it. When questioned by a Commons Committee they insisted their families had sold milk in this corner of the park since the mid-seventeenth century. Researchers got to work and uncovered a long history of milk selling in St James's Park. References in obscure documents dating back centuries did indeed make occasional reference to the sale of milk. It was becoming increasingly difficult to justify the removal of the two milkmaids and their cows.

At last the planners relented and the ladies were allowed to stay but they were told they would have to move away from The Mall and closer to the lake. They were also told that the right to sell milk would die with them. In the end this did not happen, however. The last of the two women died in about 1920 but the sale of refreshments did not die with them. The right to sell refreshments in the park seems to have become a right defined simply by long use and the present kiosk, situated where the two women and their cows once plied their trade, exists under that ancient right.

CHEEKY PORTER IN BUCKINGHAM PALACE

1905

There is a long tradition of mighty magnates rewarding their courtiers, friends and mistresses, either with dukedoms, knighthoods, vast tracts of land or monetary gifts, but instances of complete strangers being rewarded by monarchs are far more rare.

Edward VII, a bloated and unattractive figure whose life was permanently overshadowed by his mother Queen Victoria, was a bit of practical joker, so when he came across a cheeky porter in Buckingham Palace he was delighted by the man's audacity.

It all began when a picture ordered for the palace was delivered by a porter from a local art gallery. He was directed into the king's study and left alone to unwrap the painting. It took just ten minutes or so to remove the picture from its elaborate protective wrapping but somehow the official who'd led him into the room had forgotten all about him and he was left there. Clearly bored and unsure about what to do next, the porter eventually sat at a rather untidy desk in the corner of the room where he spotted a mass of writing paper – each sheet had the words Buckingham Palace emblazoned across the top.

The porter sat down, took a sheet of paper and, to pass the time, began to write a letter. At that precise moment Edward VII waddled into the room and the embarrassed porter leaped to his feet. The king walked over to the desk, looked down at the writing paper and hooted with laughter. He gave the porter a guinea – a great deal of money in 1905 – and showed him the door.

What so amused the king was the porter's opening few words which read:

'Dear Dad, Please note change of address...'

The story became and remained one of the king's favourites and he dined out on it for the rest of his life.

HIDDEN FIGURES ON THE BRIDGE

1906

The modernist movement in architecture seems largely to have consisted of a move to ban all forms of decoration from buildings. For the man on the Clapham omnibus, of course, this meant that the built environment that was once designed to delight and entertain both passers-by and those who lived or worked in a particular building suddenly came to look increasingly dull and utilitarian. It is no accident that critics of modernist architecture see it as a close ally of fascism – cold cruel lines, brutal in their conception and execution came to epitomise the most famous architecture of the 1930s onwards and most famously in the work of Le Corbusier and his followers.

The last great flowering of architecture that could be witty and decorative, playful even, came at the end of the much maligned Victorian era. We tend to think of the Victorians as lacking in grace and humour – an entirely false idea. Their builders and architects loved to embellish and decorate even in areas of a building that would only rarely be seen – much as the builders of medieval churches would encourage their carpenters to carve the underside of pews, the Victorians encouraged a riot of decorative stone, wood and brickwork.

One of the most unusual structures in London came about as a result of just this kind of impulse – in 1906 the present Vauxhall Bridge was finally completed. Like all Victorian and earlier bridges across the Thames it is enlivened with decorative detail, but what strange impulse persuaded the designers to add eight sculptures that can only be seen with great difficulty?

On the downstream side of the bridge the figures represent science, local government, education and the fine arts; on the upstream side they represent agriculture, sculpture, pottery and engineering.

Among these extraordinary sculptures is a perfect miniature version of St Paul's held in an outstretched hand!

Little St Paul's on the Water, as it has long been affectionately known among watermen, is very difficult to see from the bridge itself – you have to lean over the parapet, but it is worth it!

ONE-LEGGED ESCALATOR TESTER

1910

London's underground railway system is the oldest in the world and many of the tunnels we travel through today are relatively unchanged from when they were first built late in the nineteenth or early in the twentieth century.

When the Piccadilly line opened in 1906 it was the longest underground line in the world, covering more than ten miles. It was later extended to thirty-two and then finally covered more than forty miles, but even at ten miles it was one of the wonders of the world – it was also rather terrifying for passengers unused to travelling below ground.

But hardly had the public got used to this remarkable long-distance underground railway than the company that ran the trains introduced something even more remarkable.

When London's first railway escalator began operating at Earl's Court Station on the Piccadilly line in 1910 the passengers, to a man, were too terrified to use it. The railway company was aghast – they'd paid huge sums to have the revolutionary equipment fitted but it was all wasted if no one would dare use it. Then a bright spark had an idea – why not employ someone to use the escalator throughout the day to give the public confidence? The idea was accepted and Bumper Harris, a man with a wooden leg, was thereafter employed for a number of years to go up and down the escalator all day. Soon the public began to realise that if a man with one leg could use this remarkable new transportation system safely there was no reason why they shouldn't be able to. Of course Bumper, about whom almost nothing else is known, did his job too well – the public soon thought nothing of using the new moving staircase and he was out of a job.

MYSTERY CLOCK IN THE STRAND

1910

With its vast number of churches and older public buildings, London is a great place for public clocks – although, sadly, architects of modern buildings usually think it beneath their dignity to include clocks on their glass and steel cubes.

Remarkably accurate clocks and watches are now cheap to buy and available to all, but it was not always thus and in order that apprentices, schoolboys and others should be able to get to work on time city ordinances required church clocks to be kept well maintained – particularly their striking mechanisms, which carried news of the hour far beyond those who were close enough to the church to see the clock.

A law was passed by Henry VIII that all church and other official clocks in the city must be painted blue and gold and, officially at least, that law has never been rescinded, which is why city clocks are still mostly painted in the king's colours.

London has numerous highly eccentric clocks – the clock at St Dunstan's in the West with its giants beating the hours on a bell with their clubs, for example; or Fortnum and Mason's clock outside their famous shop. But perhaps the most bizarre and least known is the Law Courts' clock in the Strand.

What makes this clock so unusual is that it was built by an illiterate Irishman who only made clocks as a hobby, yet it is supremely accurate – in fact when completed it was said to be the most accurate clock in London. The difficulty arose when a second clock was needed and the court authorities wanted something of similar quality. Only then was it discovered that the original had been made by a man who – because he could not write – had kept no record of how he did it, which is why the Law Courts' clock is unique and always will be.

THE KING WHO NEVER GREW UP

1911

In the modern world princes try at least to seem to be in touch with their people. They haven't a clue how to do it, largely because they still insist on sending their sons to Eton and teaching them to shoot red deer, but they pay lip service to the idea that we are all equal. In the past the son of a king or queen did as much as he could to lead a life utterly different from that of his subjects and if you as much as suggested that he was no better than his footman he'd have had you arrested. The democratic principle is very much a recent phenomenon.

Horribly treated by his mother Queen Victoria, the future Edward VII was a prince who felt that he could let go of the reins entirely when the old Queen finally died in 1901. The pious, serious son she had hoped to create by telling him how hopeless he was in comparison with her late husband, had turned into a grossly overweight sensualist who enjoyed the favours of a string of mistresses and spent the relatively short time during which he was king indulging his passion for eating, drinking, shooting – and of course womanising.

But with all this there was a difficulty. No whiff of scandal was allowed to attach itself to the King of England, so despite the vast hypocrisy of the whole thing, elaborate efforts were made by the King's courtiers to make sure he could do what he liked while appearing to stick to the rules of decorum and good behaviour. How did they do it? Well, at the two-hundred-year-old Rules restaurant in Maiden Lane they built a special side door that led to a private room where the King could entertain his mistresses and when he went to the theatre he was ushered into a private, well-screened box far away from the public gaze. He was like a little boy who, long deprived of sweets, is let loose in a sweet shop.

Much of this is of course well known, but less well known is Edward VII's passion for fire engines, a passion that led to some very odd behaviour at No. 13 Rupert Street, Soho. Here the King would enter as king and emerge disguised as a fireman sitting on top of a fire engine. No one knows quite how often he indulged this passion but it certainly continued until within a few months of his death.

THE STATUE THAT ISN'T THERE

1912

When Peter Llewellyn Davies, a successful publisher, killed himself in 1960 by throwing himself under a train at Sloane Square, the newspaper headlines were all variations on a theme and that theme was Peter Pan.

Llewellyn Davies, like his four brothers, had been the inspiration for what is one of the most famous characters in children's fiction.

Peter Pan came into existence almost by accident when author J.M. Barrie (1860–1937) met the Llewellyn Davies boys in Kensington Gardens in 1900. He befriended their mother and father and when both died of cancer, Barrie virtually took over the boys' upbringing. He showered them with gifts and paid for their education. The games they played together in Kensington Gardens inspired the story of the boy who never grew up.

Years later the only surviving brother, Nico, told an interviewer that Barrie's motives were not sexual. But there is no doubt that Barrie was an unhappy man who wished to live vicariously, as it were, through the boys he idolised. Certainly his own marriage was a disaster and there were rumours that it was never consummated, for Barrie seems to have loved the idea of being in love – particularly with young actresses – rather than the reality of it.

When *Peter Pan* was first performed in London in 1904 it made Barrie famous – and very rich. In 1912 he conceived the idea of a statue of Peter Pan in the park where he had first played with the Llewellyn Davies boys, but this proved difficult and complex. Statues in the royal parks are permitted only following agreement by Royal Commission or, at the least, a parliamentary committee. But Barrie was world famous by now and not an easy man to refuse. After making enquiries he received an extremely odd reply to his request to erect the statue. He was told that he would not receive permission, but at the same time there would be no objection. On that basis Barrie assumed he could go ahead so he commissioned Sir George Frampton (1860–1928) to make the statue we see today.

Barrie himself unveiled the new statue at midnight and on his own – he liked the idea that children would see it the next morning and assume it had simply appeared as if by magic.

Initially the statue was hated (though not by children) but by 1921 it was the most popular statue in London, a position it almost certainly retains to this day.

But the lives of the boys who inspired the story and the statue were curiously unhappy – despite material wealth and expensive private educations provided by the ever generous Barrie, they seem to have been deeply troubled. Michael Llewellyn Davies, Barrie's favourite of the five brothers, drowned with a close friend during his last year at Oxford. There were rumours that it was a suicide pact and it is certainly true that Michael drowned at a spot on the river where only a good swimmer should have been – Michael could not swim at all. George was killed in action during the First World War and Peter, as we have seen, committed suicide. In Peter's case the connection with Barrie and the story of Peter Pan was almost certainly central to his decision to end his life.

In 1952 he had burned more than two thousand letters between his brother Michael and Barrie – he called the collection of letters 'The Morgue' and told friends that he absolutely loathed the connection with Barrie. It is odd that something that has brought so much pleasure to countless thousands of children across the world should have brought

only sorrow to the five children who inspired it. Curious too
that their memorial, the statue of Peter Pan, is a statue that,
officially at least, isn't even there.

THE PALACE THAT FACES
THE WRONG WAY

1912

Buckingham Palace is known throughout the world as the London home of the royal family, but it has a curious and less well-known history. The present building is the fourth on the site and it started life as a small, rather unpretentious house lived in by the Duke of Buckingham.

Built at the end of the seventeenth century, the original house bore no resemblance to the present building. Buckingham sold it in 1761 to George III, who wanted it for his wife Charlotte. Some fourteen of George's fifteen children were born in the house.

William Chambers (1723–1796) was brought in to partly rebuild and remodel the house in 1762 and it was left alone then until the 1820s when John Nash (1752–1835) doubled the size of the main block and refaced the house with Bath stone. He demolished a couple of wings and had Marble Arch made as a triumphal entrance to a new courtyard – Marble Arch was then discovered to be too narrow for the royal coach.

One would have thought that the designers would have measured a coach or two before going ahead – they didn't because they wanted the arch to be an exact copy of the Roman Triumphal Arch of Constantine. George IV and his architect John Nash wanted to reflect the dignity of ancient Rome, but in their obsession with ancient precedent they forgot modern practicality. The width of the arch itself is perfect for a Roman chariot but far too narrow for a Georgian coach. The embarrassing arch was moved in 1851 to an isolated spot at the end of the Edgware Road and there it has stayed ever since. And still to this day only royal coaches are allowed to go through the arch – except, of course, they don't fit so it remains unused.

But back to Buckingham House. After spending more than half a million pounds of taxpayers' money (the budget was £150,000) on it George IV died in 1830 having never actually lived in the house. His 'improvements' were still unfinished. The new king, William IV, spent more money on the house.

It's easy to forget that before Queen Victoria and the growth in which they took part of newspapers, which brought a sense of the monarch as a public figure, the royal family did not care what the general public thought of them. They lived private lives and the grand public ceremonies were only ever seen by other important people. If a king spent too much money on a project no one would dare criticise them anyway, although Parliament might grumble.

But as the monarchy realised that its public role was developing and that it had to show its face to the world, a decision was taken to turn Buckingham Palace around so that instead of facing into its private park it would face down The Mall in a decidedly public manner. This is why what we think of as the front of the palace is actually the back – the 'real' front faces the private park as it has always done.

It was Victoria who had the east front added in the 1840s by Edward Blore (1787–1879). For the first time the house faced down The Mall.

But the endless tampering with the house didn't end there – Blore's French stone was considered too soft so it was replaced a few decades later by the architect Sir Aston Webb (1849–1930) using the rather harsh Portland stone we see today.

A CARRIAGE PULLED BY ZEBRAS

1920

Aristocrats traditionally have the time and the money to indulge the most obscure, eccentric tastes. And the combination of money and eccentricity has always produced Londoners of exceptional lunacy.

Take Walter Rothschild (1868–1937), for example. Decidedly but brilliantly eccentric, he hated speaking to people, was blackmailed out of a fortune by his mistress and trained three zebras to pull his carriage along Pall Mall. Unfitted for the normal routes into public life that Rothschild elder sons tended to take, he set up a natural history museum that eventually grew into the biggest private museum in the world.

Throughout his life he was prepared to pay almost anything for a rare or unusual specimen, and by 1920, after working in virtual seclusion for years for eighteen hours a day, he had amassed some two thousand complete mounted animals, two hundred animal heads, three hundred sets of antlers, three thousand stuffed birds, seven hundred reptiles, one thousand stuffed fish, three hundred thousand bird skins and two hundred thousand birds' eggs. He was a brilliant if utterly obsessive zoological classifier – his enthusiasm and dedication was eventually rewarded when a subspecies of giraffe was named after him.

The stories of his madcap adventures in London are legion. Among the best is the story of his motorcar outing in Hyde

Park. He was hurtling through the park and had reached the bridge over the Serpentine when he spotted a chauffeur standing outside a stationary car with a folded rug over his arm. Rothschild immediately shouted at his own driver to stop. He leaped from the car, explaining that the rug in the other chauffeur's arms was made from the pelts of extremely rare tree kangaroos. Having waited till the owner of the rug arrived he refused to leave until the rug had been sold to him – the owner of the rug was shrewd enough to demand an absurdly high price but Rothschild would have paid almost anything.

ILLEGAL WHISKY FROM RESPECTABLE LONDON

1922

The attempt to ban alcohol completely in America – the Prohibition Era, 1920–33 – was one of the greatest disasters of twentieth-century social policy. Alcohol may be bad for you; it may be the cause of motoring and other accidents, not to mention numerous other social problems, but banning the world's oldest and most popular drug was never going to work.

Once alcohol was outlawed the pleasure-loving people of America simply got their supplies from illegal sources, thus turning millions of law-abiding Americans into criminals overnight.

Alcohol supply became central to the huge fortunes amassed by American criminals like Al Capone, but the curious thing is that since alcohol was perfectly respectable in much of the rest of the world, American criminal gangs could buy it perfectly legitimately even though it was destined for the sleazy underworld of US gangland.

Which is how one of London's most respectable and ancient wine merchants is said to have become involved in keeping America supplied with whisky during the thirteen years prohibition lasted.

Berry Bros and Rudd in London's St James has been supplying wine and spirits since the seventeenth century, so when an American walked into the shop and ordered several hundred cases of whisky they probably thought nothing of it.

But Jack 'Legs' Diamond was planning to take his whisky where whisky drinking was no longer allowed.

Ironically, during Prohibition demand for whisky in America increased, which meant a boost in business for many of Britain's whisky sellers, including the highly respectable Berry Bros, who didn't think twice about selling their wares to Americans since such sales – so long as the sale itself was carried out in England – were perfectly legal.

There is evidence to suggest that big orders for whisky and other alcoholic drinks were delivered by British suppliers to Nassau in the Bahamas, which was still then a British colony. Certainly Berry Bros shipped a great deal of Cutty Sark Whisky into the Bahamas at this time and – according to legend – that whisky was then taken out into international waters off the New Jersey coast where it was sold on in the dead of night to American gangsters like Al Capone.

Scottish distillers did a roaring trade, as did the London-based merchants, and since they were shipping to a British colony it was all perfectly legal. Those who think it's all a myth need only look at the figures – in 1918, before prohibition, the citizens of the Bahamas were knocking back some 944 gallons of whisky a year. By 1922 they were apparently drinking more than 386,000 gallons a year! Whisky sales via London ports to other British islands near the US mainland also increased – islands like the Turks and Caycos and Grand Cayman suddenly became inordinately fond of alcohol.

The American Government complained bitterly to the British Government about the exports of whisky to their colonies but nothing was done simply because the trade as far as the islands was legal and one suspects that the British Government knew that the American law against alcohol was ultimately unenforceable.

ANCIENT HALL GOES TO CHELSEA

1925

London is constantly changing and in various periods the pace of that change may increase or decrease, but in essence it never stops, which is why buildings built before 1700 are so rare.

Perhaps the most interesting, bizarre and least-known early building is Crosby Hall, which was built near Bishopsgate in the City of London by Sir John Crosby, a wealthy wool merchant. The house was completed between 1466 and 1475 and though it is no longer in Bishopsgate it survives because of the enthusiasm of a group of preservationists in the 1920s.

Crosby Hall now stands in Chelsea near the site of Sir Thomas More's (1478–1535) former home. The hall is largely complete – it has its original roof and oriel window and is the only remaining tangible evidence of how the wealthy built in fifteenth-century London.

It was moved stone by stone in 1925, but is substantially unaltered and the last example left of a medieval London merchant's house. The casual visitor may think as he passes the house on the north bank of the Thames near Cheyne Walk that it is a piece of fake Gothic architecture but he'd be mistaken – this is the real thing.

PRIME MINISTER CAUGHT
IN A BROTHEL?

1926

No one really knows why clubs started in London, but the whole idea of like-minded people getting together regularly to discuss mutual interests seems to have been, in its origins, peculiarly British and the very first clubs were certainly based in London.

The first clubs included the Wolf Club, whose only qualification for membership was that a man had to have been forbidden to sing in the bath by his wife (see page 170); the Lunar Society (whose scientifically minded members met when there was a full moon); the Fly Fishers' Club, whose members were addicted to pursuing trout by the most difficult means possible; the Garrick, where actors and those in the media were able to boast to each other about how wonderful they were; the Macaroni Club, whose members, according to one critic, were 'upper-class effeminate practitioners of sodomy, a crime imported from Italy by our spindle-shanked Gentry, who make the grand Tour but to bring home the vices of our Neighbours, and return, if possible, greater Coxcombs than they were before Embarkation'; and the Beefsteak, originally known as the Sublime Society of Steaks. It began in 1735 and is still based in Irving Street. Its founder members met – bizarrely enough – to discuss the disgraceful tendencies of 'levelling' – by which they meant the tendency, which cannot have been that common in early eighteenth-century London, for different classes to mix.

Beefsteak members were the supreme reactionaries who believed that birth conferred a status that neither success nor failure in life could change.

By 1926 the club was still meeting and some of Britain's most powerful reactionaries were members. Unfortunately, they met in an old rather seedy house on the edge of Soho and at a time when the police were taking a more than usually enthusiastic interest in local brothels.

On one particular summer evening a policeman saw four elderly and rather disreputable-looking men enter a house. The policeman made a written note to the effect that 'They looked highly suspicious and eager not to be observed'. The policeman called for reinforcements, convinced that they were about to raid a brothel. They forced their way into the house and arrested the four men, who happened to be the Governor of the Bank of England, the Chancellor of the Exchequer, the Prime Minister and the Archbishop of Canterbury.

When their identities were revealed the arresting policemen refused to believe them and threatened them with further prosecution for attempting to impersonate their betters! Despite the best efforts of the Beefsteak Club it seems that class isn't always that obvious!

THE WORLD'S MOST
FAMOUS PARROT

1926

Archaeology is not just about discovering how the great lived or worshipped. It's also about how the poor lived – but as the poor tend to have less they have tended to leave fewer artifacts in the archaeological record. Which is why an occasional commonplace survival from an earlier era deserves the attention it often gets. One such survival is the Cheshire Cheese public house just off London's Fleet Street.

In 1666 the Great Fire of London destroyed Old St Paul's, crept down Ludgate Hill towards the River Fleet and even destroyed a number of houses on the west of the river in what is today Fleet Street. But a few houses did escape the flames only to be destroyed – for example – when the hideous modern buildings of King's College were built.

Fleet Street was always famously bordered by a mass of tangled courts and alleyways typical of a crowded city that had grown slowly over many centuries.

Most of these courts and alleys are now built over or lined with dull office buildings but in Wine Office Court there is a most surprising survivor – a late seventeenth-century pub that looks exactly inside as it would have looked when it was first built. What's more, the interior is not a re-creation – the tables in the public bar, the fireplace, the décor and the pictures on the wall have all been here for at least two hundred years.

If we compare the interior of the Cheshire Cheese to prints

311

and drawings of early London coffee houses we realise that the Cheese is the last of these long-vanished and once hugely popular features of London life.

The fame of the Cheshire Cheese spread far and wide and from the 1850s it was on the itinerary of most visitors to London.

And by 1900 the pub had a resident who was to become almost as famous as the Cheese itself – this was Polly the Eccentric Parrot. Polly was known across the world for her bizarre antics and for her intelligence and abilities as a mimic. Famously garrulous and rude about visitors she didn't like, Polly celebrated the end of the First World War in 1918 in her own way. She imitated the noise of champagne corks popping an estimated four hundred times and then fell off her perch suffering from exhaustion.

When she died in 1926 she was estimated to be over forty and her antics over the years she spent at the Cheshire Cheese earned her an accolade unique in the animal kingdom – her obituary appeared in more than two hundred newspapers worldwide.

Polly lived at the Cheese during its most famous days but the list of celebrities who drank here is extraordinary: mostly literary figures are associated with the pub – Dr Johnson, who lived just two minutes' walk away in Gough Square, is reported to have come here every night for years along with his friend and biographer James Boswell (1740–1795); Dickens sat through many long evenings in the corner by the door in the room opposite the public bar; in the eighteenth century the actor and impresario David Garrick (1717–1779) came here with his friends the painter Sir Joshua Reynolds (1723–1792) and Edward Gibbon (1737–1794), author of *The Decline and Fall of the Roman Empire*; in the nineteenth century as well as Dickens, Wilkie Collins (1824–1889) was a regular together with Tennyson (1809–1892) and Carlyle (1795–1881); by the twentieth century everyone from Theodore Roosevelt (1858–1919) to Mark Twain (1835–1910) and Conan Doyle (1859–1930) came.

Above the fireplace in the public bar is a fascinating portrait dating from 1829, darkened by the smoke from countless candles and coal fires, of the waiter William Simpson. Apart from the fact that paintings of servants are rare the picture is interesting because the very table on which Simpson leans in his portrait is still in the bar nearby.

In the nineteenth century, the Cheese had one other claim to eccentricity: its landlord made some of the biggest pies in London. Filled with beef, oysters and lark each pie weighed between fifty and eighty pounds! Each was big enough to feed about 100 people and among those who ceremonially dished up the first serving were Sir Arthur Conan Doyle and future Prime Minister Stanley Baldwin (1867–1947).

THE GIANT OF FLEET STREET

1928

London's Inns of Court, home of lawyers since the Middle Ages, have produced vast numbers of eccentrics, oddballs and criminal lunatics over the centuries.

One of the strangest of these legal loonies was Judge James Crespi. Christened Caesar James, Crespi was born in 1928 and educated at Cambridge. He was a remarkable eccentric by any standards, although by profession he became a quite brilliant advocate. He claimed that he saved his most eloquent speeches for the Fleet Street wine bar El Vino's, where apparently the wine waiter always greeted him with a clenched fist across his breast and the words 'Ave, Mr Crespi'. He also became enormously fat, though luckily all the taxi drivers knew him by sight so he never walked anywhere – his huge bulk made it virtually impossible anyway – except one novice cabby who once mistook Crespi's wing collar for the dress of a waiter, and dropped him at the staff entrance to the Savoy.

He married a woman he met in a nightclub, but for reasons he was never able to recall. The marriage was described by Crespi as 'Obviously a case of mistaken identity' and it lasted less than a week. When asked if he regretted anything in life he simply said, 'Being mistaken for Lord Goodman, whoever he is.'

THE CHURCH THAT MOVED

1928

Whatever one might think of its superstitious aspects the Church of England has been pretty good at preserving the historic past. Among the few buildings that survive from the distant past in London today, for example, are the churches (most heavily restored after the carnage of the Second World War), but even the church has occasionally let the side down and allowed wonderful historic buildings to be destroyed.

During the Reformation vast quantities of English art was destroyed largely because most of it was religious art – the iconoclasts of the Reformation decided that plain white churches were far more interesting than highly decorated churches, so wall paintings were destroyed or covered up; statues and other decorative sculptures hurled on to the bonfire. London undoubtedly suffered particularly badly from this kind of thing – churches in remote rural districts were sometimes left alone – but anyone who thinks church destruction ended with the Reformation would be mistaken.

As late as the 1920s the then Bishop of London (clearly something of a philistine) decided that London had far too many Wren churches. No doubt he decided that Wren was a little dated and not much of an architect anyway, and promptly demolished half a dozen.

But astonishingly one of the churches earmarked for destruction was taken down carefully stone by stone and rebuilt out at Twickenham where it – or at least its tower – can still be seen as you drive out of London on the left-hand side of the A306: a rare ghost from the medieval City on a suburban bypass.

DEMOLISHED CAFÉ RETURNS

1929

Everyone talks about Regent Street as if it were one of London's most famous and architecturally important thoroughfares, but that judgment is based on a complete misunderstanding – it's based on the mistaken notion that what we see today is the work of that genius of Regency architecture, John Nash (1752–1835).

The great sweep of this magnificent thoroughfare remains as Nash, the man who built Carlton House and the exquisite terraces of Regent's Park envisaged it, but though the route of Regent Street is as it was conceived by Nash, none of the buildings we see today in Regent Street has anything to do with him.

Despite the beauty of the street that he created here, developers in the 1920s demolished every Nash building (with the exception of All Souls' Church, which was very badly damaged by German bombs) as well as the ornate colonnade that kept the rain off shoppers. The big ugly buildings that we now see in Regent Street are the work of a justly forgotten third-rate architect. However, amid all the devastation one feature of the vanished Regent Street that Nash built did survive: the Grill Room at the Café Royal.

The Café Royal was originally opened – in one of Nash's now lost buildings – by Daniel Thevenon, a Paris wine merchant, in 1870. The café he created became so famous that

317

artists, writers and film stars rarely visited London without insisting on a trip to the Royal.

When the new Regent Street was proposed the architects had every intention of building a new Café Royal and they were astonished when there was an outcry from across the world at the prospect of the beautiful Café Royal being destroyed. After a long campaign, which included representations from the royal family, a compromise was reached – the interior of the dining room, with its magnificent decorative scheme, would be carefully removed and then when a room the exact size of the old room had been built in the new Café Royal the old interior would be slotted back into place – and that's exactly what happened.

Today – if you are wealthy enough to be able to afford lunch at the Café Royal – you can dine in an interior of deep red plush and golden cherubs that is identical to the interior known and loved by everyone from Oscar Wilde to Augustus John, Lillie Langtry, Duncan Grant, J.M. Barrie and George Bernard Shaw.

ENTERTAINER WITH A POTATO HEAD

1929

In his famous book *Down and Out in Paris and London* (published in 1933) George Orwell recounts the extraordinary number of ways in which London's destitute managed to earn a living, from the screevers who drew pictures on the paving stones outside galleries and public buildings to the singers, acrobats, jugglers and escapologists. Orwell – himself an old Etonian – met several other old Etonians who were destitute and sleeping rough on London's streets.

But among the odd characters he meets none is perhaps more extraordinary than the big bald-headed Irishman who made a very decent living outside London's theatres using nothing more than a large potato.

We have to remember that before the telephone was widely available many theatregoers if not most would queue outside the theatre to buy tickets for that evening's performance. This meant that street entertainers had something of a captive audience.

The Irishman with the potato had a very simple and effective routine. He attracted the attention of the crowd, threw his potato (the biggest he could find) high into the air and then manoeuvred himself until he was directly underneath it. When the potato hit his bald head it splattered into tiny pieces and the Irishman immediately went along the queue with his hat.

Hard though it may be to believe, the audiences loved it.

A STATUE WITH ITS OWN INCOME

1929

St Dunstan's Church in Fleet Street is one of London's oddest churches. For a start it is octagonal in shape – the result of an oddly shaped site – and for many years it provided a home to a number of strange Christian sects: the Coptic Ethiopian Church, the Assyrian Church, the Romanian Orthodox Church and the Old Catholic Church of Utrecht.

Now hemmed in on all sides by later rebuilding, the churchyard was once a thriving place of business. Anyone who has a collection of seventeenth- and eighteenth-century books will see on the title page again and again the address 'Published at St Dunstan's in the West' followed by the date, for St Dunstan's, like St Paul's less than a mile away, was once a great centre of book publishing.

The most reprinted book after the Bible was first printed here – Izaak Walton's *The Compleat Angler* (far more a book about the contemplative life than about fishing) was sold here by Walton himself, who lived here and was St Dunstan's churchwarden for many years.

But the strangest feature of St Dunstan's is the statue of Elizabeth I that stands just in front of the church. Carved in the 1580s while the Queen was still alive it stood for many years on Ludgate where the Queen would regularly have seen it on her progresses from Westminster to the City and back. When Ludgate was demolished at the end of the eighteenth century the statue was brought to St Dunstan's.

The statue has been here ever since and it is the only statue in London (probably the only statue in the world) that has its own income.

In 1929 the philanthropist Lady Millicent Fawcett, concerned that the statue should be properly looked after, left enough money in trust for it to be cleaned and repaired in perpetuity.

FISHING FROM THE ROOF OF THE SAVOY

1930

The Savoy Hotel and surrounding area is rich in history, much of it bizarre in the extreme, but there are also odd endearing tales that attach themselves to the modern hotel and the ancient palace that once stood on the Thameside site.

One of the best of these tales concerns two guests staying at the hotel back in the 1930s.

Like the English, Americans are obsessed with fishing with rod and line and to the enthusiast half the pleasure of fishing is arguing about flies and lines and the various techniques for casting them.

Two Americans staying at the Savoy in London were particularly keen on fishing and over dinner one evening they had an argument over whether or not it would be possible to cast a fly, using a salmon rod, from the roof of their hotel over the gardens and the busy Embankment and into the Thames.

They were so determined to settle the dispute that they went along to Hardy Brothers, the tackle-makers in Pall Mall, and asked them to decide if such a thing was possible. Hardy Brothers approached the angler and author Esmond Drury who agreed to attempt the feat on condition that he was tied securely to a chimney on the hotel roof.

Early one Sunday morning, and with the help of a policeman who stopped all the traffic on the Embankment, he proved that

322

it was indeed possible to cast a fly into the Thames from the roof of the Savoy.

But the Savoy has always been a place that generates eccentricities. Take the short street at the front where taxis pull up to pick up hotel guests – this short stretch of roadway is the only place in the country where traffic is allowed to drive on the wrong side of the road. No one knows why this is but cars and taxis here must drive on the right.

The Savoy stands on the site of the old medieval Savoy Palace built by Henry III's friend Count Peter of Savoy in 1264. The courtyard at the front of the present hotel is said to follow the lines of the original medieval courtyard palace. The present building, completed in 1889, was commissioned and paid for by Richard D'Oyly Carte (1844–1901) using the vast sums he made putting on Gilbert and Sullivan operas. The famous Peach Melba was invented here (in honour of the great opera diva Nellie Melba), as was the dry martini. And legend has it that if thirteen guests find themselves about to sit down to supper the hotel will provide a fourteenth guest (a black cat) to avoid the bad luck inherent in the number 13.

And there is a long tradition at the hotel that if the guest is important enough they will put up with almost anything – one guest turned up with her pet crocodile, others have appeared with monkeys; marmosets and parrots are virtually commonplace. Two final strange tales about the Savoy: an American guest once took pot shots with his 12-bore shotgun from the roof at geese flying towards Green Park, and the great violinist Jascha Heifetz once had bagpipe lessons on the roof.

A little further west along the Strand from the Savoy is a short street that once ran down to the river. Savoy Street will take you to the Savoy Chapel, parts of which certainly date back to the original foundation, which is contemporaneous with Count Peter's twelfth-century palace. Most of the present building is relatively recent but it was once the cause of a bizarre legal suit. Having reverted to the Crown following the death of Peter of Savoy (1203–1268) the chapel was given to the Duke of Lancaster – who also happened to be the king. This meant the chapel was owned both by the king and by the Duke of Lancaster, but as they were one and the same person confusion reigned. The difficulty was only eliminated in the early eighteenth century when the king sued the Duke (i.e. he sued himself) to establish who had the right to the chapel and the land on which it was built. Not surprisingly the king won.

THE BUILDING THAT'S REALLY AN ADVERTISEMENT

1930

In the early part of the twentieth century, London was still a rather strait-laced place where advertising was considered rather vulgar – to the extent that it was banned on the sides of buildings. Partly this was an attempt to tidy up after the chaos of earlier centuries when shopkeepers and tradesmen put signs outside their shops and then tried to outdo each other by gradually making their signs bigger or attaching them to long poles until narrow streets would be dark all day because of the shadows cast by countless signs.

The first buses were also covered in ads, which then began to creep up the sides of buildings until the authorities called a halt. Tall buildings began to appear and though they would have provided magnificent sites for advertisements the authorities were horrified at the prospect. But one or two advertisers were determined to get round the ban and in at least one strange instance they got away with it.

On the south bank near Blackfriars Bridge a tower was built above a warehouse. The tower still survives and is now home to a very fashionable restaurant which offers diners a magnificent view from their tables along the river. At the top of the tower and visible from miles away there is an advertisement for the famous Oxo beef cube. The ad has been here since the building was first put up and it escaped the ban to which all such similar ads would have been subject. It did it by incorporating the advertisement – the letters OXO – into the very structure of the building. What look like three big letters are in fact three gigantic windows filled with red glass.

COWS IN THE STRAND

1930

Until relatively recently all London's food supplies had to be brought fresh to the capital – in the days before refrigeration there was no alternative, which explains why live animals were driven to Smithfield well into the twentieth century and milk was sold in various parks around London straight from the cow. Until 1900 you might often have seen a flock of geese marching towards London, each bird wearing a pair of tar boots (their feet were dipped in tar to prevent the long walk causing bleeding and pain).

But London was also a curiously unregulated place and the authorities were often more astonished than anyone to discover that odd trades and crafts were still being carried on long after everyone had assumed they were extinct.

Down by the river about halfway between Waterloo and Charing Cross Bridges was the world's first block of flats. Adelphi Terrace, completed in 1768, was built by the Adam brothers and was split into apartments – to the utter astonishment of Londoners who had never seen anything like it before.

Sadly little remains of this marvellous scheme and the superb buildings that once stood here. Most were demolished in the 1930s (one part survives in nearby Adam Street) but it was discovered as demolition got under way that an elderly woman was still living in the building along with half a dozen cows whose milk she sold in the Strand!

327

Dozens of other curious tales attach to this most historic and relatively little-altered part of London – J. M. Barrie of *Peter Pan* fame and George Bernard Shaw, for example, lived opposite each other for a while in Robert Street and when they wanted a break from writing they would throw biscuits or cherry stones at each other's windows to attract attention.

Another story tells how the Adam brothers wanted the building work on the Adelphi carried out as cheaply as possible so they brought workers down from Scotland. The workers quickly found out how much less than the going rate they were being paid and went on strike, so the brothers set off for Ireland where they employed Irish labourers, but only those who could speak no English! But the canny Irish, though they spoke only Gaelic, were not so easily fooled. Within days of their starting work in London they knew they were being swindled – the Adam brothers forgot that many of the workers would have had had relatives in London and they quickly discovered what they should have been paid. In the face of another threat of strike action the Adam brothers quietly gave in and paid up.

MAX MILLER'S LAST
PERFORMANCE

1936

Much of what once made London a truly fascinating place has been destroyed in the name of profit. The Victorians were particularly bad at knocking anything and everything down for this reason but we have not learned by their bad example. When the grossly overpaid and incompetent officials at the Royal Opera House wanted to make their theatre bigger and therefore more profitable in the 1980s they destroyed a row of eighteenth-century buildings, including the house in which Tom's Coffee Shop – one of the best-known coffee houses in eighteenth-century London – opened in 1722.

The much-loved buildings of the old Covent Garden Market were only just saved following a campaign by local residents in the late 1970s. Developers didn't care a fig for the historic fabric of the area. In the 1930s a similar campaign to save the world-famous old Alhambra Theatre in Leicester Square was not so successful, but the destruction of this splendid old building led to one of the oddest and saddest of all goodbyes.

The great comedian Max Miller (1894–1963), who was banned by the BBC for telling rude jokes, heard that the Alhambra, one of his favourite theatres, was being demolished so he went along to have a last look at the building in which he'd performed on numerous occasions. He arrived at lunchtime and hearing that the famous stage was to be taken down that afternoon he climbed on to the boards and gave the workmen an impromptu – and by all accounts hilarious – one-hour performance. Ten minutes after he'd finished, the stage was gone for ever.

Towards the end of his life Miller confessed that in a distinguished career his proudest moment was not appearing on the BBC or at the Theatre Royal but, as he put it, 'closing the old Alhambra'.

DOGS BEFORE NAZIS

1938

The British are famous, among other things, for tolerance – while Europe, from France to Poland and beyond, persecuted the Jews during the years leading up to and through the Second World War, Britain provided a haven for Jewish refugees; in the 1970s when Idi Amin expelled every Asian from Uganda, Britain offered them a home; and in recent years more migrants have targeted the UK precisely because of its reputation for tolerance.

But if the British are tolerant of foreigners they love their dogs even more. Indeed the British love of dogs is legendary – visitors to Britain over the past three hundred years have commented again and again on the fact that the average Briton is much fonder of his dog than of his friends and family. A long-forgotten magazine once printed the results of a survey of its readers: the survey revealed that given the choice of sleeping with their wives or their dogs the majority (the figures worked out roughly three to one) would prefer the dog!

One dog that enjoyed the tolerant affection of the British belonged to Hitler's ambassador to Britain in the 1930s, Joachim Von Ribbentrop (1893–1946). In 1938 Ribbentrop's dog Giro died and as a gesture of goodwill he was allowed to bury it in the gardens to the left of the Duke of York's monument just off The Mall.

Despite the fact that when war came Von Ribbentrop immediately became a hate figure for the British no one would

331

have dreamed of disturbing the grave of his dog – probably because they had always preferred the dog anyway. The dog's little headstone can still be seen today.

WHERE THE DUTCH DECLARED WAR

1940

A relatively small hotel just off Piccadilly, Brown's came into existence as early as 1837 when former servant James Brown and his wife Sarah opened their hotel at number 23. The Browns hung on until the late 1850s before selling for a handsome profit – by this time the hotel had expanded to include several neighbouring houses. Over the next century the hotel provided a temporary home for numerous celebrities including Cecil Rhodes, Rudyard Kipling and American President Franklin Roosevelt, who chose the hotel for his honeymoon.

In 1940 the Dutch government in exile – which seems to have consisted quite literally of two men and a dog – solemnly declared war on Japan from room 36. Since the announcement wasn't broadcast it is difficult to imagine that the Japanese Emperor was quaking in his boots.

TOP-SECRET GRASS-CUTTING SERVICE

1940

In its present triumphal form The Mall was laid out in the nineteenth century to emulate the triumphal routes of various other capitals – for example, Paris and Rome. It joins Trafalgar Square to Buckingham Palace, passing Horse Guards Parade on the way. The Mall is a familiar thoroughfare, but just where it passes Horse Guards Parade there is a very odd building that most people completely fail to notice.

Built from dark-red bricks and almost always covered in ivy, the building has a fortress feel about it – there is no decorative brickwork and not a ground-floor window in sight.

The building was made to protect the admiralty communications centre from bombs during the Second World War and almost nothing about it appears in any guide book about London.

When it was first put up the press was forbidden to mention it and everything possible was done to make sure it was undetectable, particularly from the air, and impregnable. The walls are incredibly thick and there is no doubt that it would withstand a conventional bomb or two, but just to be on the safe side the military decided that the best way to hide the building from the air would be to plant grass on top of it.

However, this led to one extremely eccentric proceeding which continues to this day – every morning in summer an employee carrying his top-secret pass presents himself to the

334

officials within the building and is allowed to enter. He carries with him a lawn mower – this has to be carried out through an upstairs window onto a set of steps that lead to the roof. He mows the grass, carries his mower back downstairs across the office floor and out of the building.

HOW ST PAUL'S HAD A
MIRACULOUS ESCAPE

1940

The Blitz on London – the word is from the German *Blitzkrieg* meaning lightning war – destroyed almost as much of the beautiful ancient City as the planners and developers of the 1950s and 1960s.

Despite its great size and the fact that, from the air, St Paul's Cathedral was an easy target, London's greatest church was not destroyed during the Blitz – in fact it was scarcely touched at all, despite the rain of bombs that fell in the area month after month. The fact of St Paul's survival is well known, but it is only when we look in detail at the number and size of bombs that fell that we realise quite what a miraculous escape the church had.

The bombing began in September 1940. Before that date Hitler had concentrated his attacks on British RAF fields and more obviously military targets, but the indiscriminate bombing of London that began in September showed that Hitler would stop at nothing to win the war. His actions over London and later Coventry were to lead ultimately to the fire bombing of Dresden and other horrors.

For 57 nights London was bombed every night and frequently also during the day. Between September 1940 and May 1941 almost nineteen thousand tonnes of high explosive rained down on the capital. Largely residential areas such as Southwark and Holborn were very badly damaged.

Through the early weeks of the Blitz the historic area of smaller houses and offices that were in many cases just yards from St Paul's in a warren of tiny ancient streets were completely flattened by direct hits. The whole of the historic booksellers area of Paternoster Row vanished forever, but right in the midst of this firestorm St Paul's remained unscathed for reasons that really cannot be adequately explained – expert fire watching certainly helped and the cathedral was also just very lucky. Disaster came very close indeed when on 12 September a bomb fell right next to the southwest tower but failed to explode. It buried itself deep underground and hard up against the church foundations – only the skill and bravery of the firefighters who spent three days extricating the bomb prevented disaster. When the bomb was finally removed it was still live. It was placed on the back of a truck and carried at a snail's pace to Hackney Marshes where it was detonated – the resulting crater measured more than one hundred feet across.

SAVED BY A BATHTUB

1941

During the savage, relentless bombing of London in 1941 there were numerous tales of extraordinary escapes from what really should have been certain death – in one case a man was blown out of the upstairs bedroom of a house into a bush in his garden. He emerged entirely unscathed despite the fact that his house had been completely demolished. In at least one case a man was found unharmed still in his sitting room, still in an armchair but with the whole house demolished around him.

Perhaps the most extraordinary example of survival against all the odds during the Blitz was the nineteen-year-old woman – later described by her rescuers as extremely attractive – who was taking a bath when a huge bomb scored a direct hit on her house in Poplar.

The explosion blew the house to pieces but somehow in the moment of destruction the young woman's bath was turned over on top of her, and as the rubble crashed down she was protected completely by the cast iron. It took several hours to dig her out but she emerged completely unscathed – though naked and highly embarrassed!

LONDON BRIDGE GOES TO WAR

1944

When Charles Rennie's Waterloo Bridge – completed in 1817 and named to commemorate Wellington's great victory – was destroyed by a stupid decision made by the London planning authorities, London lost what was generally agreed to be one of the most beautiful structures in Europe.

The ghastly modern bridge that replaced it has nothing to recommend it other than the fact that it is part of a bizarre and little-known story.

London's bridges generally were so busy by the mid-1930s – a direct result of a vast increase in car ownership – that the decision was taken to rebuild Waterloo Bridge, but while it was being rebuilt a way had to be found to keep the Waterloo crossing open, so a temporary metal bridge was built alongside the old one.

Finally the new (and very ugly) bridge was opened and the metal bridge taken down, but rather than destroy this useful temporary structure it was carefully packed away and stored for future use.

By now the war was on and by the time the Allies invaded Germany in 1944 only one bridge remained over the Rhine. When that was destroyed the old metal Waterloo Bridge was put on a train and taken to the Rhine where it was quickly put together and thrown out across the river. It became an absolutely vital part of the war effort. When hostilities came to an end it vanished without trace – just a small part of the vast pile of twisted metal strewn across Europe.

A CURIOUS CORRESPONDENCE

1949

Charing Cross Road has been famous for its second-hand and antiquarian booksellers for more than a century and it was in a small, now vanished shop here that a fascinating and bizarre relationship developed between a customer of the bookshop and one of the staff.

The story – published in 1970 – was eventually to be made into a film. It captured the imagination of the public because it seemed so ordinary and yet somehow romantic and even, ultimately, tragic.

It all began in 1949 when New York writer Helen Hanff (1920–1979) decided to order a number of rather obscure books of English literature from the London bookseller Marks & Company. She wrote to the bookseller at 84 Charing Cross Road and received a helpful reply from Frank Doel, an employee who was able to send her the books she needed. She replied and became a regular customer, but as the books were ordered, wrapped and dispatched something else was developing. The brief letters ordering various volumes began to take on a new character and soon Doel and Hanff were exchanging letters filled with jokes, news and gossip. She wrote mostly to Doel but also to other members of staff and when she heard that post-war austerity meant shortages of a number of basic food items she even sent the bookshop staff food parcels.

By the mid-1950s Doel and Hanff were on intimate terms yet they had never met. They exchanged birthday presents and

Christmas gifts and wrote extensively to each other about their interests in everything from the poetry of John Donne to the best recipe for Yorkshire pudding.

The correspondence lasted almost twenty years. On several occasions Hannf planned to visit London but somehow it never happened and in 1968 Hannf's regular letters from London ceased. Doel had died.

Hanff visited England at last in the early 1970s but with Doel's death Marks & Company had closed and the shop that Hanff visited stood empty and bare. She was able to look through the window but the rich life she had enjoyed through her correspondence had died with the man who inspired it.

The touching and curious story was immortalised in Hanff's book *84 Charing Cross Road* (1970) and in the later volume *The Duchess of Bloomsbury Street* (1973) that recorded her sad visit to the empty shop.

In 1987 the story was made into a successful film.

WHY THE AMERICANS DON'T OWN THEIR EMBASSY

1950

Despite London's apparent pride in its built heritage, early buildings are still demolished to make way for the bland and the mediocre. Most recently the Mappin and Webb site – a group of attractive Victorian City buildings from the nineteenth century – was destroyed to make way for yet more bland office buildings; in the 1970s and 1980s Georgian and earlier houses in central London were frequently pulled down for no good reason. But even while the authorities were allowing the destruction to go ahead they were extolling the virtues to tourists of London's historic architecture – the very architecture they were allowing to be demolished at every opportunity.

But it was far worse in the past. In the 1920s all of John Nash's magnificent Regent Street was demolished; in the 1870s the last great Jacobean mansion in central London – Northumberland House – was destroyed to build, of all things, a cut-through road.

In the 1930s Norfolk House, an exquisite building in St James's Square, was knocked down to build something of absolutely no merit whatsoever. The list goes on almost indefinitely.

Grosvenor Square, between Piccadilly and Oxford Street, suffered particularly badly from this mania for destruction. By the 1940s most of the original houses in the square – many relatively unaltered since the late seventeenth century – had gone to be replaced by flats and shops.

Then in the late 1950s the Duke of Westminster agreed to allow the Americans to demolish the whole of the west side of the square so they could put up the terrible building we see today; but the siting of the American Embassy led to one of the most bizarre and protracted processes of negotiation ever seen in London.

The Americans have embassies all over the world and in every single case they buy the land first and then build their embassy. They assumed that this would be possible in England so they asked the Duke of Westminster – who owned Grosvenor Square – how much they would have to pay to buy the freehold of the land. What they didn't know is that the Grosvenor family never sell. Their vast wealth is based precisely on this simple fact: they own three hundred acres of central London including most of Belgravia and Mayfair, not to mention land holdings all over the world. All the houses and offices on this land are leased; their freeholds are never sold.

When the Americans were told they could not buy their land they insisted that was unacceptable and that they would petition Parliament to force the Duke to sell. Questions were asked in Parliament; the Grosvenor family were heavily leaned on but all to no avail.

Then the Duke thought of a good compromise. He told the furious Americans that if they were prepared to return to the Grosvenor family all those lands in the United States stolen after the American War of Independence then he would allow the Americans to buy their site on the west side of Grosvenor Square. The Americans knew when they were beaten (they would have had to give the Duke most of Maine and New York!) and being unwilling to hand over land they themselves had stolen from the Indians anyway, they backed down and the Duke of Westminster allowed them a 999-year lease. And that explains why the embassy in London is the only American embassy built on land not owned by the United States.

A PIGEON SHOOTER IN
FLEET STREET

1950

It's easy to forget that Fleet Street was once not just the home of Britain's national newspapers but also of a substantial part of its book-publishing effort. And the most obscure magazines had their offices either in the main thoroughfare or in one of the numerous courts and alleys that run north and south of Fleet Street.

After the Second World War *Shooting Times* magazine, an eccentric weekly beloved of old colonels who liked to read how many pheasants or grouse had been shot in a particular week, was still being published from a tiny upstairs office in Fleet Street, an office it had started life in more than fifty years earlier. At that time, and for many years afterwards, the magazine was staffed almost entirely by dull-witted public schoolboys who had almost no knowledge of journalism but were absolute experts at all matters to do with hunting, shooting and fishing.

They were also terrific drinkers and practical jokers.

One editor – who stayed in the editor's chair for nearly thirty years – was cautioned by the police on several occasions for playing practical jokes on passers-by that could have had serious consequences.

He regularly took pot shots at pigeon out of the window or slipped out at lunchtime when the street was crowded and left his bowler hat on the ground with a live pigeon trapped underneath it just to see the fright it would give the first person who picked the hat up.

Another favourite trick was to drop nets from the first floor window on to unsuspecting passers-by, but long before the newspapers all moved away small magazines like *Shooting Times* found they could no longer afford high London rents and they moved away, leaving Fleet Street a quieter but perhaps less interesting place.

WINE CELLAR SURVIVES THE CENTURIES

1952

It is difficult now to visualise Whitehall and the Palace of Westminster as they were before the building of Parliament Square and the present House of Lords and Commons.

All along the river here was once a warren of royal buildings stretching from the Thames to Westminster Abbey and up Whitehall to the Banqueting Hall.

But the Palace of Westminster was never a palace in the modern sense of one great building – it was a mass of small ramshackle buildings dating back to the time of William the Conqueror.

Henry VIII got so fed up with its shabby appearance that when Cardinal Wolsey (1473–1530) fell from grace he appropriated the Cardinal's huge house further up Whitehall and changed its name from York Place to Whitehall Palace.

Many of the old royal buildings along Whitehall had been demolished by the time a huge fire destroyed almost everything in 1834, but the Banqueting Hall (1610) survived as did the Jewel Tower and what is now known as Henry VIII's wine cellar.

The cellars are in fact an astonishing survival – they are the only remaining part of Wolsey's old palace and were probably built as early as the end of the fifteenth century. What makes the vault's survival even more extraordinary and exciting, however, is the fact that when Whitehall was being rebuilt in

346

the 1950s the vaults were spared the demolition normally suffered by anything old that got in the way of modern redevelopment. Instead the vaulted undercroft supported by four massive octagonal pillars and weighing more than 800 tons was carefully lowered eighteen feet to preserve it beneath the foundations of the modern office building.

Not a brick or stone was damaged during this remarkable operation. The move cost more than £100,000, which would equate to tens of millions of pounds in today's terms.

A GIFT TO LONDON – A GERMAN LAMPPOST!

1963

The practice of town twinning is bizarre – for many it simply provides an excuse for local officials to enjoy all-expenses-paid trips to foreign countries; for those who enjoy such trips, twinning represents (perhaps) a hand of friendship extended across the seas to nations with whom we are already friendly.

Perhaps the odd, slightly dubious, nature of twinning explains one of the strangest gifts ever given by one nation to another.

Anyone who walks along the north side of the Thames above Hammersmith Bridge will see the old inns and boathouses that have characterised the area for centuries, but tucked away against the wall of an old house the eagle-eyed may spot something very different – a worn rectangular metal plaque. The plaque records that in 1963 Herr Willy Brandt (1913–1992), later the German Chancellor, gave the good citizens of Hammersmith a lamppost. The gift was to mark the twinning of Hammersmith with the borough of Neukollen in Berlin.

The plaque solemnly declares that 'The lamp above this plaque was formerly used to light a street in West Berlin. It was presented by Herr Willy Brandt, the Mayor of West Berlin, to councillor Stanley Atkins as a token of friendship.'

Whether the lamp has some symbolic significance – perhaps to shed light on the relationship or to illuminate the dark past of European history is anyone's guess. One wonders what Hammersmith gave West Berlin – perhaps a manhole cover or a stretch of municipal railing!

CAMPAIGNING AGAINST PEANUTS AND SITTING

1965

Strange stories and strange characters are not entirely a feature of London's more distant past. Anyone over fifty who knows London well will remember a very odd character who haunted Oxford Street and Regent Street for several decades.

Stanley Green died at the age of seventy-eight in 1992, having spent nearly thirty years parading the West End carrying a placard warning mostly against the dangers of protein.

Over the years he sold tens of thousands of hand-printed leaflets (at 12p each) explaining why lustful feelings were induced by 'fish, birds, meat, cheese, egg, peas, beans, nuts and sitting'. He had worked for many years in a perfectly ordinary job in the civil service before starting his one-man campaign against lust and peanut eating in the early 1960s.

No one really knows why he decided that protein was the root of all the world's evils but once he'd made his decision he never gave up.

'Protein makes passion,' he would say to anyone who would listen. 'If we eat less of it, the world will be a happier place.'

He produced his leaflets on a small press in his tiny flat in north west London; the tenants below often complained about the terrific sounds of thumping and crashing on print day. Until he qualified for a free bus pass he would cycle each day to Oxford Street in his raincoat, cap and wire-rimmed spectacles, and always recalled with pleasure that motorists reading the board on the back of his bicycle would toot their horns and wave. 'I've known coaches pass,' he said, 'and everyone has stood up and cheered me.'

He was occasionally spat at, but he was rarely upset by abuse, explaining that people only attacked him because they thought he was a religious person, which he most clearly was not. He would often concentrate his efforts on cinema queues, using such opening gambits as 'You cannot deceive your groom that you are a virgin on your wedding night.'

CABMAN'S REVENGE

1965

For centuries London's cabmen and porters were vital to the efficient running of the city, but as long as they continued their work nothing much was thought of them. In the eighteenth century this began to change when a porter's rest was put up in Piccadilly – this strange–looking contraption is a broad thick plank of wood set on two cast-iron pillars. The plank would be at chest or even shoulder height for the average man. The reason it was fixed at this height is that it allowed the porters to ease any load off their shoulders and on to the plank, which was almost at the same height, rather than have to lower it to any significant extent. The porter's rest allowed them to slip their load off and on again easily.

Hansom cabs were the great feature of the second half of the nineteenth century (particularly after Poet Laureate Sir John Betjeman's grandfather invented a new lock for their doors) and they grew massively in numbers until the advent of the First World War – after 1918 they rapidly disappeared as motor cabs took over.

But the harsh conditions under which the Victorian hansom-cab drivers had to work – out in all weathers for twelve or more hours a day, seven days a week – came to the attention of a group of philanthropists who started the cabmen's shelter fund in 1874. Their money was used to establish a set of green timber buildings – usually set in the middle of broad thoroughfares – where the cabmen could stop for a cup of tea or lunch or dinner. Many of these cabmen's shelters have now disappeared but thankfully those that remain are now protected. They are always painted green and look rather like large slightly ornate garden sheds with small windows and a pitched roof.

One such cabmen's shelter survives in the Brompton Road near Knightsbridge. Another can be found just off Sloane Street. A third, in Temple Place just north of the Embankment, was the cause of one of the oddest building disputes of the past two centuries.

When in the 1960s a proposal was lodged by developers to knock down four ancient streets running down to Temple Place, officials at the Greater London Council agreed to allow the demolition despite the fact that the hotel planned for the site was designed to house tourists who presumably were coming to London to see the sort of sites their hotel was about to destroy.

The disgraceful demolition plan got the go-ahead and the vast hotel was built but as it neared completion the dozy architects realised that just at the spot they'd planned to put their grand hotel entrance there was a green cabmen's shelter.

With typical corporate stupidity they tried to use their financial might to have the shelter removed by the authorities, but they were told that the shelter had been there since 1880 and it was staying put. Filled with horror that their rich American clients would baulk at the sight of a ramshackle old cab shelter in front of their new hotel, the directors of the building firm had to approach the cabmen cap in hand and ask if they would mind if their shelter were moved a few yards down the street. The cabmen – far more civilised than the corporate bigwigs – agreed provided that the hotel owners paid for the shelter to be moved and made a donation to the cabmen's shelter fund. No doubt the hotel paid as little into the fund as they could, but the shelter was duly – and very carefully – moved a few yards along the road.

'HOW NOT TO GET LOST IN LIBERTY'S'

1970

One of London's most famous shops since it was opened by Arthur Liberty, a Buckinghamshire draper, in 1875, Liberty's was the ultimate in fashion between 1880 and 1920 and it has always been associated with the Arts and Crafts movement. The shop originally sold Japanese fans – Mr Liberty was one of the first to import oriental goods as well as silks and other fabrics in bulk.

Then in 1925, flushed with success, the company, which had by now acquired three adjacent shops, decided to rebuild. The result was the extraordinary mock Tudor building we see today, but this is only visible in Great Marlborough Street. On the side of the store that faces Regent Street, Liberty had to stick to the Portland stone from which the rest of Regent Street is built, but in Great Marlborough Street he could do what he liked. And in the great tradition of craftsmanship and individuality championed by William Morris (1834–1896), the man behind the Arts and Crafts movement, Liberty really let himself go in Great Marlborough Street.

Built around an interior courtyard, Liberty's conceals a remarkable and bizarre secret – it is made almost entirely from the magnificent oak timbers from two dismantled ships, HMS *Hindustan* and HMS *Impregnable*.

Not content with this, the owners of what was and still is one of London's most successful shops employed the best craftsmen – including several brought here specially from Italy – to install stained glass, magnificent staircases and superb carvings. Everything is handmade and unique.

What really ensured the success of Liberty's, however, was not the spectacular building, but the decision made much earlier by Gilbert and Sullivan to use Liberty fabrics for the costumes in their light opera *Patience* (1881).

Perhaps the most delightfully eccentric thing about Liberty's is that its staircases are built in such an odd way that at one time customers were always getting lost. All was resolved when, in the 1970s the then owners published a booklet which was available free to all regular customers entitled 'How Not To Get Lost In Liberty's'!

LONDON FISH LOVE SEWAGE

1972

As a general rule there is no arguing with the fact that fish thrive in clean water and die in heavily polluted water, but London fish have regularly proved themselves an exception to this rule. In one or two instances the survival of fish in London's rivers is quite extraordinary.

The old River Lea that runs from Hertfordshire down into north London and from there joins the Thames in the East End was once one of the cleanest rivers in the country. It was also a river valley that was so rich in wildlife that when Elizabeth I went hunting – which was something she liked to do often – she would set off for the Lea Valley. It was here too that the great Izaak Walton (1593–1683) fished and many of the experiences described in his famous book *The Compleat Angler* took place on this once glorious waterway. But as the city expanded and industry flourished much of the river became too dirty to support much worth fishing for. By the early decades of the twentieth century the River Lea in London was little more than an open sewer.

Then rumours began to spread that in one or two places fish had been seen again in the London reaches of the river. This was remarkable enough, but local fishermen simply shook their heads in disbelief when it was also reported that the fish that had been seen were actually seen in greatest numbers precisely at those places where sewer outfalls entered the river.

In Tottenham a journalist from a fishing magazine went

356

along to see what all the fuss was about. He found a gin-clear fast-flowing stream that ran between high solid-concrete banks. In fact it wasn't a stream at all. It was the sewage outfall, but the water that ran through it looked cleaner than the water that ran, at that time, through Hampshire's famous River Test.

Even more exciting was that great shoals of fish could be seen in the fast water. They were difficult to catch, but each fish was enormous – far bigger than the general run of these species in most rivers.

In the two years that followed the discovery of the sewage outfall fishery the British records for gudgeon, bleak and dace were all broken by fish taken from that tiny water.

When scientists investigated they discovered that the effluent was being so efficiently cleaned up that it was actually providing the fish with a protein-rich diet – hence their enormous average size.

Hardly surprising then that very few fish were knocked on the head and taken home for supper!

PENIS FOR SALE AT CHRISTIE'S

1972

When Napoleon Bonaparte died in May 1821 there were fears that rumours would spread about the manner of his death (recent claims include the suggestion that he was poisoned), which may explain why no fewer than seventeen witnesses were invited to observe the autopsy which was carried out the day after he died by the Emperor's own doctor, Francesco Antommarchi.

On the Emperor's own instructions, his heart was removed first. Napoleon had asked that it be sent to his wife Marie-Louise, though the heart apparently vanished before it could be delivered.

The stomach was carefully examined and at the time it was agreed that cancer was the cause of death. Nothing else is recorded as having been removed. However within a few decades it was commonly supposed that Napoleon's penis had been cut off and stored away carefully during the autopsy. Oddly this was not mentioned by any of the seventeen witnesses present at the time of the autopsy. But several commentators have suggested that the body was not guarded at all times during the procedure and while everyone's backs were turned Napoleon's organ could have been quickly snipped off.

Napoleon's friend Vignali, who administered the last rites, was left a large sum of money in Napoleon's will as well as numerous 'personal effects' – these were not specified. Thirty years later Napoleon's manservant claimed that Vignali had indeed removed various parts of Napoleon's body, but this was not corroborated.

By 1916 the material bequeathed to Vignali had been sold *en masse* to a London collector, who some years later sold the collection on to an American. It was at this point that the penis story became more substantial. The description of the collection included the curious phrase mentioning 'the mummified tendon taken from Napoleon's body during the post-mortem'.

By the 1930s A. S. Rosenbach, an American collector, was displaying the 'tendon' in a blue velvet case and describing it as Napoleon's penis. It travelled to France and was later the centrepiece of a grand display at the Museum of French Art in New York.

A newspaper report described the organ as looking 'something like a maltreated strip of buckskin shoelace or shriveled eel'. Reports – largely stemming from Napoleon himself – that he was particularly well endowed seem to be contradicted by the fact that the organ was also described as 'one inch long and resembling a grape'.

The most extraordinary part of the story occurred in London in 1972 when the putative penis was put up for sale – complete with magnificent velvet-lined case – at the London auction house Christie's along with the rest of the Vignali collection. The collection failed to reach its reserve and was withdrawn. A few years later the penis popped up again, this time in Paris and unencumbered by all the other paraphernalia of the collection.

The penis was bought by John Lattimer, a retired professor of urology (apropriately enough) at the University of Columbia, for around $3,000. The penis is still, as it were, in Professor Lattimer's hands.

FAMILY MONEY ARRIVES AFTER TWO HUNDRED YEARS

1976

Right across London ancient bequests are still being distributed to various good – and perhaps not so good – causes. Guy's Hospital enjoys the financial benefits of a number of bequests, some of which are centuries old. The British Library is another beneficiary of some odd legacies – it still receives upwards of half a million pounds a year as a result of a decision by George Bernard Shaw to leave his copyright fees to the library. He left the money because as a penniless author back in the 1880s he had been able to work free of charge (and despite the holes in his shoes) every day in the warmth of the library with access to every book he needed.

The bizarre thing about that bequest is that it was not properly honoured. When the British Library separated from the British Museum in the early 1990s something very odd and rather scandalous happened to Shaw's money. Museum officials are still cagey about the whole subject, but it looks as if Shaw's money goes to British Museum coffers rather than to the British Library, which of course goes entirely against Shaw's own wishes.

Other more ancient bequests are far more strictly administered, even when the amounts of money involved now seem tiny.

Among the most extraordinary ancient bequests was that made by a member of the Society of Antiquaries, whose base has been in Burlington House in Piccadilly for nearly two hundred years. In 1776 the member left a considerable sum of money in a trust fund that benefited his family, but he stipulated that if his family should die out then the money should go to the Society of Antiquaries. In 1976 the last member of the family died and the money was duly paid over to the society, much to their astonishment.

BIZARRE RAILWAY
ADVERTISEMENTS

1977

One of the strangest things about London is that the authorities claim to be proud of the capital's historic sites and traditions yet they do their best at every turn to destroy them.

The City of London Corporation is one of the worst offenders – it is generally believed that German bombs did most to destroy the historic heart of old London, a city in which substantial areas of Tudor and Elizabethan housing survived until the war, but the fact is that far more of old London was destroyed and has continued to be destroyed by developers than by the Luftwaffe.

One of the most inexplicable acts of vandalism occurred at Blackfriars Station when in 1977 the station was rebuilt. Londoners and visitors alike had always loved the oddball carved Victorian panels in the station that placed the most exotic destinations side by side with the most prosaic as if each would appeal equally to commuters. Thus Sittingbourne was right next to Constantinople; Paris next to Sevenoaks. But when the decision was taken to rebuild the station and it became clear that the developers intended to destroy the much-loved panels, worldwide protests astonished the philistine developers, who were forced to keep at least a few of the old panels in the new booking office.

Sadly Euston Station, one of the glories of Victorian railway architecture, was not so lucky. In 1963 despite the protests, the whole station was destroyed to make way for the architectural disaster that we see now.

TEARING UP £80,000

1979

Before he became rich and famous the painter Francis Bacon (1909–92) used to take his friends several times a week to Wheeler's Oyster Bar in Soho. He almost always insisted on paying despite having no regular income at all, which meant that he often had to ask the owner to allow him to run up a tab. Such was Bacon's astonishing charisma that the restaurant owner allowed the bill to reach more than ten thousand pounds before he began to complain. Bacon had become quite well known by this time and the restaurant owner begrudgingly accepted a small Bacon painting as a sort of surety that the bill would eventually be paid. It was paid long before Bacon became a multimillionaire but the restaurateur kept the picture and eventually sold it for more than a quarter of a million pounds. A rare case of justified faith in an artist!

Bacon – a famous and outrageous habitué of Soho bars (most especially The Colony and the French House) – was for decades at the centre of an outrageous clique of artists and writers around whom strange stories swirled like a dangerous mist. Among the most delightful stories is that he once spotted one of his own paintings in a shop in Bond Street and decided he didn't like it. He stepped into the shop, wrote a cheque for something in the region of £80,000, stepped back outside with the carefully wrapped picture under his arm and then smashed it to pieces on the roadway, grinding the canvas underfoot until it was beyond the powers of any restorer to recover it.

364

HOW THE GOVERNMENT LOST A HOSPITAL

1980

Foreigners always find the systems of land ownership and tenure in the UK completely baffling. The idea of leasehold, for example, is unknown in many countries, but in the UK it is combined with flying freeholds, tenants in common and a host of other bizarre methods of ownership.

In London until relatively recently titles that proved ownership of land were not registered – that meant that if you lost the paper that proved your ownership (your title) to land you also lost the land. These days land is registered with a government department so even if the title deeds are lost it is possible to look up the owner of a particular plot of land in official documents. But those buying leasehold property in London still frequently find that the freeholder has long vanished and they are advised by their lawyers that the freeholder may never be found – which produces the odd situation that a leaseholder can inherit a freehold at absolutely no cost.

One of the strangest tales of landownership in London concerns the famous St George's Hospital on London's Hyde Park Corner. The shell of the building remains to this day – the façade was preserved for a new hotel when the hospital finally closed in 1980 having been run continuously as a hospital since 1783.

When it closed, the government of the day looked forward to selling the land for development. They simply assumed that

365

they owned the land as the hospital was by then part of the National Health Service and all hospital sites were government owned. As they prepared to sell the site – which was and is enormously valuable – they received a polite letter from the Duke of Westminster, whose family, the Grosvenors, own much of the land in Belgravia and Mayfair. The letter pointed out that the land on which the hospital was built was owned by the Grosvenors and not by the government. The government thought they were safe when they realised they had a nine-hundred-year lease on the ground, but again they were thwarted by the Grosvenor Estate, whose representatives had carefully kept the original deeds for more than two centuries.

The government certainly did own a very long lease on the land on which the hospital was built; that much was agreed, but when government officials were invited to take a careful look at the terms of the lease they discovered that it remained valid only if the land continued to be used for a hospital. Since a hospital was no longer required, the land reverted to the Grosvenors and the government was left with nothing.

ENDLESS SECRET TUNNELS

1980

When journalist Duncan Campbell found an entrance to a shaft in the middle of a traffic island in Bethnal Green in London's East End, he was astonished to discover a large tunnel at the bottom that led away into the distance apparently heading towards central London some half a dozen miles distant.

Campbell went home, collected his folding bike, and some time later returned to the shaft entrance. He carried the bike down the shaft and started pedalling towards central London along a series of extraordinary tunnels.

Over the centuries the curious have regularly come across underground tunnels beneath London's streets – some are ancient, others, as Campbell discovered, more modern. But the oddest thing is that there are almost certainly far more tunnels – many-layered and interconnecting – than we imagine.

Campbell's tunnel started about one hundred feet down and he rode around the tunnels for hours covering in excess of a dozen miles in total, but it was clear to him, as it has been to others, that he had barely scratched the surface of London's extraordinary underground tunnel network.

Beautifully built brick-lined sewers, some dating back to medieval times, certainly exist in the oldest parts of the city and it is still possible to walk along the old bed of the Fleet River, which is now buried beneath Farringdon Street at the bottom of Ludgate Hill. The river – reduced to little more than a trickle

367

– runs along the bottom of a giant pipe but there is plenty of room to walk.

In Victorian times the vast network of ancient sewers provided a living for hundreds of men and children – intimate knowledge of the tunnel routes was passed from one generation to the next and a team of sewer searchers might travel from the city to the West End and back in a day and always entirely underground, but they had to be careful: a sudden storm in Highgate or Hampstead could lead to flooding – a torrent of water hurtling along the tunnels would sweep the men to their deaths. Experienced sewer men knew the dangers and posted lookouts before they went down as well as trying to restrict their activities to days when the weather was fine. In the thick layers of human fat that lined the tunnels they would often find a rich store of lost gold trinkets and coins.

Those sewers are still there and beneath them, far deeper and almost as deep as London's water table, is a vast array of tunnels that some believe are part of a nuclear network of bunkers centred on Whitehall. There is some evidence for this too. We know, for example, that when the Jubilee line was built planning permission for certain routes was refused but officials would not say why. The same happens when telecommunications tunnels have to be dug – certain areas and depths and routes are always out of bounds because London under London is still the capital's greatest and most complex secret.

DARWIN ON THE UNDERGROUND

1985

Only the very superstitious – meaning the religious – now seriously question the validity of Darwin's theory of evolution. Darwin's idea about the survival of the fittest has been widely misinterpreted it is true – by fittest Darwin meant best adapted for survival in a particular environment, not strongest or toughest.

Darwin also explained that time was the great factor in evolution: when groups of individuals of the same species are separated by some physical barrier – say a mountain range or an ocean – for long enough they will gradually change to such an extent that they would no longer be able to breed if they were brought together again. They would, in short, have become two different species.

Astonishingly, London's Underground provides a splendid example of Darwinism in action. In the mid-1980s scientists noticed that as well as the numerous rats and mice living in the Victorian tunnels deep under the streets of the capital there were also large numbers of mosquitoes.

Nothing particularly unusual about that, except that studies quickly revealed that the mosquitoes were very different from other known mosquitoes. Comparisons were made with similar insects from Africa and Asia and with all the known subspecies of mosquito and the London mosquito was sufficiently different to be labelled a new species.

How on earth could this happen? The answer is evolution by natural selection but in a speeded-up form.

Scientists pieced together the likely history of the London mosquito.

When the tunnels of the Underground were first being built at the end of the nineteenth century mosquitoes would have been more common than they are now, although they are still common enough. The pools of stagnant water inevitable in and around building sites would have provided perfect breeding grounds for the insects and when the tunnels were finally closed in the mosquitoes found themselves underground. As the years passed they reproduced and gradually migrated all along the system wherever there was water. Today mosquitoes exist in the deepest parts of the system and tests have shown that they can no longer interbreed with any other known species of mosquito – physical isolation has made them change to the point where they have become a separate species, exactly as Darwin predicted.

The reason they have changed in a relatively short time is that a century is not in fact a short time at all when seen in relation to the lifespan of a mosquito. Those tunnel mosquitoes have probably gone through thousands of generations in the time they have been isolated.

LOST LAVATORIES

1985

One of the great tragedies of the past fifty years is the gradual disappearance of London's magnificent public lavatories. Built into the fabric of the environment by nineteenth-century urban planners who were concerned (unlike modern developers) that their buildings should be decorative as well as functional, public lavatories tended to be built at major street junctions and below ground.

But, much as the Victorian pub builder wanted to celebrate his skill in the sumptuousness of gin palaces with their sparkling cut glass, fabulous mirrors and huge ornate ceilings and walls, so the lavatory builders created splendid subterranean palaces of gleaming copper pipework, hugely decorative tiles and basins, and lavatories with delicate flower decoration. Heavy mahogany doors were used for each lavatory cubicle and the overall impression was always one of spacious loftiness, for these were palaces to ease and bodily contentment.

As it cost a penny to use these grand public conveniences the Victorian lavatory also gave us the splendid euphemism that survives to this day: the phrase 'I'm going to spend a penny' being among the politest and most delicate indications that one wishes to use the loo.

The grand Victorian lavatories were gradually taken out of use by penny-pinching local authorities who simply assumed that the growth in cafés and restaurants would fill the gap – if the modern city dweller needs to spend a penny she has to go

371

into an expensive restaurant for a cup of coffee she may well not want simply to use the loo.

But oddly, though many of the old public loos were closed and their entrances sealed over, many still exist complete with all their magnificent pipework below ground, buried like Egyptian tombs and awaiting some enthusiastic future lavatorial archaeologist.

One of the last lavatories to go was the splendid example in Covent Garden just outside the church in the piazza. Here in its dying days in the 1980s you could spend a penny and listen to opera, for the lavatory attendant was a keen opera buff who also decorated the walls with reproductions of some of the National Gallery's most famous pictures. Tourists and Londoners flocked to this eccentric destination, and rightly so, until it was closed by unimaginative local officials.

Odder still than the Covent Garden lavatory was the public loo that once stood in the middle of the road about halfway along High Holborn.

So magnificent were the fittings in this the ultimate public lavatory that they are now in the Victoria and Albert Museum, a testament to the public-spiritedness and architectural pride of our Victorian ancestors.

The brass and mahogany fittings of the Holborn public loo were surmounted by a set of superb cut-glass cisterns. These were spectacular enough to provoke comment in numerous newspapers but the enthusiasm of the public for them knew no bounds when an attendant in the 1930s decided that each cistern would be far more interesting stocked with goldfish. He duly stocked them and the fish lived happily in the sparkling clean water to the delight of patrons for many years – until in fact the Holborn public loo suffered the fate of almost every other public loo in London.

HOW CRIME BECAME ART

1995

In 1962 the future playwright Joe Orton, whose plays *Loot* and *Entertaining Mr Sloane* were later to astonish theatregoers, was arrested along with his lover for defacing library books.

Contrast that with the last year of Orton's extraordinary – and sadly rather short – life. The year 1967 saw the first performance of his play *What the Butler Saw*, the latest in a string of theatrical successes. But Kenneth Halliwell, Orton's lover since 1951, found it difficult to cope with his partner's increasing fame and in a fit of depression killed Orton with a hammer while he slept and then took a massive overdose of sleeping pills.

The newspaper obituaries tended to dwell on what was then described as Orton's 'unnatural relationship' with Halliwell and his outrageous behaviour.

The incident of the 1962 book-defacing offence was also dredged up. After the court trial of 1962 both Orton and Halliwell had been sentenced to six months' imprisonment but the public was outraged – not by the severity of the sentence, but by its lenity.

One commentator said: 'People who deface library books must be dead to all sense of shame; six months' imprisonment, the severest sentence that the law allowed, is totally inadequate for a crime of that kind.'

Yet how strange is the world that over thirty years later Islington Library – the very library that instituted the prosecution against Orton and Halliwell – could proudly proclaim that an exhibition of the books defaced was to be held. Anyone wanting to visit the exhibition and see the images that outraged an earlier generation now had to pay an entrance fee. The defaced books – showing among other things Winston Churchill's head on an ape – had become enormously valuable and still are. They are now among the library's most prized possessions. If Orton had never become famous the books no doubt would have been thrown away long ago – such is the extraordinary power of celebrity.

CAMILLA – DESCENDED FROM THE ROYAL MISTRESS

2004

One of the best-known things about the British is our obsession with class. In the past it was extremely rare for class barriers to be breached – in the seventeenth century and earlier the idea, for example, that a bricklayer might marry the daughter of an earl would have seemed not just outrageous but quite simply impossible. Her family would not allow it under any circumstances and any environment in which a bricklayer might meet the daughter of an earl on anything like terms of equality or intimacy simply didn't exist.

But with the rise of the mercantile middle classes in the eighteenth century the rules began to relax – Hogarth's famous *Marriage à la Mode* series explains the new realities well. The old landed aristocracy frequently found itself with status, and no cash. The merchant classes had cash but not status, so they helped each other out by marrying their children off to each other.

Despite these changes royalty was and still is very little affected by ideas of equality. When Prince Charles – the descendant of a minor German Prince – married Lady Diana Spencer there were complaints that he had married a commoner. In fact she was at least as nobly born as Charles, being descended from countless generations of English aristocrats with close ties to the pre-Hanoverian royal family.

But when Prince Albert decided to employ the builder

Thomas Cubbitt (1788–1855) to create Osborne House, the royal palace on the Isle of Wight, he would have been shocked and horrified to be told that a descendant of Cubbitt – who famously built the squares of London's Belgravia – would marry one of his own royal descendants.

In fact this happened in 2004 when Prince Charles married Camilla Parker Bowles. He is the great-great-great-grandson of Prince Albert; she is a descendant of both Thomas Cubbitt and, even more extraordinarily, Edward VII's mistress Alice Keppel (1869–1947).

DEATH BY PELICAN

2006

There have been pelicans on the lake at St James's Park since the first few were presented to Charles II by the Czar of Russia in 1660. Nothing so exotic had ever been seen in the capital and Londoners flocked to the park to see the new arrivals.

By the early 1970s disease and bad luck had reduced the St James's flock of pelicans to just one bird. Something had to be done and with a sense of tradition typical of the Court of St James, it was recalled that the original birds had been presented by the Imperial Russian Court.

Despite the Cold War the British Government approached the Russian Government and asked if they could spare a few more birds. When the birds arrived everyone was delighted – except the other birds in the park.

The newspapers were filled with stories of songbirds and more especially pigeons being eaten by the pelicans – the stories were not generally believed because pelicans are not carnivores, but the experts had not reckoned on these new and very ferocious Communist pelicans. Proof was difficult to obtain until in 2006 a photographer managed to get a close-up picture of a plump woodpigeon disappearing into a pelican's gaping maw!

GOING DUTCH

2007

Dutch ships that land their cargoes in the City of London –
admittedly a rare event today when most cargo is unloaded
miles downriver at Tilbury – are never charged harbour fees.

In fact they have paid no fees since the plague year of 1665
when London was virtually cut off from the rest of the world.

No other nation would land its cargoes at that time for fear
of catching the terrible disease; only the Dutch kept trading
with London, dropping supplies of food and other goods vital
to the survival of a city which has shown its gratitude ever since
by waiving the charges that apply to all other nations.

Created in 2007, Portico publishes a range of books that are fresh, funny and forthright.

portico

An imprint of **Anova** Books

THE
STRANGEST
SERIES

The *Strangest* Series has been delighting
and enthralling readers for decades with
weird, exotic, spooky and baffling tales of
the absurd, ridiculous and the bizarre.
This bestselling range of fascinating books
– from the Ashes to Fishing, Football to
London and Motor Racing to the World Cup,
detail the very curious history of each subject
area's funniest, oddest and most compelling
characters, locations and events.
For all things weird and wonderful, pick
up a *Strangest* from Portico Books today…

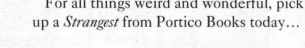

9781861052933

9781861055354

9781861052926

9781861051844

9781905798162

9781861054111

9781861057457

9781861056795

9781907554339

9781907554971

9781861059765

9781861058270

9781907554131

9781861059383

9781906032906

9781905798285

AND NOW FOR SOMETHING EVEN STRANGER!

9781906032760   9781906032913   9781907554476

The Strangest Series has now introduced even stranger delights for its readers. With *The Ashes' Strangest*, *World Cup's Strangest* and *Olympics' Strangest*, fans of this unique and extraordinary series can delve even deeper into the world of the bizarre and utterly ridiculous with these special sport-related *Strangests*. A great read no matter where you are, these fascinating books highlight the bizarre, weird and downright bonkers events, characters and locations of each particular sport.

Just don't read them all at once though – you might start acting all peculiar! You have been warned.

WROTTEN ENGLISH

A Celebration of Literary Misprints, Mistakes and Mishaps

Peter Haining

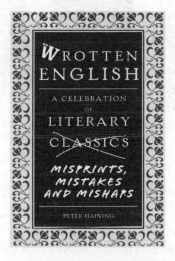

'An absolute gem of a book'

booksmonthly.co.uk

Following on from the hilarious collection of typos, gaffes and howlers in Portico's *A Steroid Hit the Earth*, comes *Wrotten English* – a fabulously funny collection of literary blunders from classic, and not-so classic, works of literature. This book is an anthology of side-splitting authors' errors, publishers' boobs, printers' devils, terrible titles, comical clangers and all manner of literary lunacy dating back since the invention of the printing press.

£9.99 • Hardback • 9781907554100

THE HIDDEN MATHEMATICS OF SPORT

Rob Eastaway & John Haigh

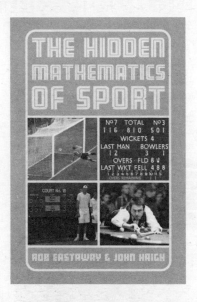

*'A fascinating mixture of analysis, trivia and sporting history,
with plenty to appeal to any sports fan.'*
Ed Smith, *The Times*

The Hidden Mathematics of Sport takes a novel and intriguing
look at sport, by exploring the mathematics behind the action.
Discover the best tactics for taking a penalty, the pros and cons of
being a consistent golfer, the surprising link between boxing and
figure skating, the unusual location of England's earliest 'football'
game (in a parish church), and the formula for always winning a
game of tennis. Whatever your sporting interests, you will find
plenty to absorb and amuse you in this entertaining and unique
book – and maybe you will even find some new strategies for
beating the odds.

£9.99 • Hardback • 9781907554223

WHATEVER HAPPENED TO TANGANYIKA?

The Place Names that History Left Behind

Harry Campbell

*'Marvellous and intriguing, Campbell has
created a whole new discipline – one which
we may perhaps call nostalgic geography.'*
Alexander McCall Smith

In this fascinating trawl through the atlas of yesteryear, Harry
Campbell explains how and why the names of countries, cities
and counties have changed over time, and tells the extraordinary
tales behind places from Rangoon to Rutland and Affpiddle to
Zaire. *Whatever Happened to Tanganyika?* is a treasure trove of
stories to delight armchair travellers and history fans alike.

£9.99 • Hardback • 9781906032050

365 REASONS TO BE CHEERFUL

Magical Moments to Cheer Up Miserable Sods ...
One Day at a Time

Richard Happer

It's a well-observed fact that human beings can be a grumpy old bunch, always choosing to see that infamous metaphorical glass as constantly half empty rather than half full. Where's the fun in that? *365 Reasons To Be Cheerful* is, well, it's exactly that. It's a whole year's worth of funny and unique events that happened on each and every day – a wild, weird and wonderful journey through the year highlighting the moments that changed the world for the better as well as the delightfully quirky stories that will simply make you smile. 365 Reasons To Be Cheerful is designed specifically to look on the bright side of life every day of the year – the perfect pint-sized pick-me-up in these sobering, sombre times.

£7.99 • Hardback • 9781906032968